AMERICAN TRAVELER

ALSO BY JAMES ZUG

Squash: A History of the Game

AMERICAN
TRAVELER

The Life and Adventures of

John Ledyard, the Man Who

Dreamed of Walking the World

JAMES ZUG

BASIC
BOOKS

A Member of the Perseus Books Group
New York

Published by Basic Books
A Member of the Perseus Books Group

Books published by Basic Books are available at special discounts for bulk purchases in the United States by corporations, institutions, and other organizations. For more information, please contact the Special Markets Department at the Perseus Books Group, 11 Cambridge Center, Cambridge, MA 02142, or call (617) 252-5298, (800) 255-1514 or e-mail special.markets@perseusbooks.com.

Cataloging-in-Publication data for this book is available from the Library of Congress.

ISBN 0-465-09405-8

05   06   07   /   10   9   8   7   6   5   4   3   2   1

For Rebecca

Contents

Captain Cook's
Third Voyage: 1776–1780
to the North Pacific
in the *Resolution* and *Discovery*

⟵——— Outgoing voyage

----➤ Return voyage
after Cook's death

Oblique Azimuthal Equidistant Projection
central latitude: 40° N
central meridian: 90° W

JOHN LEDYARD'S ROUTE ACROSS THE
RUSSIAN EMPIRE: 1786–1788

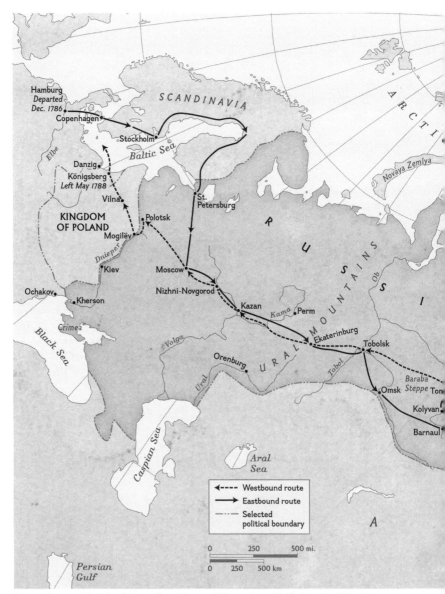

Primary Source: *John Ledyard's Journey Through Russia and Siberia 1787–1788, The Journal and Selected Letters*, Stephen D. Watrous, editor, University of Wisconsin Press, Madison, 1966.

We are pensioners of the wind.

—Ralph Waldo Emerson

Prologue

Under the gray roof of a wintry sky, two sloops furled their topgallant sails and bore towards land. The sailors stared at the deeply forested hills and snow-capped mountains in the distance and the streams in the foreground that cascaded through moss-covered cliffs into the sea.

Three times in this voyage, they had made landfall on unknown shores only to find no inhabitants, and however mighty the king and country under which they sailed, they still needed native people to supply food and water, advice about tides and shoals, and knowledge about what lay beyond the horizon.

"It was a matter of doubt with many of us whether we should find any inhabitants here," wrote John Ledyard, "but we had scarcely entered the inlet before we saw that hardy, that intrepid, that glorious creature man approaching us from the shore." As the sailors drew closer, they also smelled land. The breeze brought wet soil, cedar, spruce, yew and woodsmoke to the sailors. It had been two months since they had walked on solid ground, and now they were about to land on the west coast of North America.

Native people usually gave the ships a tumultuous reception. Everywhere from Tonga to Tahiti to Hawaii, throngs of men and women swarmed onto the ships, climbed into the rigging, wandered below decks, gestured, laughed, stole, ate and even offered sex. On this day on this new shore, however, the natives gave a more formal welcome. More than thirty dugout canoes appeared. Each was forty or fifty feet long, made of cedar and carrying two or three dozen people. The Native Americans encircled the sloops, but not a single one could be persuaded to board.

Facing this restrained response, the mariners feared an attack and loaded their muskets. The natives instead performed a singular ceremony. One man stood upright in his canoe—a remarkable feat, considering the heavy western swell and his thin canoe—and gave an oration punctuated by the tossing of feathers and red ochre powder into the sea and the shaking of a wooden, pebble-filled rattle. He was "dressed like a harlequin in many-colored garments," wrote a sailor. "He changed these garments, holding different masks before his face, and went through all kinds of farcical acting." Reaching the heart of the ritual, he started to sing. The men on board the ships found the song astonishingly polished. According to the captain of the expedition, it was "a very agreeable air, with a degree of softness and melody which we could not have expected." His aria became a thundering anthem, as the entire procession joined in, everyone keeping time by lightly tapping their paddles on the sides of their canoes. The song resembled a chant, with each line ending, as the captain wrote, "in a loud and deep sigh uttered in such a manner as to have a very pleasing effect." The sailors, "greatly astonished at the exactness of their rhythm and the charm of their song," put down their guns and watched as these strange people, with painted faces, white powdered hair and fur-clad bodies, sang their way into something almost familiar. Their songs reminded one officer, the son of a highly regarded music critic, of a village church service: "What they sung was composed of a few notes, and wild as could have been expected, yet was solemn and in unison, and what I thought most extraordinary, they were all well in tune with each other. The words were at times given out by one man, as a parish clerk gives out the first line of a psalm." He added that "the halloo is a single note in which they all join, swelling it out in the middle and letting the sound die away. In a Calm with the hills around us, it had an effect infinitely superior to what might be imagined from any thing so simple."

Moved by this striking welcome, the sailors returned the favor. "We judg'd they might like our musick, & we orderd the Fife & drum to play a tune," wrote a lieutenant. The natives' reaction was as astonishing as their welcome had been. "These were the only people we had seen that ever paid the smallest attention to those or any of our musical Instruments, if we except the drum, & that only I supposed from its Noise & resemblance to their own drums; they Observd the Profoundest silence, & we were sorry that the Dark hind'red our seeing the effect of this musick on their coutenances." After the band stopped, the natives sang another song. In reply, the sailors added the French horn to their band and played a benedictory tune.

Night fell and the concert ended. The fleet of natives departed for the shore. Five canoes filled with unarmed men stayed and quietly circled the ships. The natives and sailors watched each other under the glimmering light of a nearly full moon. It was a cold night. "The Ther'[momete]r in the morning being 34," wrote the lieutenant, "the Decks & shore coverd with a hoar frost."

A day later, March 31, 1779, the two ships moved into a small cove in the tightly bound bay. Unfathomably deep, "far beyond the limits of European Geography," wrote one sailor, the bottom of the bay could not be reached by the ships' anchors. The mariners fastened hawser lines, both stern and bow, to trees on the shore. Under the watchful eye and helping hand of the natives, the sailors disembarked onto the tiny, rock-strewn beach. At that moment, John Ledyard became the first American citizen to touch the west coast of North America.

Tethered to old and new worlds, his ship moored on unknown shores, his eyes glimpsing vast sights, his ears hearing songs strange and beautiful, his hands grasping the hands of the native people of his homeland, John Ledyard that day changed the history of the United States.

Known as Ledyard the Traveler, John Ledyard inaugurated a tradition of Americans roaming the world's wild, unmapped regions.

He had the uncanny ability to appear in the most exciting places with the most amazing people of his time. He sailed with Captain James Cook on Cook's third voyage and wrote vividly of Cook's murder on a Hawaiian beach. He formed fur-trading companies with Robert Morris, the Philadelphian financier, and John Paul Jones, America's notorious sea captain. He helped launch the China trade and the Northwest fur trade, bringing the U.S. economy into the Pacific for the first time. He visited Egypt before Napoleon's invasion opened the country up to Western travelers. Sir Joseph Banks, the celebrated botanist, engaged Ledyard as the first explorer for his African Association, a society for which such legends as Mungo Park and Johann Burckhardt later traveled. He delighted Paris's pre-revolutionary expatriate society in the 1780s, becoming close friends with the Marquis de Lafayette and the U.S. ambassador, Thomas Jefferson. He so thoroughly convinced Jefferson of the need to explore the American continent that Jefferson asked him to do the job twenty years before Lewis & Clark. The plan called for Ledyard to go overland through Russia, cross at the Bering Strait and head south through Alaska and across the American West to Virginia. This expedition failed after fifteen months of traveling when Catherine the Great had him arrested in eastern Siberia, but Ledyard's trip across Russia was historic: it was one of the three failed attempts that preceded the Lewis & Clark expedition and one of the first known attempts by a person to walk around the world.

With his magnetism, resourcefulness, unbridled imagination and rare ability to endure hardship, Ledyard epitomized the bold new American republic. He used a capacious intellect to theorize about his travels, regularly debunking the beliefs of the day. He published a classic memoir of Cook's fatal expedition, his 1783 *Journal of Captain Cook's Last Voyage*, a book famous for being the sole account that blamed Cook as much as the islanders for his death on a Hawaiian beach in 1779. His focus was not on landscape but the people in it. His letters and journals sparkled with descriptions of customs and habits. He compiled lists of vocabularies of various languages in hopes of unraveling the mysteries of migration. Almost alone among travelers of his age, he wrote from the viewpoint of indigenous men and women.

An early version of Ernest Shackleton, Ledyard brimmed with courage but failed at his appointed tasks. He was incurably restless and hot tempered. He left Dartmouth at the end of his freshman year. An eldest son, he abandoned his widowed mother and six siblings, leaving them without support. He deserted from the British navy. He did not fulfill his goal of setting up a fur-trading company in the Pacific Northwest, he did not cross the American continent and he did not reach the source of the Niger. He courted women on three continents but never married. He did not have a job for the last six years of his life, living off the largesse of friends. He got into fistfights in London, started a shoving match in Tonga and challenged a Siberian provincial governor to a duel.

Despite his impulsive, elusive personality, Ledyard created a lasting legacy. He was more than a footnote to the Lewis & Clark expedition or the China trade, more than a curious American artifact on the Cook voyages or an also-ran in the annals of European exploration in Africa. As the first American to report on exactly where North America ended, he generated a continental dream. Like the photographs of earth the astronauts brought back in the 1960s, Ledyard's writings changed how America viewed itself. The United States was not a baker's dozen of struggling British colonies on the eastern seaboard, but one nation, immense and inevitably stretching coast to coast.

Fame not fortune was his shibboleth. He was well educated and well connected and shamelessly courted the rich and powerful to make a name for himself. He viewed his 1783 *Journal* largely as a marketing tool. Like any modern professional explorer, he constantly looked for sponsorship and spent more time courting donors than actually exploring.

In his lifetime he became a legendary figure. When he died newspapers across America and Europe published his obituary and he was mourned around the world. His public moniker—Ledyard the Traveler—was suffused with a romantic tinge because he had lived up to his well-tended reputation. He supped with cannibals and kings. He sailed the South Seas and became the first American to return to the country with a Tahitian tattoo. He touched at fabled cities like Cape Town, Cairo, and St. Petersburg and lands like Hawaii and Alaska that would one day remember him as the first American to step on their soil. He had astounding adventures—paddling the Connecticut River in a dugout canoe and hiking through Lapland in the dead of winter—but he always looked toward the next challenge.

While he was a patriotic American and loved "the Genius of my noble country," he also articulated an early manifesto for a boundary-less, global citizenship: "For no State's, no Monarch's Minister am I, but travel under the common flag of humanity, commissioned by myself to serve the world at large." Such was his faith in native peoples that for his attempt to circumambulate the globe he outfitted himself with just two dogs for company, an axe to cut firewood, and a peace pipe to make friends.

He completed the prerequisites for enduring fame by dying young on the trail towards further glory. When he succumbed to a combination of dysentery and exhaustion along the banks of the Nile in January 1789, John Ledyard became immortalized as America's first great explorer.

1

Ocean's Briny Waves—
A Connecticut Childhood

HE GREW UP WITH THE SEA. Salt was in the air of the first breath he took. Gray-green tidal water lashed rocks within sight of his first house. The sounds of his childhood were the smack of ropes on wood, the rumble of barrels rolling steady across wharves, the hesitating flap of a sail unfurling and the cadence of the tides. The official seal of his town was a full-rigged ship, with sails spread and the motto *Mare liberum*. As a young boy he unloaded cargo brought from a dozen nations for the family store. Each ship that moored in the harbor brought tantalizing news from distant lands. When his father, a sea captain, died young and his grandfather disinherited him, he turned to the sea, because it was familiar and because it was the way to discovery.

John Ledyard was born in Groton and always referred to himself as a Connecticut man, yet his family roots were in Long Island. In 1637 the Reverend John Youngs, a graduate of Oxford who had converted to Calvinism, emigrated from England with his brother Joseph to Salem, Massachusetts. There he married a widow named Mary Gardner, the sister of his brother's wife. Youngs chafed under the Puritan strictures in Salem, and after three years he took his family to a new colony. They landed near the far eastern tip of the North Fork of Long Island. The Corchaugs who lived there called the spot Yennecock or Yennecott; Reverend Youngs named it Southold, after the village of Southwold in Suffolk, England, where his wife was born. Southold was the first English settlement in what would become the state of New York. Situated on a narrow, windswept spit of land, with Peconic Bay and Shelter Island to the south and Long Island Sound to the north, Southold prospered and became an important port in what was then the colony of Connecticut.

The reverend's grandson, Benjamin, born in 1689, was the leading judge on the North Fork and a captain in the local militia. Young lawyers came from around the colonies to apprentice under him. They also courted his beautiful, smart daughters. One protégé, Robert Hempstead from New London, Connecticut, married Benjamin's daughter Mary, inherited his practice and built a grand house on the northeast corner of Youngs Avenue and Town Road. A younger daughter, Deborah, also fell in love with a visiting apprentice lawyer, John Ledyard, who had recently emigrated from Bristol, England. In 1727 John Ledyard and Deborah Youngs married and moved across the Sound to Groton.

The village of Groton lay two miles up the Thames estuary across from the town of New London. Founded by John Winthrop, Jr., the son of the leader of the Massachusetts Bay Colony, New London was one of the major ports in North America. Groton, named after Winthrop's family seat in Suffolk, England, had officially separated from New London in 1705 but was considered more of an outlying industrial district than a separate town. Besides farming and salt works, the main industry for the few hundred people on Groton Bank was the shipping industry. Warehouses and wharves crowded the shoreline, and shipbuilding became Groton's signature industry after an Englishman named John Jeffreys transplanted his shipyard there. On a rainy Tuesday in October 1725, Jeffreys launched a seven-hundred-ton ship, the largest ship ever built in North America.

John Ledyard flourished in Groton. He started his own merchant house, became a justice of the peace, represented Groton in Connecticut's General Assembly, was a deacon at the First Church of Christ in Groton and was soon known as Squire John. He stocked his warehouse on the Thames with goods from around the world: Gloucester cheese, Bristol beer and Herefordshire cider from England; cinnamon from India; rum and muscovado sugar from the Caribbean; flour from New York; and coats from Philadelphia. Starting with John, III, in 1729—Squire John had been named after his grandfather John, who upon his death in 1685 willed £100 to his younger son, Squire John's father, Ebenezer—Deborah Ledyard bore ten children in sixteen years before dying of measles—at age forty-three in March 1747, just days after giving birth to her tenth child. Within months, Squire John married Mary Austin Ellery and moved to Hartford, the capital of the colony. Widowed herself, Ellery had a substantial estate and a position in the upper reaches of Hartford society. With Squire John, she bore five children in rapid succession.

Once he moved to Hartford, a two-day horse ride away, the paterfamilias exerted less influence over his Groton brood. This became apparent in the spring of 1750. John, III, had worked in his father's warehouse as a clerk until old enough to sail on Groton merchant ships. He also spent time in Southold and fell in love with his first cousin Abigail Hempstead. Their mothers were sisters, and everyone strongly disapproved of the relationship. One night in early May, John, III, and Abigail, both twenty years old, secretly left Southold together. Abigail's father, Robert, rushed across the Sound to track them down. For three days he and his father and brother looked in vain for the love-crossed couple, visiting churches to "take the evidence" of ministers and talking to neighbors. They finally found the missing couple sailing into Groton in a boat manned by a cousin. They were husband and wife. Instead of crossing to Groton, John and Abigail had traveled to Setauket, a Long Island village nearly halfway to New York City. There a doctor, whose father-in-law was the Southold minister, used an extra marriage license to perform a civil ceremony.

Despite eloping, the young couple managed to return into their families' good graces. Soon enough Abigail's grandfather, Joshua Hempstead, who was an assiduous diary keeper, mentioned visiting with his granddaughter and having Sunday dinners with her at his grand house in New London. Joshua was absent, though, on 10 November 1751, when at the little Congregational meetinghouse in Groton, Reverend John Owen wrote in the church ledger, "John, son of John Ledyard, was baptized in infancy."

John Ledyard, IV, was probably born in his parents' new home on Broad Street in Groton, and for the first decade of his life he was nestled in a cozy, close-knit family. In the small triangle of Groton, New London and Southold, dozens of cousins, uncles and aunts and in-laws lived, especially as Ledyards had married into extensive New London clans like the Averys and Saltonstalls. John, III, and his brother Youngs Ledyard, with the help of their father, formed a merchant company and piloted ships in the West Indies trade, earning the title Captain.

Youngs had four children within three years of John, IV's birth, and so while the fathers were away at sea, the Ledyard cousins ran about Groton Bank. John, IV became particularly close with Benjamin and Isaac, eighteen months and three years younger. "We have a language of our own," John later wrote to his cousin Isaac, "& you so well know my soul that should Language fail in the communication you would still understand me." The boys played in the Ledyard warehouses, peeking out from richly scented sacks and barrels. They prowled for coyote and bear that still lived outside town. They climbed Lantern Hill, the highest spot in the area and the first bit of land that sailors saw coming into the Sound. They spent hours paddling canoes and rowboats, riding ferries and taking day trips in little smacks up the Thames or the Mystic River or out to Fishers Island. In winter they sledded; in spring they fished for smelt that ran in silvery schools up the Thames to spawn; in autumn they lit bonfires on Guy Fawkes Day. They visited the construction site of the New London lighthouse, which when it was finished in 1760 was the first lighthouse on the Connecticut coast. They searched Cedar Swamp for Spanish gold. A year after Ledyard was born a Spanish galleon struck a reef west of the harbor. The town helped unload the ship's chests of gold, but one night the local men guarding it in New London spirited the chests into the swamp outside town. For decades afterwards gold coins materialized in the woods.

The Ledyard boys schooled at the meetinghouse in the center of Groton. They studied under Daniel Kirkland, who had replaced Reverend Owen. A graduate of Yale, Kirkland stayed at Groton for just four years. Jonathan Barber, another Eli man, took over and brought the Great Awakening revivalist fervor of Methodist evangelist George Whitefield to the little meetinghouse. Whitefield himself preached twice in Groton to enormous crowds.

The Seven Years' War of 1754–1763 (or the French & Indian War, as Americans later called it) was a prosperous time for the Ledyards. The British forced the American colonies to buy high-priced sugar from the

British West Indies rather than from the cheaper French West Indies. False papers, sham swearing of goods, fake unloadings, bribing of customs officials and a constant, intricate game of selling and buying—all washed down by the universal solvent of rum—was the order of the day. More than three times as many ships stopped at sugar-producing St. Kitts than at its neighbor Nevis, for example, because St. Kitts specialized in issuing the right paperwork. Captain John profited from the clandestine smuggling and privateering, although in 1757 he got caught while sailing his ship, *Greyhound*—named for the animal on the Ledyard family crest. In quick succession the French and then the English captured the *Greyhound*, and Captain John had to ransom the ship in Antigua in order to return to Groton.

While young Ledyard considered his cousins Ben and Isaac his brothers, his own family grew apace. His sister Frances arrived in 1754, then Thomas in July 1756, Charles in September 1759 and George in September 1761. Charlie tragically died at just three and a half months old and was buried in the northeast corner of the Groton cemetery. The loss of a baby brother was saddening, but the shattering event of Ledyard's childhood came in the spring of 1762. Within three weeks time, both Captain John and Captain Youngs, on voyages to St. Eustatius, died at sea, John of malaria and Youngs of smallpox. The dangers of the sea were well known to the family, especially after 1753, when a storm blew Captain John's cargo of horses and sheep overboard. But for John, IV, a ten-year-old boy living a charmed life, the death of his father stunned him. With the gulls cawing overhead, the Ledyards laid Captain John to rest in the Groton cemetery in front of his infant son. On a gravestone adorned with a bursting sun, his eloquent epitaph read, "Once did I stand amid Life's busy throng/Healthy and active, vigorous & strong/Oft' did I traverse Ocean's briny waves/And safe escape a thousand gaping graves/Yet dire disease has stop'd my vital breath/And here I lie, the prisoner of Death/Reader, expect not lengthened days to see/Or if thou dost, think, think, ah think of me."

Compounding the loss was a rupture in the family. Abigail Ledyard had not completely gotten along with the Ledyard clan since the elopement, and after her husband's death the tensions broke into the open. Captain John's estate, in particular the deed to the Groton house, was thrown into a complicated morass of legal dealings, and the house legally reverted to Squire John, who gave it to his son William. That summer Abigail took her four children and moved across the Sound to Southold. It was not a horrible exile. They lived in the Hempstead family home. Ledyard could still paddle and sail on the Sound, but he missed his cousins and the life he had led.

On the Feast of the Epiphany in 1765, Abigail married Micah Moore. The town doctor of Southold, Moore was a fifty-two-year-old widower (Abigail was thirty-five) with a daughter named Jerusha. The new family moved into a saltbox house along the King's Highway at the eastern side of town, and soon added three daughters, Julia, Phebe and Abigail.

Ledyard never knew the girls that well, for in 1765 he moved to Hartford. Squire John had invited three of his fatherless grandsons to come to Hartford and prepare for a life in business. Reunited with Ben and Isaac, Ledyard found his third home in three years quite comfortable. The boys lived in a garret on the top floor of Squire John's imposing house on Arch Street. With three aunts, an uncle, numerous cousins and the Squire's five young children from his second marriage all living there, the house burbled with footsteps. The family slaves lived in quarters in the back.

The boys went through their arithmetic at the redbrick Hartford Grammar School and learned about business at Squire John's complex of farms, shops and mills along Hartford's Little River. They worked closely with their uncle, Colonel Thomas Seymour, who was a Yale man, lawyer, representative in Connecticut's colonial assembly and later mayor of Hartford for twenty-eight years; Seymour swam every day in the Little River, breaking ice in winter if necessary, and died at age ninety-four. Hartford, with four thousand citizens, was a larger version of New London, but the Ledyard clan was even more prominent. Squire John was the head of an ever-growing family (he had more than seventy grandchildren), a representative in the colonial assembly and one of the wealthiest merchants in the colony.

Ledyard worked earnestly at his studies. "Under the tuition of a tender Uncle," he wrote to his mother in December 1767, "I shall be Diligent and in time Be able to make Some proficiency in My business. Uncle Seymour Promises me as far and kindly as an Uncle Can he sayeth that if I will (which I hope I will be steady and mind my business) That he will do well by me & if my life should be spared he will let me be chosen up to the Law Businesses (as Docs) and to follow the Business long and leave room for us."

Despite his assurances, Ledyard never felt entirely at home in Hartford, and tragedy struck soon after his arrival. In May 1766 during a celebration at the repeal of the hated Stamp Act, John's uncle Nathaniel Ledyard was killed in a fireworks explosion. Furthermore, Ledyard and his grandfather never saw eye to eye. The great patriarch held decided views on matters of business and politics and considered his grandson a bit of a fool. Ledyard's cousin Henry Seymour later recalled that one day Ledyard met a drover bringing some horses for sale in Hartford: "Being pleased with one of them & ready for sport, he bought the whole drove, & drew on his grandfather for the amount. He came with the horses to Hartford, and, arriving in the night, he drove the horses to his grandfather's yard, where they remained till morning, when the owner called for his money, & found that they had been dealing with a boy, & was glad to receive his horses again." No doubt this stunt did not amuse Squire John. In response Ledyard regularly went back to Groton, often finding himself so wrapped up with family and friends that he would not cross the Sound and visit his mother and siblings. He corresponded regularly with them, though, begging for letters from them and complaining when they arrived that they were too short.

In September 1771 Squire John died. The minister who presided over his funeral at South Church gave a sermon titled "The death of good men compared to a sweet, refreshing sleep." It was so noteworthy that it was printed as a pamphlet. When Squire John's sons Ebenezer and William opened his last will and testament three days later, the news staggered young John Ledyard. Squire John gave his wife his "Negro called Didge," half his livestock, half of the family furnishings and kitchenware and a £20 annual legacy unless she remarried. He gave each of his sons £200 and each of his daughters £120. Instead of giving the rest of his estate to the eldest son of his eldest son, as tradition required, he almost ignored John, IV. The will read, "I consider my son John, deceased, as having a large portion out of my estate," referring to Squire John's assistance in bankrolling Captain John's merchant company. Squire John gave £60 to John Ledyard, IV, and £30 to the other three children, to come to them when they turned twenty-one or got married. "This is the whole that I may (consistent with what I suppose to be just toward my children) give to the heirs of my son John." Squire John instead gave Austin Ledyard, the eldest son by his second marriage, the balance of his estate. Five years later when Austin died, his share was valued at £1,285 (equivalent to $200,000 in 2005). To pour salt in the wound, Squire John also ignored Ledyard's right to his grandmother's money. Squire John's first wife, Deborah Youngs, was an heiress to a considerable estate which he should have passed on to John, IV.

With the death of Squire John, the Ledyard cousins broke up. Ben and Isaac moved to New York to live with their aunt Sarah; Ben entered into Sarah's husband's merchant business, and Isaac started medical studies. Ledyard moved into his aunt Mary and uncle Thomas Seymour's home down Arch Street. Seymour tried to get his young nephew interested in business and law, but it did not appeal to him, as Ledyard wrote to his mother:

> I was in hope that you had got over y^r. illness & was in a way to Spend the remainder of y^r. Days Some What happy—But Happiness I more & more Perceive is not to be found in any Perfect Manner in this World. I am not a Stranger to such discomforts—for I have the unhappiness to See a great many of them (if False it is) in the Transaction of Uncle Seymour's Business—After the decease of persons—people that are left to such things will forge Counterfeit, or do anything. They Don't seem to have the fear of God before their Eyes—But will sell their Immortal Souls for 'a Little Dust.'

Despite a lack of enthusiasm for the bare-knuckle world of commerce, he told his mother that he was still content in Hartford: "I am well & hearty. I last had above one Day Sickness since I left you (and that nothing worse than a Head-ache) & then Aunt Seymour was so kind & Uncle too that it did not seem to last long. I am very Sensible & ought to say I am Surrounded by Kind Parents great and small." But he was now twenty and had no definite prospects. In mid-March 1772 he wrote his favorite aunt, Elizabeth, a spinster living in New York, "I have no news—I mean no new affair to acquaint you."

Yet within days, everything changed. With his mean-spirited disinheritance—in startling contrast to how his own grandfather had treated his father—Squire John had liberated, for better or worse, his grandson from a life as a Hartford merchant or lawyer. He forced young John to make his own way through life and granted him the option to follow his dreams rather than the family business. Ledyard's first step was to get out of Connecticut. Cashing in on one of his grandfather's connections he arranged to gain admittance to a new college in New Hampshire called Dartmouth.

2

Saucy Enough—Dartmouth

IN APRIL 1772 JOHN LEDYARD DEPARTED for college in style.
Instead of traveling by horseback or walking, as most other students did,
he took one of the family's sulkies. A sulky was a one-horse, two-wheeled
carriage with room on top for just one aloof-looking, or sulking, passenger.
Ledyard's sulky, however, carried more than just the young scholar. He
packed trunk-loads of colorful calico bolts, destined, he hoped, to become
curtains and costumes for Dartmouth's stage.

The journey took more than two weeks, for winter was going out with
a vengeance. Snow, ice and frozen mud blocked the roads. On 24 March
the *Connecticut Courant* in Hartford reported: "Since the first of March instant, there have been no less than four heavy storms of snow which is very
much drifted and has rendered travelling almost impracticable. The snow
upon the level in these parts is upwards of three feet. It is said the winter
past has been the most severe of any since the year 1740." Once the weather
abated in early April, Ledyard slowly traveled along standard routes. From
Hartford, a stone-wall-lined coach road ran along the eastern bank of the
Connecticut River through the Massachusetts border town of Deerfield. At
Charlestown, New Hampshire, Fort No. 4 stood as the northernmost for-
tified outpost in northwest New England. Indians had harried and attacked

the fort just over a decade before. After a few miles on the New Crown Point Road, Ledyard headed into the wilderness bouncing along old corduroy log roads, drover's trails and Indian paths. Nearing Hanover, he joined a road built just the summer before for Governor John Wentworth so that he and sixty attendants could attend Dartmouth's first commencement. The last hurdle was coming down the steep side of Moose Mountain northeast of campus.

As he joggled and jolted into Hanover around the twenty-third of April, Ledyard created a stir. James Wheelock, a classmate, later wrote, "I remember when he first came, he came in a sulkey the first carriage of the kind ever on Dartmouth plain, which then, considering the Wilderness, the new & almost impassable state of the roads, want of bridges &c displayed in him a fortitude, & something of that spirit of enterprize, for which his after life was so highly distinguished." Besides revealing fortitude and enterprise, Ledyard had demonstrated a sophomoric spirit of foolishness, and he matriculated with a reputation as an eccentric fool. His clothes were odd—he wore baggy Turkish pantaloons—and his trunk of calico bolts odder, but on the Hanover Plain the sulky was absurd. The village was days beyond the frontier. There were no good roads in town and, as Ledyard well knew, no good roads out of town. Only one other carriage, that of the president's wife, had ever made it to Hanover. Ledyard had imagined that Dartmouth maintained a fashionable society where expensive breeches, elaborate stage props, and a sulky would be necessary accouterments for a gentleman scholar. He realized as he wheeled into the muddy grounds of Hanover that he was sadly mistaken.

Dartmouth College at the time was an experiment on the verge of failure. Eleazar Wheelock, a 1733 graduate of Yale, was a quiet Congregationalist minister in Lebanon, Connecticut, when the Great Awakening swept him into a tide of manic preaching—in 1741 he gave more than five hundred sermons. Wheelock soon channeled his revivalist passions into education. He started tutoring English boys to supplement his small salary. A prominent early protégé was Samuel Kirkland, who had grown up in Groton while his father was minister at the local congregational church. Kirkland went on to Princeton and founded Hamilton College; his son became president of Harvard. An even more illustrious student of Wheelock's was a twenty-year-old Mohegan named Samuel Occom. A recent convert to Christianity, Occom moved to Wheelock's house for a two-week course of study. He stayed for four years. Despite weak eyesight, Occom became proficient in Latin, Greek, French and Hebrew and upon finishing became a well-known Indian figure and a missionary among the Montauks in Long Island.

Moved by his work with Occom, Wheelock founded a high school to educate Indians. It was soon named after Colonel Joshua More, a wealthy farmer who donated two acres of land and buildings adjacent to Wheelock's house to the school. Moor's Indian Charity School (the deed misspelled More's name) achieved a modicum of success. Over the next fifteen years, nearly seventy Indians studied and prayed in a sky-blue meetinghouse. The student body was admirably diverse, with thirty-two pupils hailing from Western nations, mostly Mohawk and Oneida, and thirty-one from New England tribes like the Pequot, Narragansett and Algonquian. More than twenty of the students were girls. The first Moor's student, an eleven-year-old Delaware named Jacob Woolley, eventually went to Princeton.

The pool of potential students, with the forced migration of Native Americans away from the East Coast, was too small to sustain the school, and Wheelock dreamed of creating a university to educate and ordain Indians and send them back to their villages as missionaries. In 1765 he decided to send Samuel Occom on a fundraising mission to Great Britain. Squire John Ledyard hosted a meeting in Hartford devoted to finding a suitable minister to accompany Occom. They chose Nathaniel Whitaker, a Norwich minister, and, after a delay because of Stamp Act rioting, the two sailed that winter. Occom took Great Britain by storm. Over the next two years, he delivered four hundred sermons, including one for three thousand people. He became a darling of the London social scene, Mason Chamberlain painted his portrait and Covent Garden parodied him on stage. He gave Indian curiosities to his hosts, everything from a stone pipe covered with porcupine quills to a strip of elm bark used to bind captives. When he returned in 1768, he had raised a trust fund of £12,026, with donations from King George III (£200) and William Legge, the second Earl of Dartmouth (£50), who soon became the Secretary of State for the American colonies. The fund was administered from London by a board of British trustees chaired by Legge.

In December 1769, with Squire John giving legal advice, Wheelock obtained a charter from King George III for a college named after the Earl of

Dartmouth (the ninth and last university in the colonies to receive a royal charter). In the summer of 1770, after considering and dismissing several sites, Wheelock chose an undeveloped New Hampshire district called Hanover. With the help of his slaves Exeter, Brister, Chloe and Peggy, along with two Narragansett men, Abraham and Daniel Simons, who were the only Indians at Moor's to come north, the determined minister went to the wilderness. They cleared six acres of forest and built, as he wrote in his diary, "a Hutt of Loggs about 18 feet square, without stone, brick, glass or nail." That winter food ran short and he sent home ten of his thirty students. In August 1771 Wheelock presented four men, including his son and his son-in-law, with bachelor's degrees—they had studied at Yale for their first three years.

When Ledyard arrived, the college was nineteen months old and still painfully rudimentary. Enormous old-growth pines, marked with the King's broad arrow as masts and spars for the Royal Navy, lay scattered across the stumpy fields. Three log cabins on the southeast corner of the main pasture, or green, made up the college buildings: the original hut of Wheelock's called Old College; a house for Wheelock, his family and slaves; and Commons Hall, a two-story, east-facing house, with eighteen rooms, a kitchen and sleeping quarters.

A bitter wind blew that April. Hungry coyotes howled in the deep snow around the sheep pens. Provisions grew scarce, and just days before Ledyard pulled into town Wheelock had dispatched students to Walpole by canoe to fetch food—he was so desperate that he armed them with a pass to travel on the Sabbath. On 12 June Wheelock noted in his diary that after he cleared a layer of woodchips and cow dung from the entrance to Commons Hall, he uncovered ice an inch thick.

Ledyard settled into the life of a college student. There were twenty-three other men enrolled, as well as seventeen "sub-freshmen" preparing to enter Dartmouth. More than half the students, including the school's six Indian students, were on charity; they did not pay the annual tuition fee of £4 and worked in lieu of the weekly room & board charge of five shillings sixpence. Of the twenty-four matriculates, seventeen were from Connecticut, and Ledyard probably already knew some of the men. He roomed with a Connecticut man named Thomas Walcutt. His bed was a box of boards, with a thin mattress filled with pine shavings. The schedule included prayers at dawn and then recitations of mathematics, geography, logic, English, Latin and Greek. The primary tutors, Bezaleel Woodward and Silvanus Ripley, both of whom had married daughters of Wheelock, guided Ledyard through Virgil, Homer and Cicero. From the tuck shop run by the college Ledyard bought common necessities such as thread, handkerchiefs, pipes, ink, quills, linen, soap, knee buckles and candles.

One respite from his studies was Dartmouth's second commencement. Held on the last Wednesday in August, the ceremony for Dartmouth's meager graduating class of two scholars turned into a festival. Hundreds of neighbors and curiosity seekers poured onto the green and drank, sang, gambled, danced and ate all day. The party was briefly interrupted by men giving orations from a rough stage of hemlock planks or, in the case of Indian speakers, from the branches of a nearby pine tree. As in the first commencement a year earlier, the college cooks got so insensible with rum and hard cider that, when the time came for the trustees' dinner at Wheelock's house, no food emerged from the kitchen.

Five days earlier, Ledyard had settled his account with Wheelock, paying a total of almost £7 for five months of tuition and room & board. After commencement, he disappeared.

In September 1822 Jared Sparks, John Ledyard's first biographer, discovered an explanation. Sparks's notes from an interview with Ledyard's cousin Henry Seymour began with his first memory of Ledyard's college experience: "While Ledyard was at Dartmouth he absented himself without permission of the College Govt. and made a tour among the Six Nations of Indians on the borders of Canada. During this period he made some progress in learning their languages, & becoming acquainted with their manners and inured himself also to hardship and fatigue."

But it probably was not true. None of Ledyard's classmates mentioned this extraordinary journey. Eleazar Wheelock's diary, which often noted the comings and goings of students, especially those without permission, revealed nothing. In reality, Ledyard's knowledge and experience with Indians came primarily through his classmates. While growing up in Connecticut, he had befriended Indians, especially the Pequots living on the edges of Groton, and had read through the standard books on Indians and Indian country: John Bartram's *Observations* (1751); Cadwallader Colden's *The History of the Five Indian Nations* (1755); reports by Sir William Johnson, the New York superintendent of Indian affairs; and the many "Faithful Narratives" of captivity stories. But what Ledyard knew of Indians he learned living with them on Dartmouth's campus. In 1773 the college boasted seventeen matriculated Indians, as well as a dozen sub-freshman Indians, many of whom had come to Dartmouth as a result of intensive recruiting drives Wheelock had organized in Indian country.

Ledyard may have gone to visit the families of his classmates. He had about two months. The last notation in the college ledger referencing Ledyard was 21 August, and according to a letter from William Patten, a Dartmouth trustee and Wheelock's son-in-law, he was in Hartford in late October. Ledyard was back on campus in mid-November, and on the first of December, he resumed buying sundries from the college store when he took five and three-quarters yards of green baize for seventeen shillings, threepence. Attendance at Dartmouth was fluid. There was no fixed calendar of terms, no exam dates, no credit requirements for graduation. Students came and went constantly. Ledyard himself had arrived midterm. In May 1773, a month after he matriculated, two white and two Indian students left for Canada; three other white students left in June, one of whom, founding an Indian school in Canada, did not return to Hanover until October. In March 1774 Wheelock noted in his diary that "Fairbanks [Phineas, a junior] returned in ye. Evening from his Tour up the River wc. he took wth out Leave." Ledyard may have made a similar tour upriver.

Ledyard, who was congenitally adverse to hiding his tales of adventure, never referred to any junior year abroad. Later in life, while in Alaska with Captain James Cook, he compared the Inuit language to the ones "which I very well remember to have heard pronounced by the American Indians from the frontiers of the northern American States." Hanover was on the frontier; there was no mention of Canada. The supposed tour of the Six Nations was part of the nineteenth-century construction of the Ledyard myth. Because the Connecticut lad later exhibited an unusual affinity towards native peoples around the world and an ability to endure incredible discomfort, biographers had tended to paint a James Fenimore Cooperesque picture of kind Native Americans patiently guiding the earnest Dartmouth student through the mysteries of Indian life.

When Wheelock arrived in Hanover to educate Indians, his ox-cart contained, according to Dartmouth lore, a Bible, a drum and five hundred gallons of rum, a combination Ledyard came to abhor. He learned from his Indian classmates that a missionary often did more harm than good, that Native Americans had a strong and vibrant society and that European religion was unnecessary. He later called Indians "glorious," and "intrepid," and declared that Ben Uncas, the celebrated seventeenth-century chief of the Pequot tribe near Groton, should be considered an equal of Isaac Newton. A missionary armed with a Bible and rum offered nothing Native Americans needed. Ledyard realized he had no appetite for the purpose of Dartmouth.

The intellectual benefits of college did not carry with Ledyard. As a scholar he was mediocre. From his schooling in Groton and Hartford, he had developed an appetite for history and literature. One classmate remembered how "he was much addicted to reading plays." For six shillings he hired an alcove in the second-story library in Commons Hall, and some afternoons he sat by a window and read Sterne, Cervantes and Richardson until the sun set over the Vermont hills. He tried to buckle down—his first two purchases from Wheelock's store were writing paper—and he even briefly tutored a sub-freshman named Bailey. But he did not apply himself with fervor to the stultifying tasks of reciting Latin declensions. A classmate later wrote diplomatically that "he was respectable, tho he did not excel" in his studies, adding "that his mind was not adapted to close application."

Souring on Dartmouth, Ledyard discovered that the college was simply too restrictive to handle his outsized personality. His friend and cousin by marriage, Philip Freneau, remembered that he was "disgusted with the austerity of those regulations which he foresaw must control him and disappointed as to the extent of the travails which it proposed." He tried repeatedly to liven up the scene in Commons Hall. Dartmouth did not have a bell to announce meal and class times, and it was the job of freshmen to blow on a conch shell. Whenever it was Ledyard's turn, he blew it with exaggerated force and rhythm until everyone laughed. He was fond of practical jokes, even those played on him. Ledyard had the unusual habit of leaving his shirt open, instead of buttoning it up to his throat as was the fashion. One frosty morning Eleazar Wheelock, Jr. took advantage of this habit. As his brother James Wheelock remembered, Eleazar "unobserved by

Ledyard took a cold frosty iron wedge & ran it down his back, between the shirt & skin—at which Ledyard screamed out in a loud voice, "come come, Wheelock, is the D[evi]l in you?"

Eager to add extracurricular activities to the schedule, Ledyard, along with two other students, composed a whimsical petition to Wheelock: "We consider our Well beloved Dartmouth as in her Infancy & from the nature of her Character & the general disposition of her inhabitants envy'd by many . . . & so being we are desirous, (having Taken into consideration our Sister Cambridge & Jersy & Their serveral approved practices—as well as what they have done in this particular) of having liberty allowed us by our Worthy & very dear President to spend certain Leisure hours alloted to us for the relaxation of our mind,—in such sort as, stepping the Minuet & Learning To use the sword." Wheelock deigned not to reply to the sassy request.

Using his bolts of calico, Ledyard directed the first play at Dartmouth, Joseph Addison's *Cato*, the blank verse tragedy about the failed attempt of a selfless Roman statesman to resist the tyranny of Julius Caesar. It was a popular play at the time—George Washington's favorite—and five years later Continental Army soldiers would perform it at Valley Forge. Ledyard made costumes and curtains and one afternoon turned Commons Hall into the governor's palace in Utica. He played the part of old Syphax, the Nubian prince, and wore a long, gray beard, much to the amusement of his classmates.

Suffering from a case of cabin fever, or perhaps hoping to avoid the epidemic of measles afflicting the college, Ledyard organized a midwinter backpacking expedition. With the permission of Wheelock, he persuaded a dozen men to join him. One afternoon they marched out of Commons Hall to the east toward Velvet Rocks. Hiking in pairs, they tromped through knee-high snow on what would become the Appalachian Trail. Towards sunset they reached the summit and built a fire. After a cold supper they went to bed. No one except Ledyard, it seemed, got any sleep. They returned by the same trail and reached the campus at noon, "all of us," James Wheelock wrote, "unless it might be Ledyard, well satisfied not to take such another jaunt."

His Dartmouth colleagues found Ledyard amusing, inspiring and preternaturally strange. He was older than most of the other students but not necessarily more mature. "He was gentlemanly, & had an independence & singularity in his manners, his dress, & appearance that commanded the particular notice & attention of his fellow students," wrote James Wheelock, adding that "he was too restless to be long in any one place." Ledyard was a bit of a dandy. He wore white linen trousers and Turkish pantaloons that, according to Ebenezer Avery, his tailor in Groton, he ordered cut in an unusual style, bellowing out at the leg but "snug withal" at the hips. He rang up a bill of £7 ($1,000 in 2005) for frivolous items at the tuck shop: a one-shilling chocolate cake, a ninepence skein of silk and a five-shilling, fourpence two-yard bolt of camlet, a rich camel-hair and silk fabric. He frequented the taverns in the area, especially John Payne's, a notorious establishment at the northern end of the green. Nathaniel Adams, class of 1775, said, "His manners were singular." His roommate Oliver Wolcott was even more blunt. He told Jared Sparks that "Mr. Ledyard was a Locomotive Machine."

Trains are meant to move, and at some point late in his freshman year the Ledyard Locomotive began to rumble out of Hanover. The catalyst was a financial misunderstanding. In January 1773, when Wheelock asked for more tuition payments, Ledyard told him that his uncle Thomas Seymour would be paying his bills. Wheelock immediately wrote to Seymour asking for money: "When I was last at Hartford and discoursed with you of John Ledyards coming into this school, I told you I could not take him on Charity. You told me he had something then in his Hands particularly a Horse, and that there was a legacy left him which was (as I understood) coming to him soon, upon which it was concluded that I was safe in letting him go on for the present. You told me you would talk with those concerned and write me what I might depend upon accordingly." Wheelock added that if the legacy was not there, he "supposed you have seen some good prospects for him or you would not thus neglect to advise in the affair."

In March, frustrated at the delay, Wheelock sent a friend with power of attorney to Connecticut to collect the money. Later that month Thomas Seymour finally replied to Wheelock. He explained that while on his long autumn vacation Ledyard had secretly obtained his legacy and spent it all. Wheelock wrote a testy reply five weeks later, blaming Seymour as much as Ledyard for the sudden loss of his small patrimony.

I am far, very far, from thinking y° clear of blame . . . & yᵗ y° shod let him run such lengths intirely without my knowledge is indeed wᵗ I canᵗ accoᵗ for. . . . And indeed Sir had y° faithfully done wᵗ I expected & joinᵈ yʳ Ends with mine I don't yet conclude we might not have effected so great a good as the humbling of that youth, & fittᵍ him for usefulness in yᵉ world—but as he Secretly got his Legacy into his own Hands to waste as his Pride & Extravagant Humor dictated, & all out of my Sight and without my knowledge, it was not possible for me to restrain him.

Three times in the letter, Wheelock said he had tried and failed to save young Ledyard from total ruin.

Eleazar Wheelock and John Ledyard never got along. Ledyard called him "the Sanguine Divine." Wheelock, out of loyalty "and Respect to the Family of my deceased Friend his Grandfather," had initially pinned some hope on Ledyard. Soon after Ledyard matriculated, Wheelock told Seymour that the young man had "been pritty steady, & bids fair to make a good scholar." Wheelock was pleased to receive a sober letter from Ledyard and nine other students asking for a prayer of thanksgiving after Lewis Vincent, a Huron student at Dartmouth, had courageously plunged thirty feet to rescue a professor's little daughter who had accidentally fallen down the college well. Yet, with his "Extravagant Humor," Ledyard exasperated the college president. He requested dancing and fencing lessons, blew the conch shell in a disrespectful manner, swore out loud, put on plays and led midwinter camping trips. Ledyard and a half dozen other classmates wrote a cheeky letter to Wheelock on New Year's Day 1773, thanking him for being "a wise President and able Representative of us in evʳʸ scene, to our great tranquility, & prosperity." The L of Ledyard's signature had a particularly large flourish.

Once the news of the spent legacy reached him, Wheelock called Ledyard into his smoky office in the attic of his home and played his trump card. He informed Ledyard that he would not admit him to the church in Hanover and ordain him, telling him that it would "dishonor the profession." This blocked Ledyard's career as a missionary. He tried to make amends. He offered Wheelock a bill of sale for a horse he owned in Hartford and on 20 April paid a portion of his tuition and room & board. If he had wanted to stay, he could have easily paid back the rest by tutoring the sub-freshman, working in the college grist mill or even babysitting the Indian children on campus. But, as his classmate John Sherburne said years later, "Ledyard's high unbending spirit could not brook the authority, which the Pres' attempted to exercise over him." Ledyard wanted to go.

In late April Ledyard selected one of the pine trees, felled by Wheelock's ever-energetic team of loggers and left lying next to its stump along the bank of the Connecticut, and hollowed out a dugout canoe. It took many weeks and great skill to make a birch bark canoe, the most common boat among Native Americans in New England, but crafting a dugout canoe, on the other hand, took much less time. (The men on the Lewis & Clark expedition, for example, spent just four days, including an interruption to chase Crow horse thieves, to dig out two twenty-eight-foot cottonwood canoes.) Ledyard was helped by many of his classmates "for the frolick's sake," remembered James Wheelock. Once the blade of Ledyard's axe bounced off the wood and sliced into his leg, "of which he was so lame for several days," wrote Wheelock, "as to occasion a suspension of his enterprize."

One day in early May, Ledyard launched his argosy. His classmates, who had kept the work a secret from Eleazar Wheelock, provisioned him with smoked meat, bread, cheese, tobacco, candles and a big bearskin. Ledyard in return donated all of his books to them, except for a Bible and a copy of Ovid. There was no final confrontation with Wheelock, who was not in Hanover when his most famous student departed.

Ledyard put in and paddled south. As he passed Titcomb Island, Hanover fell away and he was alone. What might have started as a lark was now a dangerous expedition. The Connecticut River, the longest in New England, runs from the Canadian border to Long Island Sound. When Ledyard put in his dugout canoe, there had never been a recorded running of it. Yet this journey was not completely foolhardy. Besides having lived on its banks for many years, Ledyard had seen sections of the river while traveling from Hartford, so he knew some of its hazards and some of the villages along the way. After he paddled the first thirty-five miles to Fort No. 4, he was more or less back in European civilization. The river was never empty. Indians still plied their canoes on its waters and white settlers floated timber down to saw mills. The first bridge across the Connecticut was not built until 1785, in Bellows Falls, so Ledyard passed many a ferry boat shuttling people and goods from one bank to another.

Still, for a young man without any long-distance canoeing experience, Ledyard had taken a giant leap of faith in attempting to run the Connecticut. It was a beautiful cruise. He coasted under the toothy shadow of Mount Ascutney and through the snake-like ox-bow near Northampton. With the curling mist at dawn and the deep green reflections of tree branches, the surface of the water constantly varied. But behind the beauty—and the ever-present swarm of mosquitoes—were real risks. With no map or guide, Ledyard had to vigilantly read the river below, looking for hidden rocks and fallen trees and listening for upcoming rapids. Despite a crude shelter of willow branches in the stern of the canoe, he was exposed to the elements. The river water, especially on the first few days of his journey, was still full of snow melt and very cold. If he tipped over, especially during a storm, he might become hypothermic and die.

Years later he laughed about his canoe trip down the Connecticut, but at the time he almost did not make it. There were a number of significant rapids on the Connecticut, especially at Hartland and Turner's Falls, that boosted by spring freshets were wild and unpredictable. No one in an unwieldy dugout would normally try to canoe them, yet Ledyard managed either to careen through them or to portage them in time. But at Bellows Falls he lost control. Bellows Falls was the greatest waterfall on the entire river, with a fifty-foot drop onto craggy rocks. It was impossible to run. Ledyard did not decipher the danger early enough and panicked when he heard the telltale roar of the oncoming falls. In his hurry to reach the shore, his canoe capsized. Villagers saw him flailing in the river as he and his canoe hurtled towards the falls. They rushed into the water and pulled him and his canoe to safety. He lost most of his provisions and, if only momentarily, his dignity. After drying out, he portaged the falls and continued on his way.

After a week of such drama, he paddled into Hartford, canoeing up the Little River to his grandfather's old farm. His cousin Henry remembered that day: "Nothing had been heard from him for many months, when, early one morning several persons were attracted to the shore of the river by the appearance of a canoe of unusual length coming up the river propelled by a person, who was totally concealed by a bearskin drawn close around his neck. The canoe slowly approached the shore. Nor was the person with the paddle at the stern recognized by any of the spectators, till he leaped upon a rock in the margin of the stream, threw off the bearskin, and greeted his friends in the person, and character of John Ledyard."

A year earlier he had left Hartford in elegant style, a gentleman scholar atop his sulky carriage; now he returned half-animal, with his rough-hewn canoe, soggy bits of venison and his shape-shifting bear skin.

A few weeks later Ledyard penned a seven-page letter to Eleazar Wheelock. It was a difficult letter to compose. He repeatedly crossed out and re-phrased sentences, added underlining for emphasis, inserted sentences and parenthetical statements and, after sealing it, reopened it to make more alterations. "When I set down to write, I confess I know not where to begin or where to end, or what to say," he began. He was still burning with anger from two of Wheelock's letters sent to his uncle Thomas. He accused the reverend of violating his position as a man of God by harshly condemning an errant youth while preaching kindness, benevolence and charity. Referring to some of Wheelock's more vehement accusations, Ledyard asked what his own child or grandchild would think when he came across Wheelock's letters: "You surely are very sensible S^r that they would think that I was one of the most openly vile, far-spent Volunteers of Hell." He called Wheelock "very ill natured, very unkind" for scolding him about his extravagant "Coat & breeches." He spent more than a page haranguing Wheelock for his refusal to ordain him. "I was shut out . . . I was thrust back" he wrote. "This one affair Rev^d S^r with the consequences shocked me more, & did me more real Damage than otherwise lay in your power to have done."

Eventually, he mentioned the cause of the rupture and his stealthy exit from the college. "You begin S^r with a surprize that my Legacy was so exhausted—Justly might you S^r, but no more so than my unfortunate self. . . . I was not aware of it, & when I saw the Letters & Acc^t, I was ever after so asham^d of my inadvertancy & so justly culpable before you S^r that I could not compose myself to come before you & answer—for my misconduct—but from that moment with such anxiety & care studied to remedy the mater, as my life was concerned & at stake." He had apparently misunderstood his grandfather's will and expected to be included in the profits from the disposing of the rest of Squire John's property. Somehow he thought he might receive more than the £60 his grandfather had willed him.

He concluded with Dartmouth's first blessing:

A few words & farewell.—So far as I know myself I came to your College under the influences of the good kind—whether you Sʳ believe it or not,— the Acquaintance I have gaind there is dearer than I can possibly express!— farewel dear Dartmᵒ—delightful repose for Innocence & true felicity—sweet society, love, & peace,—that you may flourish like the Bay tree, be like an Apple Tree in the midst of the Woods—of whose fruit I was so happy as to taste but now no more—that you may flourish in immortal green—that you may be the Sinai to this Continent & give her examples of that kind of Education that the World knows not of—that you may surmount, yea, far transcend the fondest hopes & sanguine desires of the nearest concern'ᵈ—that you may be Blessed indeed with that which is better than Corn & Wine— New Covnant increas—is certainly, tho' the weak yet constant & ardent supplication of your beloved tho' unfortunate Son., Doctʳ my heart is chaste as new fallen Snow. farewell!—ye, thro' Time & Eternity farewell! & may the God of Abraham Isaac & Jacob Bless you & yours.—I am Honᵈ & Revᵈ Sʳ Tho' sorely besett, yʳ obliged & dutifull young Servant John Ledyard.

On the back of the letter, Wheelock totted up a number of figures, apparently adding up what Ledyard still owed the college. Wheelock then endorsed it "From John Ledyard, May 23, 1773," and added below what perhaps was the most perceptive and succinct summation of John Ledyard's personality: "Saucy Enough."

His alma mater never forgot the zesty member of the class of 1776. During the ensuing years, as he catapulted from a wayward freshman into a world-renowned celebrity, Ledyard became the first Dartmouth icon. Other early graduates rose to great prominence, and two of Ledyard's classmates became members of Congress. But until the rise of Daniel Webster, class of 1801, Ledyard was the college's most famous alumni. His midwinter camping trip anticipated the Dartmouth Outing Club, and his legendary farewell letter to Wheelock gave the new college its signature color when he wrote that it would "flourish in immortal green." His relics, like those of a medieval saint, were cherished in Hanover. On the old chapel wall there was a pencil sketch of Ledyard—perhaps a self-portrait—that undergraduates enjoyed until it was whitewashed over. A fragment of the oaken keel of one of Captain Cook's ships, apparently collected by Ledyard, was a treasured memento in the college museum. "I remembered, with great clearness, the college anecdotes, which were numerous in my time, of this singular being," recalled one man who went to Dartmouth at the turn of the nineteenth century. "His genius and eccentricities, with his fine animal spirits, were topics of discussion in my day. Two of the college professors, in my time, had been intimately acquainted with him, and often spoke of him with delight, as a shrewd, restless, inquisitive, brave man, who, it was then thought, would make better traveller than divine."

In 1920 members of the Dartmouth Outing Club founded the Ledyard Canoe Club. The first activity of the new club was to reenact Ledyard's trip down the Connecticut River. In May that year fourteen men put in seven canoes at Hanover and paddled down past Hartford, two hundred and twenty miles to Old Saybrook and Long Island Sound. Called the "Ledyard Trail to the Sea" or "Trip to the Sea," it became an annual spring custom for Dartmouth undergraduates. In honor of Ledyard's exit in Hartford, recent trips have paddled through downtown Hartford in the nude.

The Ledyard shrine in Hanover was the spot where he took the pine tree, hollowed out his canoe and launched onto the Connecticut. After Ledyard's death, some students placed a fence around the stump of the tree. In time the fence deteriorated and the earth subsumed the stump. In 1859 a covered bridge connecting Hanover to Norwich was erected near the spot and named after Ledyard. (Today the bridge, in its third incarnation, is still called Ledyard Bridge.) On commencement weekend 1907, two alumni, Melvin Adams and John Aiken, placed a granite and bronze plaque for Ledyard on a boulder where the stump had been.

Robert Frost, class of 1896, left Dartmouth after his freshman year and thereafter felt a special kinship with Ledyard. In 1955 Frost started his Dartmouth commencement address by saying, "I'm one of the original members of the Outing Club—me and Ledyard. You don't know it, and I shouldn't tell it perhaps, but I go every year, once a year, to touch Ledyard's monument down there, as the patron saint of freshmen who run away."

The image of a stooped, white-haired New Englander going on a Ledyard pilgrimage to the banks of the Connecticut was something that had appeared once before. In 1839 Ebenezer Mattoon returned to Hanover for commencement and the sixty-third reunion of the class of 1776. The

Revolutionary War general was now eighty-four and blind. It was his first visit to Hanover since his senior year, and he had just one request: to once more lay his hands on the stump of the tree Ledyard used for his canoe. Mattoon said he had helped build the dugout and wanted again to commune with the spirit of his classmate. Guided by a local farmer, he slowly walked along the bank until he came to the stump. With the Connecticut quietly flowing past, the sole surviving witness to the end of John Ledyard's Dartmouth year felt the weathered remains of the tree that had carried him into the wide, wide world.

3

Before the Mast— A Sailor and a Marine

HARTFORD WAS NOW a distressingly unpleasant place for John Ledyard. His family questioned his motives for leaving college and his friends attacked his character. A Hartford neighbor reported to Eleazar Wheelock, "he seems to avoid all Company and Conversation." Depressed and beset on all sides, Ledyard pined for the happy days of his childhood. "It is to you that I will turn and for a while forget the curses of those ills I cannot shun, but by the secret raptures, of imagining myself in the presence of the youth I love," he wrote to his cousin Isaac. "How fondly do I ruminate on the pleasing, the sad imagery of times past—the hours we spent from infancy together. Shall I ever spend such hours again? Will fortune renew the pleasurable scenes? My fears dictate an unfortunate reply."

Guilty of abandoning one possible route towards becoming a minister, Ledyard tried to make amends by privately earning his ordination. He went to Preston, Connecticut, where he visited two family-friend clergymen who furnished him with letters of introduction. He crossed the Sound and surprised his mother in Southold, but he was so fired with enthusiasm for his new scheme that he stayed only one night. Armed with a third letter, from

Reverend John Storrs of Southold, Ledyard took ferries via Shelter Island to Easthampton. He lodged with Samuel Buell, the head of the Long Island synod. After a month of study under Buell, Ledyard went out to find a place as an assistant minister. "Without a moment's hesitation, wiping the sweat of care from my brow," Ledyard wrote, "I bestrided my Rosinante with a mountain of grief upon my shoulders, but a good letter in my pocket." Such an exit would become a Ledyard specialty.

He rode around Long Island like a lost fox, twisting and turning from town to town on a faint scent: Bridgetown, Southampton, Smithtown, Fireplace, Oyster Bay and finally Huntington, where he stayed with a great uncle, Reverend Ebenezer Prime, for "twelve days' feasting upon his great library." He even practiced his sermons on long walks in the woods. All to no avail, as no church would hire him. He returned to Buell. "We advised together anew," Ledyard wrote, "and it was resolved, that since I was so disappointed I should proceed with renewed vigor." Ledyard proceeded back to Preston, where the clergymen advised him to get a letter of recommendation from his Hartford minister and to write to Dartmouth "to procure a regular dismissal from the president. When we have these, we shall proceed with confidence in the face of all men and not be ashamed to introduce you anywhere." However, his unorthodox departure from Dartmouth hung like a black cloud over Ledyard's ecclesiastical career and the letters never came.

It was for the best, as Ledyard never had the patience for organized religions. Steeped in the Bible like most colonial children, Ledyard regularly referred to Old Testament figures and passages in his writings and felt simpatico with the God of Abraham, Isaac & Jacob. His was a private faith, however, unconvinced of claims of the New Testament and the public displays of religious fervor that were commonplace during the Great Awakening. He told his Aunt Elizabeth before going to Dartmouth that the crucifixion of Christ was "ungenteel Entertainment" and belittled "the tasteless repasts of—the New testament, Faith, regeneration, repentance, & whats worse than all—Humility." Fifteen years later, when his mother was leaning toward a Methodist sect that encouraged speaking in tongues, Ledyard told her: "Remember Madam, that I am ready to go out of life with this assertion, that you carry your notions of religion, to the most ridiculous & absurd lengths. May that Great and Good Being, who delights in the cheerful praises of his creatures, & who is not to be mocked by shakings, quakings, groanings, grinnings, grimaces & contortions of the Body or Mind, Bless us all."

Back in Groton, wondering what to do next, Ledyard broke away from his suffocating life as a failing divinity student and decided to travel. "I allot myself a seven year's ramble more," he wrote his cousin Isaac, "altho the past has long since wasted the means I had, and now the body becomes a substitute for Cash and pays my travelling expenses." Having churned through his legacy and exhausted his options, Ledyard did what many impoverished young men did: he went to sea.

In September 1773 John Ledyard shipped on a voyage to Europe, Africa and the West Indies. The captain was John Deshon, a respected New Londoner, a church-warden and alderman. The ship's owner was Nathaniel Shaw, Jr., New London's richest citizen, a merchant who often traded with Ledyard's uncle Peter Vandervoort. In the small town of New London, young John Ledyard was well known to Deshon and Shaw, especially with the Vandervoort connection, and a spot was available to him as he was willing to sail as a common seaman or before the mast.

When Ledyard saw the lime green peak of Lantern Hill slip beyond the horizon, he joined a floating wooden world. Ledyard's ship was a schooner. The deck was packed with horses, oxen, goats, chickens, rabbits and even cows for fresh milk and meat; while in the hold were staves, board, shingles, hoops, lumber and five hundred barrels of flour. Like a bat in a cave, he slept in a hemp hammock swaying in tight, stooped quarters below deck. Ledyard ate salt pork and salt beef (called Irish horse), and a weekly issue of two pints of peas and one pound of cheese. He never drank plain water, but instead a mixture of water and rum or brandy in what was called grog, named for the grogram breeches of Captain Edward Vernon, who in 1740 tried to stop the daily drunkenness of his sailors by diluting their daily ration of rum with water. Ledyard relieved himself into the ocean from the head, a small platform over the bowsprit. He never bathed properly, as fresh water was scarce and soap was not commonly issued to sailors. He worked in the vertiginous upper yards, battling with the topgallant and royal sails, furling and unfurling in all kinds of weather. He assisted with the weighing of the anchor, helping turn the capstan that raised the monstrous iron beast and catting it so its six-foot flukes would not strike the hull. His checked shirts, grey kersey jacket lined with red cotton and loose canvas trousers were perpetually damp with salt spray. He, like all sailors, went barefoot. With no hat or sunglasses his face grew weathered and worn by prolonged exposure to wind, water and sun; with no gloves his hands became scarred by handling ropes and cargo. The ship smelled of sweat, tar, pitch, rum, rotting cheese, dung, moldy bread, wet rope and salt water.

After a rough but quick passage of forty days, they arrived at Gibraltar and traded well. But there was a delay at the Rock, according to a story told by a Deshon nephew who was on the voyage to Jared Sparks: "There came a rumor at length, that he was among the soldiery in the barracks. A person was sent to make inquiry, who descried him in the ranks, dressed in the British uniform, armed and equipped from head to foot, and carrying himself with a martial air and attitude." Ledyard had deserted his ship and enlisted in the British Army. He told Captain Deshon that he "thought the profession of a soldier well suited to a man of honor and enterprise." Only the strenuous intervention of Deshon secured his release from a bewildered British commander. With rising tensions between Great Britain and the American colonies and the depressing history of Americans pressed against their will into the British navy, such a sophomoric stunt probably earned Ledyard a flogging from Deshon.

The ship sailed across the Mediterranean to the Barbary Coast of North Africa, where Deshon bought seventy-four mules, then returned across the Atlantic to the West Indies, landing at Dominica. "Detained so long at Gibraltar," reported Nathaniel Shaw, the ship's owner, Deshon found that "when he arrived in the West Indies, mules would not sell for cash . . . the season so far advanced." Ledyard's goofy gambit, Shaw wrote, "disappointed me very much" and Deshon had to sell the mules for credit. Deshon then sailed to Guadeloupe to load sugar and molasses and returned to New London at the end of the summer in 1774.

His sojourn on the seas over, Ledyard spent the winter in Groton. It was the last time he stayed for any length of time in the town of his childhood. He worked for his uncles in their merchant business and attended his cousin Ben's wedding in New Jersey. Matrimony also passed through his mind, as he fell in love with a Stonington woman, Rebecca Eells. The daughter of Reverend Nathaniel Eells, who was a Harvard graduate, and a friend of Eleazar Wheelock's, Rebecca was three years younger than Ledyard. They spent many happy afternoons at her house on Stonington's Hinkley Hill.

But Ledyard abandoned Groton and Rebecca Eells and headed overseas again. A decade later, living in Paris in the middle of his travels, Ledyard wrote that Rebecca Eells represented a deep loss:

> Nature, she made me a voluptuous, pensive animal, and intended for me for the tranquil scenes, of domestic life, for ease and contemplation, and a thousand other fine, soft matters, that I have thought nothing about, since I was in love, with R–E— of Stonington. What Fate intends further, I leave to Fate, but it is very certain, that there has even been a great difference between the manner of life I have actually led and that which I should have chosen, and this I do not attribute more to the irregular incidents which have alternately caressed and insulted me on my journey, than to the irregularity of my Genius.

Something deep inside impelled him to continue his "seven years' ramble."

In March 1775 Ledyard went to New York and joined a ship sailing to England. Unlike his first voyage, with a friendly captain and old neighbors for crew, Ledyard found his "situation unprofitable & unpleasant in the ship." Upon reaching Falmouth, England, he deserted. Running, as it was called, was a common event, and over 10 percent of a typical ship's crew was lost to desertion. Returning late from leave because of bad roads or weather or being arrested for a debt were such common excuses that one had to miss three full weeks of roll calls before being considered a deserter.

Accompanied by an Irishman from the ship, Ledyard walked to Bristol to find Ledyard relatives. A large city of nearly one hundred thousand, Bristol was a center of shipping and the locus of England's slave trade. His grandfather Squire John had left Bristol in the 1720s, and in the intervening years there had been little communication between the two branches of Ledyards. He spied a carriage adorned with the Ledyard family crest and asked the coachman where the owner lived. Going to the house, he talked to the owner's son, who said he never knew there was an American branch of Ledyards. Indignant at the accusation of being an imposter, Ledyard stormed out his cousin's home, declaring that they were not true Ledyards.

A few hours later a note came to his lodgings from the father of the cousin inviting him to come to his house, but stubborn pride prevented Ledyard from accepting.

In Bristol, Ledyard's luck changed for the worse, and he found himself a member of the British army. He may have joined of his own volition. In Gibraltar he evinced a leaning towards the military life, and in a 1781 letter he wrote that he "entered the Army." Perhaps he was pressed. In 1783 he said in a third-person letter to the Connecticut assembly that "he was however so unfortunate then as to be apprehended by a kind of Police in that city who obliged him either to ship himself for the coast of Guinea or to enter the British Army. Your Memorialist, young, inexperienced & destitute of friends, chose the latter as the least of two evils." A state-sanctioned method of recruitment, the press-gang swooped through cities, arresting men at saloons, coffeehouses and even jails. (It was so common that on naval enlistment papers, there was a column for "Whence and whether Press or not.") Lexington and Concord had occurred while Ledyard was at sea, and the British military, now at war with America, dispatched press gangs around the country.

Sent to Plymouth, Ledyard, according to his 1783 letter to the assembly, "was ordered to Boston in New England: to this your memorialist objected being a native of that country & desired he might be appointed to some other duty, which ultimately was granted." In the 1780s, after the American Revolution was completed, Ledyard spoke often of his loyalty and love for the United States. But one of the little-known facts about the Revolution was that in the beginning a majority of Americans favored a negotiated solution: it has often been suggested that one third of America was Tory, one third was neutral and one third was in favor of independence. It appeared that Ledyard leaned towards the first or second category. After all, not too many ardent, twenty-three-year-old Sons of Liberty shipped out to England in the spring of 1775.

On 15 July 1775, John Ledyard, permitted to switch from the British army to the navy, enlisted in the Twenty-fourth Company of Marines, Plymouth Division. The marines, officially formed during the Seven Years' War, were a unique branch of the Royal Navy. They were on a separate muster list and received the same pay as British army soldiers on land (thirty shillings a month, as opposed to an able seaman's twenty-four). On shore they were expected to help in the dockyards. At sea they slept and ate in separate quarters from the seamen. Their primary duty was to suppress mutinies, which meant they stood on guard near the captain's cabin and at the entrance to the officer's quarterdeck. Like sailors, marines wore slops, unless they were presenting themselves for Sunday inspections on the quarterdeck, when they donned spiffy red coats, white waistcoats, black stockings and polished boots. They seldom went aloft and more or less whiled away the hours on guard duty until the ship landed. One key job was playing instruments, and marines supplied the ship's band: fife, drums, violin, French horn and bagpipes if a Scot was in the contingent.

For a year, the peripatetic Ledyard chafed within the stone barracks at Plymouth Dock. He never spoke about this interlude—"matters continued thus" was the most he ever wrote about it—but his wandering spirit never acclimated to the monotony of roll calls, drills and marches of naval life. If studying at Dartmouth seemed constricting, Plymouth Dock, with its dry docks, rope houses and blacksmith shops was almost a jail.

In February 1776, the Board of Admiralty in London commissioned two ships for a voyage of discovery led by Captain James Cook. The ships would need a sizeable contingent of marines. Suddenly Ledyard had a chance to escape. He maneuvered his way into receiving the assignment: "The equipment for discovery came round from London to Plymouth & your memorialist, esteeming this a favorable conjuncture to free himself forever from coming to America as her enemy & prompted also by curiousity & disinterested enterprise, embarked in that expedition." This was not a particularly plum job. On the first Cook expedition, more than a quarter of the crew died; on the second 15 percent did not return. Men fell off the ship in storms and drowned, froze to death in Patagonia and were killed and eaten by Maori in New Zealand. Those who did not die suffered scurvy and frostbite and long periods of privation. Desertions plagued the admiralty throughout the spring of 1776 as more than fifty men signed up for the voyage and then fled. Still, for Ledyard this was a perfect opportunity and he grasped it.

On 26 June 1776, a sloop named the *Discovery* sailed into Plymouth harbor from London. Four days later the *Resolution* joined it at anchor. The ships were Whitby cats, stumpy, shallow-drafting sloops built to carry coal through the rough North Sea to London and perfect for sailing along shallow shores. (Three-masted ships were classed as sloops because they had guns on their upper deck only.) Five days later, while the ships' crew hoisted barrels of water and port wine into the hold, William Bligh, the master of the *Resolution*, wrote "John Ledyard, Corp¹," in the *Resolution*'s muster book, and Ledyard officially boarded the ship.

The *Resolution* had a complement of one hundred and twelve men; the *Discovery* seventy. The officers had tremendous leadership abilities, yet distinct personalities. Ledyard's closest friend among the officers was Lieutenant John Gore, the oldest man on the voyage besides Cook and a veteran of three previous circumnavigations. Lieutenant James King had entered the navy at age twelve and like Cook cut his sailing teeth in Newfoundland. Lieutenant John Williamson was an Irishman with a temper to match Cook's; he was court-martialed in 1797. Another officer with a checkered future was the ship's master, William Bligh, a precocious chart-maker and navigator, just twenty-one and years away from the mutiny on his ship the *Bounty*. There were a dozen midshipmen, young gentlemen in training to become lieutenants, including James Trevenen, who later died fighting as a captain in the Russian navy; Richard Hergest, who was killed in Hawaii in 1792; and John Watts, who revisited Tahiti in 1788 while sailing home from Australia. Two of the *Discovery*'s midshipmen were destined for fame: Edward Riou, who died at Copenhagen under Nelson's command, and George Vancouver, who returned to the northwest coast of America on an epic journey in the 1790s. The *Resolution*'s surgeon was William Anderson, an autodidact Scot; his mate was David Samwell, a Welshman who had an obsessive interest in writing about and sleeping with native women. "The people," as the able seaman and marines were called, were the usual rabble of twenty-year-olds. An exception was William Watman, a marine turned able seaman, who at forty-four had already retired before returning for one final voyage. Ledyard's boss, the only marine officer, was Lieutenant Molesworth Phillips, an aristocratic Irishman who married the sister of James Burney, the *Discovery*'s first lieutenant, and was jailed in France for twelve years during the Napoleonic War. Second in command was Samuel Gibson, who had sailed as a marine private on the first voyage and a corporal on the second, and was renowned for his knowledge of Polynesian languages. James Thomas was the other corporal besides Ledyard on the *Resolution,* and there were fifteen privates and a young drummer. All but Phillips came from the Plymouth division of the marines, and two hailed from Ledyard's own company. Five of the *Resolution*'s twenty marines would not survive the voyage.

The ships were a microcosm of the European sailing world, and a refreshingly cosmopolitan mix greeted John Ledyard. Men came from Inverness, Limerick, Bermuda and Germany. John Webber, the expedition's official artist, was Swiss. Seven men besides Ledyard were listed as American in the muster book. On the *Resolution*, Gore was from Virginia; William Ewin, the boatswain, was from Pennsylvania; Benjamin Whitton, an able seaman, was from Boston; George Stewart, also an able seaman, was from Charleston; and quartermaster John Davis was from "America." On the *Discovery*, Nathaniel Portlock, a master's mate, and Simeon Woodruff, an able seaman, were also from "America." All these men considered themselves British—Gore, for example, had not been in America for over twenty years—and all stayed in England after the voyage. The only exception was Woodruff, who returned to America, sailed as an officer on the *Columbia*—the first U.S. ship to circumnavigate the world—and retired to Connecticut.

The last few days before leaving were riven with excitement. After a year of stasis, Ledyard was moving again. Like everyone else he received two months' advanced wages of £1 and $^1/_2$ which he spent on provisions for the voyage and perhaps more fleeting pleasures. Yet, despite the excitement, for Ledyard there was also a troubling sight. Three massive ships-of-the-line, the *Diamond*, *Ambuscade* and *Unicorn*, and sixty-two transport ships lay at anchor in the Sound, blown there by a gale on 6 July. Their black guns glistened in the sun. Eight thousand Hessian mercenaries dressed in green and yellow uniforms prowled the decks. War horses stomped in stalls. African drummers sat on the bowsprits and tattooed an ominous, thumping beat. The fleet was bound for the city of New York in the rebellious American colonies. The British Empire, which was sending Ledyard out on a voyage of discovery, was also resolutely cracking down on his countrymen.

At eight in the evening on Friday, 12 July 1776, HMS *Resolution* sailed out of Plymouth harbor. It was an auspicious date. On 12 July four years before, the ship had left Plymouth on Captain Cook's second expedition. It was also just eight days after the congress of the agitating American colonies had voted twelve to none, with one abstention, in favor of a declaration of independence. The date of departure had a particular resonance with Ledyard. Exactly twelve days after he exited Plymouth, his alma mater held its annual commencement exercises on the green in Hanover, New Hampshire. That day Dartmouth College graduated twelve men from the class of 1776. While his classmates milled amidst the throng of neighbors and friends, holding their sheepskins, toasting each other, singing songs and bidding farewell, John Ledyard had just started his career as a famous adventurer.

4

Their Native Courage— Shipping with Captain Cook

LEDYARD AND THE OTHER SAILORS on the *Resolution* weighed anchor and unfurled her sails. A breeze from the west filled the new cuts of canvas, and they luffed out in loud, smacking flaps. Into the moonless night, the ship passed out of Plymouth Sound and moored in Cawsand Bay, the favorite anchorage for ships leaving the Sound. The next morning the *Resolution* entered the English Channel and began its eighty-thousand-mile journey.

The *Resolution* sailed alone. The *Discovery* was still at anchor at Plymouth because its captain, Charles Clerke, was in jail. Clerke, at thirty-three, was the only officer to sail on all three of Captain James Cook's expeditions. Experienced as he was with circumnavigation, Clerke was slightly naive. He wrote an article for the Royal Society, claiming that there was hardly a Patagonian man under eight feet tall. He also was too ingenuous in familial matters. He had guaranteed the debts of his brother, Sir John Clerke, a captain in the Royal Navy, who had promptly sailed off to the West Indies owing a substantial amount of money. Clerke was arrested and dispatched to the King's Bench, one of London's debtor's prisons. He wrote to Lord Sandwich, to leaders in the House of Commons, and even to Sir Joseph Banks, the legendary botanist and shipmate on the first Cook voyage. Embarrassingly for him and for the Royal Navy, it was to no avail, and Clerke had to escape the prison and flee for Plymouth. "Huzza, my boys, heave away," he yelled upon arrival on 1 August and the next day, before the King's Bench officials caught up to him, the *Discovery* sailed.

By then the *Resolution* was halfway to the equator. Heading south for Cape Town, the *Resolution* ran into its first storm in the Bay of Biscay. The caulking in the decks and sides was too thin. The sail rooms were flooded, bedding was sodden and food barrels in the storerooms bobbed in seawater. Before the first two voyages, Captain Cook had been attentive to the victualing and overhauling of the ships. But this time he had not. For one, the refitting work began in the autumn of 1775 and Cook only signed on in February of 1776. He was thereafter extremely busy. He examined charts, read travel literature and histories, selected officers, sat for portraits and dined with lords and ladies. He read a paper at the Royal Society about fish poisoning in the Pacific and prepared his journal from the second voyage for publication. He also spent time with his two sons and his wife, who was pregnant for the sixth time. (She gave birth just a few weeks after he left.) Thus the corruptible men at Deptford Yard, the London naval shipyard where the *Resolution* was refitted, found themselves free to skimp, steal and shirk their duties. The cordage was second rate, the spars old, the sheathing inexpert and the caulking shoddy. By the time they passed Portugal, it was obvious the *Resolution* was in terrible shape.

Cook's lack of supervision of the Deptford yardmen would later prove fatal. At this point, it meant an early start to Cook's renowned cleaning regimen. Fewer sailors died on Cook's voyages than on similar circumnavigations in part because he was a stickler for hygiene. He did not, as many thought at the time, solve the problem of scurvy. His portable soups, marmalade of yellow carrots, worts (inspissated malt juice), and sauerkraut dishes did not supply the necessary vitamin C. But Cook did contribute to good health by a strict schedule of pumping the bilge with fresh seawater, cleaning the decks with vinegar, airing clothes and hammocks and fumigating the holds with charcoal fires. Much to the displeasure of the crew, he insisted on refilling the water casks at every opportunity to ensure fresh drinking water, and he compulsively served fresh food throughout the trip, even when it was strange and foreign.

Normally on his way south Cook would have made for Madeira, with its famous wines, but he had, in a spurt of good will, filled the *Resolution* with farmyard animals. With the leaks, he needed hay and corn from Tenerife, one of the Canary Islands, to replace his sodden stock. The *Resolution* carried just about every domesticated animal in England, all intended for Pacific ports of call. There were cattle sent from the King's own royal herd, horses, sheep, goats, pigs, rabbits, turkeys, geese, guinea fowl, chickens and ducks. The Earl of Bessborough donated a peacock and peahen. Cook's dedication to this paternalistic project would turn into an obsession and lead to great upheaval both on board his ship and at the islands designated to receive the animals. (Cook also started gardens filled with European fruit and vegetables in a half dozen Pacific nations.) Ledyard and the rest of the crew were not enthusiastic about ferrying a farm overseas. They were used to pet dogs, cats, monkeys and goats (as well as the usual population of rats), not dozens of livestock on a one-hundred-foot ship already stuffed to the rafters with eighteen months of provisions. The smell of the beasts and their effluvia, the concatenation of hoofs, bleating and braying and absurdly crowded decks littered with cages and pens made the men uncomfortable and testy. It reminded Ledyard of Noah: "thus did we resemble the ark and appear as though we were going as well to stock, as to discover a new world."

They spent three days at St. Cruz in Tenerife. A French ship moored beside them, making astronomical observations to fixing the island's latitude and longitude. Although it was relatively easy to find one's position above or below the equator, it was extremely difficult to determine one's position east or west. For centuries the riddle of longitude had been a major stumbling block for all sailing nations. In 1714 Great Britain's Parliament offered a £20,000 reward for anyone who could solve it. Only with the recent invention of seaworthy chronometers by a Yorkshire clockmaker named John Harrison was it possible to consistently and accurately locate one's position at sea. As he did on his second voyage, Cook carried a five-inch-wide "Watch machine," made by a Harrison protégé, which lay flat in a wooden box. Its Roman numerals and delicate hands gave the time at Greenwich, England.

But not perfectly. Before checking at Porto Praya in the Cape Verde Islands off the coast of Africa to look for Clerke, Cook almost sank the ship. He had miscalculated the ship's longitude, and one evening breakers off the island of Boa Vista unexpectedly hove into view. Only quick action and some luck prevented the ship from fatally foundering on rocks off the southeastern point of the island. The whole crew was again reminded of the inherent perils of eighteenth-century deep-sea sailing.

Another peril, at least for neophytes, was crossing the equator. When ships reached the line on the first of September, all hierarchy was suspended for a day and veteran sailors took over. Sailors had initiation rites for crossing all sorts of boundaries—the Arctic Circle, the Tropic of Cancer and later the International Date Line—but the most elaborate one was for crossing the equator. A celebratory rite of passage marked the entry into a topsy-turvy world, where seasons were reversed, water funneled down a sink in the opposite direction and new stars filled the heavens. That afternoon, one of the sailors became Neptunus Rex, the king of the ocean. He climbed from the bow of the ship dripping wet, carrying a wooden trident and wearing a wig. His entourage—a page with a logbook ready to record the names of those to be baptized, a barber, a mermaid, a mendicant friar, a tailor and a soot-covered judge with bottles tied around his waist—came forward and set up a mock court. Neptune sentenced each man to a ducking from the yardarm. The only way to avoid the ducking (even one's pets were potential victims) was to pay a ransom of four day's ration of rum. "We had the vile practice of ducking put in execution to afford some fun," wrote shipmaster William Bligh in a letter, "and to my great surprise most choosed to be ducked rather than pay a bottle of Rum. The ceremony was ended without any accident and made Sail." That night the crew drank, sang and danced, all now initiated into the very small circle of people who could claim to be widely traveled.

It was otherwise an easy passage to Cape Town. Dolphins played around the ship for a few days, and one night a bright meteor streaked across the sky. One fine afternoon in the middle of October, a sailor in the shrouds called out the most lovely words for a sailor, "Land, Ho" and the honey blue-green landmark of Table Mountain came into view.

Holland had founded Cape Town in 1652 as a victualling station for Dutch East India Company ships heading to the East Indies, and the intervening time had done little to damage the beauty of the Cape of Good Hope. In the warm months, a billowing tablecloth of fog crept over Table Mountain. Sharply cut mountains, filled with incredible flora, flanked the mountain, and boulder-strewn beaches lay along the littoral. The city was awash with cultures: Dutch soldiers; British merchants; Portuguese families on holiday from Mozambique; French Huguenots; Malay slaves, some of whom had been freed and lived in a colorful quarter under pointy Lion's Head; and indigenous people like the San and the Khoikhoi. "The Cape of Good-Hope is very romantic," Ledyard wrote, "and somehow majestically great by nature: the mountains that form the promontory are as rugged as lofty. They impel the imagination to wonder rather than admire the novelty. But the town and garrison at their feet display a contrast that molifies and harmonizes so as to render the whole highly finished."

Along with many of the crew, Ledyard ventured into the town and the countryside, enjoying the mild spring weather. He climbed Table Mountain. He wandered over to Groot Constantia, the vineyard on the back slopes of the mountain, and tasted their wines "so much celebrated and so seldom drank in its purity in Europe." Some officers went on a four-day field trip to the hills beyond the Cape Flats. Others rode horses. Cook, on his fourth visit to Cape Town, traveled to Stellenbosch, a picturesque village outside of town. Many of the men spent their advance pay on the city's prostitutes. The *Resolution*'s armourer William Hunt was caught counterfeiting coins, flogged and sent home on an English ship before the Dutch could hang him. At the ship's encampment near Sea Point, a brace of local rapscallions put a dog in the ship's corral that killed four sheep and scattered the rest. To recover his flock, Cook was forced into, as he wrote, "employing some of the meanest and lowest scoundrels of this place, who, to use the phrase of the person who recommended to me this method, would for a Ductatoon cut their Masters throat, burn the house over his head and bury him and the whole family in the ashes." These roughnecks recovered some of the sheep, which Cook promptly reembarked on the ship.

On the tenth of November, to the great relief of the crew, the *Discovery* entered Table Bay. It took four days to anchor, as a stiff wind blew the ship towards Robben Island. It was a desultory end to a rough voyage. Squally weather at the equator had forced the cancellation of the baptismal ducking. While fishing off the bowsprit early one evening, Ledyard's counterpart corporal of marines, George Harrison, lurched off and fell. The *Discovery* hove to and the crew launched boats. They picked up his Dutch cap at the stern of the ship, but never saw him again.

The reunited ships sailed out of Table Bay twenty days later. The *Resolution* was still in precarious shape. "If I return in the next Resolution the next Trip I may Safely Venture in a Ship Built of Ginger Bread," John Gore, one of the officers, wrote in a letter home to England. Behind them was Cape Town, the last place of European inhabitation the sailors would see for three years.

Instead of heading directly east into the Indian Ocean, Cook steered south. Intent on clearing up one final, niggling detail from his first two expeditions, he wanted to find three groups of tiny islands: Prince Edward Islands, Iles Crozet and Iles Kerguelen.

Before Captain James Cook, the history of European exploration in the South Seas was haphazard, founded on rumors and focused on treasure. Ferdinand Magellan, the first European to sail into the Pacific, started with five ships and two hundred and thirty-seven men; only one ship and eighteen men—minus Magellan, who was killed on a beach in the Philippines—made it back to Seville. Sailing from Peru, the Spanish located the Solomons in 1567, but without being able to accurately calculate longitude, they could not find them again for the next two hundred years. Instead, they grooved an annual trading route between Acapulco and Manila and claimed the rest of the Pacific as Spanish. Britain's Francis Drake sailed up the western coast of the Americas and perhaps stopped at San Francisco. But his voyage was mostly mercenary—he raided Valparaiso and took a silver-laden Spanish galleon off of Peru. Queen Elizabeth returned much of the stolen treasure and never published his report. The Dutch East India Company sent out two men: Abel Janszoon Tasman, who circumnavigated Australia but did not know it, and Jacob Roggeveen, who found Easter Island but lost a ship, had ten of his men killed in the Tuamotus Islands, and was sued and imprisoned by his backers upon return. The pirate-turned-travel-writer William Dampier saw the northern coast of Australia and New Guinea before his ship foundered off Ascencion Island; he got court-martialed and fined his entire promised pay. George Anson circumnavigated the globe for the British, in the process losing five of his six ships and over fourteen hundred men, many of whom had been pressed into service. The British public considered the voyage a re-sounding success, though, since Anson captured an Acapulco-bound Spanish ship laden with more than a million gold coins.

The race for the Pacific accelerated in the 1760s because of a growing obsession with the blank space at the bottom of the map of the Pacific. Europeans had long imagined a great southern continent, *terra australis incognita*. With so much landmass in the northern hemisphere, everyone from Ptolemy to Marco Polo said that surely there was some large continent in the south to balance the globe. In the 1350s John Mandeville had written *Travels and Voyages*, a medieval bestseller—it was translated into eleven languages and copied thousands of times—in which he claimed to have visited inhabited lands near the South Pole. The passing centuries did not add fact to fiction. In the 1760s Alexander Dalrymple, a leading cartographer, flatly declared that *terra australis cognita* had a population of fifty million and a width of 5,323 miles.

The admiralty in London formulated a vague scheme for finding the continent. They first sent out Jack Byron, a colleague of Anson's and the grandfather of the poet. He left in June 1764, annexed the Falklands and, ignoring his instructions, sped through the Pacific, returning in May 1766 in record time for a circumnavigation. Three months later Byron's five-hundred-ton ship, the *Dolphin*, went back out under Samuel Wallis, with Philip Carteret accompanying in the leaky *Swallow*. They lost each other at Cape Horn. Carteret discovered Pitcairn Island (later the hiding place for the *Bounty* mutineers) and went home. Wallis, struggling through the Pacific with a crew wracked with scurvy, chanced upon a land with high, craggy peaks. At first he thought he had found the great southern continent. The next day it was clear it was an island, but what an island: lush valleys, abundant food and water, beaches fringed with palm trees and beautiful licentious women. They stayed for six weeks. After the *Dolphin* anchored in the Thames in May 1768, the crew spread the word about their fantasy island. Wallis called it King George's Island, but it soon was known by its native name, Otaheite or Tahiti.

The first two Cook expeditions, 1768–1771 and 1772–1775, decisively proved there was no great southern continent. Cook crisscrossed the south

Pacific in elongated, circling tacks. He wintered at Tahiti, circumnavigated New Zealand, sailed up the eastern seaboard of Australia (where he foundered on the Great Barrier Reef), landed at Easter Island, the Marquesas, South Georgia and New Caledonia and got as far as 71 degrees south, where his ships ran into the Antarctic ice pack. Other nations, not wanting to fall behind in the race for empire, also launched expeditions. While circling New Zealand in 1770, Cook almost bumped into a French ship. What separated Cook from his predecessors and contemporaries was his charts. A methodical mapmaker, Cook returned home with reams of detailed, elegant and extremely precise charts. Proving a negative—that the great southern continent did not exist—resulted in a positive: a once-empty map now teemed with islands.

One of the last mysteries in the South Seas was three tiny groups of islands south of Africa. Cook had learned of them from Julien Crozet, a French navigator from Marion du Fresne's 1771–1772 voyage whom he had met in Cape Town in 1775 on his way home from the second voyage. Cook had also heard about Yves-Joseph de Kerguelen-Tremarec, who in 1772 had found land deep in the South Pacific that he announced was the lost continent, or at least the perfect base for "La France Australe." Cook, never keen on allowing European designs on his newly charted realm, had to take a look.

The *Resolution* and *Discovery* sailed into the Roaring Forties and were blown eastward. Fog enshrouded the ships. Ledyard and the other sailors rang bells and fired signal guns every hour to keep track of each other. Some of the animals began to die in the cold. Despite the repair work in Cape Town, the *Resolution* began to leak again. On 12 December they sighted and sailed in between Marion du Fresne's islands. Cook named them after Prince Edward, King George's fourth son and later the father of Queen Victoria. Feeling confident that Crozet's second archipelago lay to east, Cook headed southeast to find Kerguelen supposed bountiful harbor.

On Christmas Eve 1776 the fog cleared. In the midst of the antipodean summer, they had found a wintry island chain. Ledyard spotted inlets, hills lost in mist and a sea that varied from dark green to milky white, but no trees and no people. One island looked like one Kerguelen had named Rendezvous, but, wrote Cook, "I know nothing that can Rendezvous at it but fowls of the air for it is certainly inaccessible to every other animal." The following day they found other animals when they pulled into a bay they named Christmas Harbour: three kinds of noisy penguins, two types of seals, cavorting sea lions, albatrosses and petrels. Ledyard and the other men worked hard for two days, hauling the seine for fish (unsuccessfully), cutting grass for the cattle, collecting fresh water, shooting birds and clubbing seals for lamp oil. On the twenty-seventh they celebrated Christmas. Ledyard and the other men received roasted rockhopper penguin and a double ration of grog. After dinner most men went ashore. "The day was spent by the common sailors," wrote John Rickman, an officer on *Discovery*, "with as much mirth and unconcern as if safely moored in Portsmouth harbour." One sailor found a message in a bottle hanging by wire from a rock and sealed with wax. Inside a piece of parchment dated 1772 declared the island to be French. Cook flattened out the paper and wrote in Latin of their visit and resealed the bottle. The next day, after replacing the bottle, Cook ignored the message he just read and formally took possession of the island for King George III.

On the last day of 1776, the ships took their leave. Ledyard and the rest of the crew were glad. Many of the goats and three heifers had died there. After hearing of the previous expeditions, Ledyard had thought a voyage of discovery implied warm waters and sun-splashed beaches. Despite the romance of a message in a bottle, the first stop after leaving Western society was a heavy disappointment. "It is ragged, detached, and almost totally barren," Ledyard wrote of "this forlorn land."

A dozen days after sailing from Kerguelen, they "were otherwise very roughly dealt with," wrote Ledyard, by the Roaring Forties. A nighttime squall slammed into the ships. In a bewildering whirl, it toppled the *Resolution's* fore topmast and main topgallant mast, and only the ship's spiderweb of rigging prevented both masts from crashing into the sea. A whole day was spent clearing the wreckage, and Cook decided to break the journey to New Zealand with a refitting stop at Van Dieman's Land. Recently visited by Marion and by Tobias Furneaux, the captain of Cook's second-voyage consort ship, the *Adventure*, Van Dieman's Land offered a reasonable climate, food and water. They sighted the coast on 24 January 1777, and two days later anchored in Adventure Bay on Bruny Island off the southern coast of Tasmania.

Life on board the *Resolution* was relatively tedious for Ledyard and the other marines. They rotated on guard duty, officially watching the entrances to the quarterdeck and Cook's cabin and otherwise lollygagged on deck gazing at the deep blue ocean. There was an almost total lack of privacy. Sleeping quarters were tightly jammed hammocks swinging below deck and the only bathroom was the exposed tip of the ship. On a sloop with a lower deck the same number of feet in length as the number of men on board, there was no place Ledyard could go and be completely alone. It was with pleasure, then, that Ledyard and the other marines landed on the sandy, half-moon beach and set up an encampment of tents. With the faint swirl of smoke seen in the distance, Cook ordered the marines to guard the parties of men getting water and trees for the masts. A cluster of marines from the *Discovery* did not perform well in their first day of real work. They smuggled some brandy ashore and, toasting their good fortune at surviving the southern Indian Ocean, got stupendously drunk. When escorted back to their ship, five had to be hoisted on board. Cook had the men flogged and ordered that the tents be struck and the ships readied to sail.

The wind died down, however, and it was three days before they could depart. In the interim the crew demonstrated their skittishness about indigenous people. The day after the marines' drunken debacle, some men were filling casks of water at a spring when seven men of the Nuenonne nation arrived. They played with the casks with "shouts of joy and laughter," according to one sailor, Heinrich Zimmermann. Another group of Aboriginals started to playfully pull one of the ship's cutters ashore. Some of the crew, "struck with Terror & Astonishment" at the laughter in the woods and the sight of natives tugging at a cutter, ran for the boats. One man, the *Discovery's* master's mate Alexander Home, fired a musket overhead. "Every soul," wrote William Ellis, a surgeon's mate on the *Discovery*, "those with the wooders and waterers, clapped their hands upon their heads, and ran off with the greatest expedition." Cook, "very indignant over this careless act," wrote Zimmermann, sent a detachment to deliver a boar and a sow as a gift, but, assuming that the Nueonne would kill the livestock, he had them secret the livestock in the woods. While the men were on the beach, a larger group of natives "issued from the thickets like herds of deer from a forest," as John Rickman, an officer with the *Discovery*, described it. They were all completely naked. Some had hair smeared with red ochre. One elderly man had a humpback. "He was not less distinguishable by his wit and humour," Cook wrote, "which he shewed on all occasions and we regreted much that we could not understand." Cook gave him a medal struck in London in honor of the voyage.

On the thirtieth a favoring westerly breeze sprang up and the two ships sailed. Tasmania had not been an entirely successful first stop. They had sufficiently restocked their larders and casks and refitted the masts, but the sailors had not found sexually receptive women or an accessible culture to amuse them. More than any other group they encountered at length, the Aboriginals of Tasmania remained a mystery to the sailors. Some men thought they were desperately passive—they seemed to have no boats or any interest in iron or fish. Ledyard said, "they appear also to be inactive, indolent and unaffected with the least appearance of curiosity." Rickman believed their poverty stemmed from being refugees. But others noted their lack of weaponry and thought they were good tempered and peaceful. "They have few, or no wants," wrote a midshipman, "& seemed perfectly Happy."

It took a mere ten days to reach New Zealand, one of the shortest legs of the entire voyage, and yet even then there was a mishap: on the night of 6 February, George Moody, a marine on the *Discovery*, washed overboard in a storm.

On 10 February 1777, they sighted the west coast of New Zealand's south island, and on the morning of the twelfth they were safely in Cook's old anchorage at Ship Cove. This was the fourth time Cook had moored in sheltered nooks of Queen Charlotte's Sound, the passage between the north and south islands. A few canoes came out to visit, but old Maori friends refused to board the ships because they thought the *Resolution* and *Discovery* were there to seek revenge.

During the second voyage, a storm had separated the *Resolution* from the *Adventure*. In December 1774 the *Adventure* pulled into their rendezvous spot at Queen Charlotte's Sound a week after the *Resolution* had departed. It was a scrappy, confrontational three weeks. On the last day Captain Furneaux sent an armed party in the cutter to Grass Cove to gather wild greens for the kitchen. They did not return. The next morning, with the cutter still missing, Furneaux sent James Burney, a respected officer, in the launch with an armed guard and a sheet of tin to repair the cutter in case it had come to grief on a reef. As the men rowed into the cove, they saw hundreds of people, as Burney said, "thronged like a Fair." The men fired their muskets, the Maori eventually retreated and the men went ashore. "We found no boat—but instead of her—Such a shocking scene of Carnage & Barbarity as can never be mentioned or thought of, but with horror," wrote Burney in his report to Furneaux. "We remained almost stupified on this spot." Strewn across the beach and roasting in fire pits were the discarded, half-eaten pieces of their ten shipmates. They recognized one hand by a tattooed "TH" that Thomas Hill had gotten in Tahiti. The men, with the Maoris threatening to come down to the beach, hurriedly gathered up their shipmates' bodies. In the darkness and a pouring rain, they rowed back to the ship, tying the remains in a hammock with ballast and shot and throwing them overboard into the black water.

Three years later, the British ships, with Burney now first lieutenant on the *Discovery*, were back in the Sound. The Maori anticipated a bloodletting. Cook promised not to seek revenge, and, when the Europeans' evident lack of aggression bore that out, the situation in the Sound became tranquil. Ledyard helped set up the tent camp on the shore and within hours a number of families arrived there to erect temporary huts alongside them. The next day the men disembarked the livestock. "These being all feeding & diverting themselves about the Tents," wrote David Samwell, "familiarized the Savage Scene & made us almost forget that we were near the antipodes of old England among a rude & barbarous people."

Even more familiar for the Englishmen was Cook's garden. Facing Ship Cove was the island of Motuara, where in May 1773 he had created an elaborate vegetable garden. Cook and an armed party rowed to Motuara, where an elderly man with a green bough in his hand welcomed them. The man spoke and sang to the sailors and marines. Cook pressed noses with the elder. The gardens were flourishing, despite the years of inattention, and the men harvested cabbages, onions, radishes, leeks, parsley and potatoes. Cook, now fully in the guise of benevolent livestock dispenser, gave local chiefs some sheep, cattle, pigs and goats and secretly released two pairs of rabbits; both the pigs and the rabbits, for better or worse, survived, and their descendents overpopulate New Zealand today.

It was a busy time for the crew. Cook ordered the brewing of spruce beer, his favorite grog substitute: the men took the needles and bark of the rimu tree, boiled it for hours, added sugar and steeped it for a few weeks.

The men boiled seal blubber from Kerguelen for oil, dried and repacked gunpowder damaged by storms and went on grass-cutting and fishing expeditions. The blacksmiths set up their forge, and carpenters worked on the spars and masts. William Bayly, the expedition's official astronomer, made a hundred calculations of longitude in the three weeks, and he found that the ship's clock was losing three seconds a day.

Generous hosts, the Maori produced fish and curiosities like jade, abalone shells, whalebones and feathered garments for trade. Ledyard found the Maori almost the polar opposite of the passive Tasmanians: "The New-Zealanders are generally well-made, strong and robust, particularly their chiefs, who among all the savage sons of war I ever saw, are the most formidable. When a New-Zealander stands forth and brandishes his spear the subsequent idea is (and nature makes the confession) there stands a man." He added that he admired "their native courage, their great personal prowess, their ineversible intrepedity and determined fixed perserverance."

Because of such ferocity, as exhibited in the Grass Cove killings, a guard of armed marines was present for every activity, except for one. News of orgiastic couplings with willing native women was rife along the waterfronts of London and Plymouth before the third voyage, and James Burney wrote that the sailors had boarded the ships "much better provided than in any former voyage." Nails had been the usual currency, and previous ships had been literally pulled apart as sailors stole even their hammock nails to pay for sex. After three previous visits, however, the terms had changed at Queen Charlotte's Sound, and the sailors' bountiful stores of nails were useless: an adze was now the accepted form of payment.

Nails or not, some of the sailors, especially those from the second voyage, refused to be intimate with people who had killed their comrades. "Their articles of commerce were Curiosities, Fish and Women the two first always came to a good market, which the latter did not: the Seamen had taken a kind of dislike to these people and were either unwilling or affraid to associate with them," wrote Cook. "A connection with Women I allow because I cannot prevent it but never encourage . . . more men are betrayed than saved by having connection with their women, and how can it be otherwise sense all their View are selfish without the least mixture of regard or attachment whatever." One young sailor on the *Discovery* did find regard and attachment. He fell in love with the daughter of a tribal leader. When the ships prepared to set sail, they ran off together. Cook sent an armed party of marines to fetch him. They found the lovers late at night, as Ledyard said, "in a profound sleep, locked in each others arms, dreaming no doubt of love, of kingdoms, and of diadems." The man was returned to the ship and Cook did not punish him.

Humane and forgiving to a star-crossed sailor, Cook's reaction to the Grass Cove killings, however, was less understandable. Less than a week after arrival, Ledyard and other men went in five boats to Grass Cove, ostensibly to collect greens but also to revisit the scene of the killings. Upon landing, they met a pair of New Zealanders who told the sailors the story of the killings. While the sailors were eating lunch ashore, they said, a trade between a Maori and a sailor had gone awry. Something was stolen and a scuffle broke out. Jack Rowe, commanding the grass-cutters, shot the Maori. In the confusion another Maori tried to steal from the cutter, and Furneaux's black servant who manned it thrashed him with a stick. A general melee ensued. Some of the sailors were killed on the spot, others were killed later in the day (and possibly tortured), and the last to die was Furneaux's black servant.

The men reacted strongly to the report of the killings and cannibalism. They thought Furneaux's black servant, as Anderson wrote, "must certainly have felt the most horrid sensations on seeing his companions murder'd before his face without the least hopes of giving them assistance or prolonging his own fate." The men openly called for revenge, especially against Kahura, a warrior chief who publicly claimed that he had clubbed Jack Rowe to death. Kahura even proudly pointed to a scar on his arm, saying it was where Rowe slashed him with his sword. Moreover, the Maori themselves urged Cook to take revenge against Kahura. They felt that the Grass Cove attack deserved immediate retribution. Otherwise, if Cook did not avenge his men and exact *utu,* or payment, the Europeans were *taurekareka,* people without *mana,* or spiritual power. To both sides, Cook's inaction was incomprehensible.

Part of the troubled equation was the voice of the translator, Mai. A tall Raiatean warrior, Mai had known the British since 1767, when he had been wounded by a fusillade of grapeshot fired by the *Dolphin* during an initial skirmish at Tahiti. During the second voyage, he had asked Furneaux if he could sail with him back to England. Mai became an able seaman and slept in the crew's quarters. After arriving in England in July 1774, Mai was inoculated for smallpox and then paraded around London high society. He was granted an audience with King George III, whom he supposedly greeted, "How do, King Tosh?" He made his rounds of balls and house-party weekends in the country. When it got cold, he skated on the "stone water" on the Serpentine in Hyde Park. He learned how to read and write English, loved playing cards and tripled his hairdresser's bill in his second year of residence.

Having been on the *Adventure* during the Grass Cove incident and aware of the deep contempt the Maori had for men who did not exact *utu*, Mai strongly urged Cook to seek revenge. Once, Mai escorted Kahura to Cook's cabin on the ship and asked him to kill the warrior. Cook dismissed Mai and asked Webber to sketch Kahura. "I must confess," Cook wrote, "I admired his courage and was not a little pleased at the confidence he put in me. Perhaps in this he placed his whole safety, for I had always declared to those who solicited his death that I had always been a friend to them all and would continue so unless they gave me cause to act otherwise; as to what was past, I should think no more of it as it was some time sence and done when I was not there." Over the course of the three voyages, Cook spent a total of 328 days in New Zealand. He understood their culture enough to know there was contempt for his passivity, but he also savored the special relationships he had with Maori chiefs. He equally loathed misbehaving sailors under his command and thieving natives. Perhaps rightly, he blamed Rowe more than Kahura for causing the attack.

If Mai did not have his way about Kahura, he did persuade Cook to allow him to take two Maori with him as servants. Te Weherua, the son of a local chief, had slept on the *Resolution* each night it was in the harbor and wanted to leave with it. A young boy named Koa, whom Cook had met on earlier visits, also asked to come. On the day of departure, Te Weherua's mother cut her scalp with a shark's tooth and, wrote William Ellis, "with tears entreated him to remain behind, telling him, among many other powerful arguments, that we should kill and eat him." The boys were unmoved and as the ship unmoored both were in fine spirits. As they sailed through

Cook Strait and out into open ocean, though, the boys began to cry and sing doleful songs of farewell. Cook ordered red jackets to be made for them, but nothing could cheer them. For a week they sat on the anchor chains, weeping and chanting. One day, "the tumult of their mind began to subside," Cook wrote, and they stopped mourning and became another part of the extraordinary panoply of life on the *Resolution*.

5

Dancing Through Life—Polynesia

ON 25 SEPTEMBER 1513, VASCO DE BALBOA spotted a vast body of water to the west from a hill on the Isthmus of Panama. He descended to a beach, waded into the water and claimed all the lands it washed upon for the King of Spain. Three decades later, Magellan, on a deceptively calm day, called it Mar del Pacifico.

The Pacific Ocean takes up third of the earth's surface, holds half the world's free water and is larger than all the land in the world combined. There are twenty thousand islands in it. Despite its name, it has raging winds, tidal waves, innumerable reefs and shoals and epic storms that in different parts off the Pacific are called cyclones, hurricanes or typhoons. It is the roughest ocean in the world. It is where, at 180 degrees of longitude, the world's day begins.

In the age of sail, a voyage of discovery depended upon the elements. Wind and current kept ships at their mercy. Nowhere was this more evident than in the Pacific, where the prevailing winds were complex and variable. After his years of experience, Cook still did not know the patterns. He had sailed in June 1773 from New Zealand to Tahiti in ten slow but steady weeks. But in February and March the winds are unfavorable for such a course. The *Resolution* and *Discovery* drifted into a hot, calm purgatory.

Breezes came from the east, died and were then constantly shifting and always light. The sails fell slack. The temperature rose.

Ledyard and the rest of the crew, angry with Cook for not seeking revenge at Queen Charlotte's Sound, grew fidgety. They watched porpoises and dolphins flash through the blue water and caught a shark pregnant with eight babies, but mostly it was a dull time. Ledyard called it a "long and distressing passage." James King, one of the lieutenants, said there was an "appearance of general disobedience among the people." Ledyard and the sailors complained about the spruce beer, which Cook had replaced their grog with for the first month after leaving New Zealand. Some stole meat from the larder. When they would not identify the culprits, Cook put all the *Resolution*'s seamen on two-thirds rations. They refused to eat their reduced allowance, which Cook called "a very mutinous proceeding."

One morning at the end of March, the *Discovery* hoisted a Dutch ensign—the signal for land—and Ledyard saw his first Polynesian island. It was Mangaia, today in the Cook Islands, a place that Europeans had never visited before. Ledyard looked upon attractive hills covered with breadfruit and coconut trees and surf-pounding coral reefs, but his hopes of finding an undiscovered Polynesian paradise were dashed. The ships bore onto the lee shore, and as they approached hundreds of warriors gathered on the beach, gesticulating and waving their spears in a threatening manner. Two men canoed out to the ships. Mai said they had come in friendship and offered them gifts, including a shirt. One man named Mourua, his arms covered with tattoos, tied the shirt around his head like a turban and demanded a gift to the gods. Mai tossed nails, beads and red cloth into the sea. He asked Mourua about a scar on his face and whether he was a cannibal. Although indignant at the suggestion, Mourua was friendly and directed the ships to a good mooring spot. Ledyard and the men anchored and launched boats, but the combination of high surf and aggressive warriors on shore persuaded them to return to the ships. Mourua went aboard the *Resolution* and, with Ledyard and the entire crew watching, talked with Cook and Mai. Mourua tripped over a goat on the deck and asked Mai what kind of creature this was. He then swam back through the reef to the shore, where the Mangaians mobbed him, eager to know what he learned on the strangers' ship.

The *Resolution* and the *Discovery* sailed on and two days later sighted Atiu. The wind was so light it took three frustrating days before they got close enough to look for a harbor. Some islanders boarded the ships and, after examining the livestock, asked for a pair of dogs, since dogs had recently gone extinct on the island. One of the *Resolution*'s officers had two dogs, a male and a female, that were "a great nuesence" according to Cook, but the officer refused to part with his pets. Mai agreed to give away his own dog, but without a mate, it would not solve Atiu's longterm canine conundrum.

The day after leaving Atiu, they spotted Takutea, a small, uninhabited island. The men landed a boat through the rough surf, gathered some greens, coconuts and pandanus branches, and prowled through several abandoned houses and burial grounds. In one of the houses, John Gore, a lieutenant on the *Resolution*, left a hatchet and nails in silent payment for the provisions. They tried one final atoll in the Cook Islands, Manuae, an uninhabited islet Cook had found on the second voyage. Surprisingly, it was now occupied and not by particularly sociable people. They stole items from the ship and even tried to take the *Discovery*'s cutter. For the third time, the ships sailed from an inhabited island without provisions. As examples of first contact, these meetings were somewhat typical of what John Ledyard would see throughout Polynesia: rituals, awkward questions, gift-giving, petty theft and proud natives who more or less controlled the proceedings.

After six weeks of ineffective sailing, something had to be done. They were 10 degrees of longitude west of Tahiti. They could not find enough food and water in the Cook Islands for the cattle. There was a light easterly wind and an easterly swell. The *Resolution* was now short of water because of the cattle. Whenever it rained the men spread awnings and channeled rainwater into empty puncheons, but it tasted of tar. Only slightly better were the results of a newfangled distilling machine that turned saltwater into potable water. When used for cooking the distilled water turned meat black. With all the thirsty livestock, Ledyard and the crew were on two-thirds water rations. Giving up on a direct passage to Tahiti, Cook sailed west with the wind and current to the Friendly Islands, where he knew he could find provisions. The men heartily foraged at uninhabited Palmerston Island en route—where Mai taught the sailors how to fish and cook the Polynesian way—and exactly two months after leaving Queen Charlotte's Sound they spotted the eastern islands of Tonga.

Cook had spent a total of eleven days in two previous visits in the Tongan archipelago. This time he stayed eleven weeks.

It was a tumultuous, exhilarating, violent and destructive sojourn. One dynamic of the Cook voyages was his decision to relax discipline while in port. It would be hard to exactly follow navy rules and regulations, but Cook, like other British sea captains in the eighteenth century permitted much carousing amongst the sailors. The officers led by example and many of them focused more on satisfying their own desires than maintaining good discipline. For Ledyard and the men, Tonga was the first of a number of unfettered, lost-in-paradise bacchanalia that cemented the stereotype of the glorious South Seas. They got blistering drunk on their grog and the local brew known as kava. They abandoned their posts when on sentry duty. They violated Tongan traditions and practices. They mowed through gigantic piles of food. They set off fireworks, boxed and wrestled. They flogged and shot Tongans. And, above all, they engaged in orgiastic sexual promiscuity.

The visit started out quietly. They anchored off the northern coast of Nomuka. Cook, trying to control the market and keep prices down, ordered that Ledyard and the other men could not trade for food or curiosities until the ships finished provisioning. One of the local chiefs was so involved in directing the operations of provisioning the ships and so apt to make long speeches that the sailors nicknamed him Lord North, after the prime minister of Britain.

Lord North was superseded by the king of Tonga, Finau, who soon arrived in a sailing canoe. Finau was about thirty-five and had a retinue of servants, including a half dozen beautiful women. He "was one of the most graceful men I ever saw in the Pacific ocean," wrote Ledyard. "He was about 5 feet 11 inches high, fleshy but not fat, and completely formed: He was open and free in his disposition, full of vivacity, enterprizing and bold, expert in all the acquirements of his country, particularly in their art of navigation. . . possessed of uncommon strength and agility; he was besides extremely handsome. . . his active soul was ever on the wing." Lord North introduced him and listed 153 islands under Finau's control. Finau became the guide for the ships. He dined every day with Cook, bringing a fish and coconut milk soup that Cook, ever the aficionado of native food, savored so much he had the *Resolution*'s cook try to replicate it.

Less than two weeks after their arrival, the mariners had eaten their way through Nomuka's food supply, Finau's fish soup and all, and Finau suggested they head north to the Ha'apai group of islands. Finau led the way in his sailing canoe, indicating the depth of water and the correct passage through reefs. Once Finau astonished the men when he effortlessly swan-dived off the deck of the *Discovery* while it was under full sail.

They coasted past Tofua, a small island with a smoking volcano, and landed at Lifuka. Here the Tongans put on a festival called a *heiva*. Finau and Lord North gave masters-of-ceremonies speeches, interpreted by Mai, to the mariners and presented mountainous heaps of the island's largesse—yams, breadfruit, plantains, coconuts, sugarcane, pigs, turtles and chickens—that took four fully-laden boats to carry out to the ships. For a crowd of a couple of thousand natives, Tongan men performed boxing, wrestling and club-fighting matches. One was a contest of two women avidly punching each other; a midshipman, his sense of chivalry offended, tried to it break up, much to the islanders' amusement. More laughter was heard when some of the sailors challenged the Tongans to wrestle and box. The Tongans easily defeated the sailors except when they, as good hosts, let the visitors win. A hundred Tongans did a paddle dance, with two hollow log drums. "It was the opinion of every one of us that such a performance would have met with universal applause on a European theatre," Cook wrote. One night there was what would eventually become a clichéd Polynesian scene, but for these men it had no historical antecedent. In a torchlit grove, with palm trees lightly waving in the breeze, Polynesian women danced. They wore red hibiscus garlands on their heads and coconut oil on their bronzed, half-naked bodies. They clapped their hands, stamped their feet, pounded bamboo sticks into the earth and gyrated their hips as they sang.

In return for these exotic entertainments, Cook ordered the marines to go through their drill. Led by Ledyard, the men marched along the beach and fired volleys. "Our soldiers were by no means examples of the best discipline," commented William Anderson, the *Resolution*'s surgeon. When they fired at a canoe set up as a target, embarrassingly only one musketball hit its mark. "In order to give them a better opinion of English amusements,"

Cook wrote, the sailors set off fireworks that night. A water rocket, fired into the sea, rose up from the water and exploded, followed by flower-pots, roses and fire-snake fireworks. The show, wrote James King, "made us perfectly satisfied that we had gaind a compleat victory in their own minds. Sky & water rockets were what affect'd them most, the water rocket exercis'd their inquisitive faculties, for they could not conceive how fire should burn under water. Mai who was always very ready to magnify our country, told them, they might now see how easy it was for us to destroy not only the earth, but the water & the Sky; & some of our sailors were seriously perswading their hearers, that by means of the sky rockets we had made stars."

Another king of Tonga arrived. Paulaho was the Tu'i Tonga, the sacred chief descended from the gods and the leader of the nation. Finau, it turned out, was the Tu'i Ha'atakalaua, who ruled on secular matters. The rulers had different areas of power, some of their authority was simply ceremonial, and each was outranked by his fathers' sisters, through whom sacred status was passed in Tonga. This political, cultural and religious system bewildered Ledyard and the other sailors, who had handled the switch of loyalties from Lord North to Finau with ease but were more skeptical of Paulaho's elevation. This was in part because Paulaho, wrote Ledyard, was twenty years older than Finau, shorter, less spirited and "excessive fat and corpulent." But the Tongans regarded Paulaho as superior to Finau, who, visibly disappointed when he arrived, bowed his head and touched the sole of Paulaho's foot. When Cook invited him into his cabin to dine, Paulaho's attendants asked that no one walk on the deck above the cabin, for it would be very *tapu* (taboo) to have someone higher than the king.

With Paulaho and Finau leading the way in their sleek sailing canoes, each carrying four dozen people and luggage and easily outdistancing the Europeans, the *Resolution* and *Discovery* inched their way south. After a three-day refueling stop in Nomuka, they continued to Tongatapu. The seat of the kings, Tongatapu boasted fertile, fenced plantations, good roads, many graveyards and artificial observation mounds. For a month, the sailors reveled in the Tongan way of life. Ledyard and the marines set up a large tent encampment for the astronomical observatory and livestock. Some of the sailors stayed there, but others wandered further afield. Paulaho gave Cook a "snug, commodious house . . . in a thick, embowring shade," wrote Ledyard. The officers and Mai slept in other nearby homes.

Except for the time he was on guard duty, Ledyard had little work to do. He talked with Tongan canoe builders, admiring the intricate designs inlaid with mother of pearl and tortoise shells. Once he led the marines through another fumbling drill, accompanied by the ship's band. It again failed to impress and again they sent up fireworks as a result. Ledyard exchanged names with a Tongan, a ritual formalization of deep friendship that joined him to a family. Through his family, Ledyard paired off with at least one Tongan woman. The islanders' attitude toward sex startled even the most jaded sailors. Women danced naked on the ships and would make love in semipublic places. The going rate for a night was an axe or a shirt.

One moonlit evening near the beginning of the stay in Tongatapu, Ledyard, on guard duty, had a conversation with Paulaho, who invited the young marine to his house. Sitting on mats placed on the grass-covered floor, they ate a meal of baked yams and fish rolled in plantain leaves. Ledyard, at ease with the great king, called for one of his servants to fetch him some of the salt he kept for seasoning at his tent. After the meal, a "fine young girl about 17 years of age" came in, kissed Paulaho's big toe and gave him a massage. It lasted for almost an hour and during it a person outside the hut played the flute. "I must confess my heart suggested other matters," wrote Ledyard. "Both the novelty of it and the situation I was in respecting a variety of objects and sentiments left me in a kind of listless reverie." He then added:

> It is true said I, rising from my reverie and walking out into the middle of the green in the full moon shine, where I could extend my prospects and where the sounds that proceeded from the circumventulating flutes would more regularly pass the ear.—It is true, that of all the animals from the polypus to man, the latter is the most happy and the most wretched, dancing through life between these two extremes, he sticks his head among the stars, or his nose in the earth, or suspended by a cobweb in some middle altitude he hangs like a being indigenous to no sphere or unfit for any, or like these Indians he is happy because he is insensible of it or takes no pain to be so.

His heart suggesting other matters, Ledyard made love to Tongan women and contracted a venereal disease. William Anderson, the *Resolution*'s doctor, treated him at a cost of fifteen shillings. There were four types of the "Venereals" or "distemper" that afflicted the sailors: lymphogranu-loma venereum, gonorrhea, chancroid and syphilis. (Tonga already had the endemic, non-sexually transmitted disease of yaws, *Framboesia tropica*, which produced raspberry-like sores on hands, feet and faces.) They caused swelling, ulcers, lesions and, at times, tremendous pain. Gonorrhea was the chief ailment at Tonga, having been first introduced by the *Resolution* and the *Adventure* during their 1773 visit. Mercury was the cure. One method was to rub a concoction of mercury, suet and lard on the lesion until the mercury was absorbed; another was to swallow a mercury pill—three parts confection of roses, two parts mercury and one part powdered licorice root; or they took a calomel pill—two parts guaiacum resin, one part mercorous chloride and one part sulfurated antimony, combined with castor oil and ninety-proof alcohol. If the doctor did not see drooling, foul breath, slurred speech or imbalance—the symptoms of mercury poisoning—he would ad-minister more. It was hard to judge whether the disease or the cure was worse.

More than a hundred of the sailors contracted venereal disease on the third voyage. Midshipmen got it, marines got it, able seamen got it. Te We-herua, the young New Zealand man, got it. Mai got it. William Peckover, the *Discovery*'s gunner, got it and "continued to sleep with different women," wrote Cook. "His companions expostulated with him without ef-fect; till it came to Captain Clerke's knowlidge who ordered him on board" the ship. Even the doctor got it. And so did many Tongans. Upon depar-ture from Tonga, William Anderson wrote with deep revulsion and guilt about the introduction of venereal disease to Tonga:

> The injury these people have receiv'd from us by communicating this certain
> destroyer of mankind is not to be repair'd by any method whatever: for it is
> not barely depriving them of life at last that forms the greatest part of the
> misfortune, but it is by rendering them completely miserable while alive from
> their not knowing how to stop its progress, and depriving them at the same
> time of the intercourse between the sexes which most probably is a principal
> ingredient of happiness in a country where custom has laid but little restraint
> upon it . . . The man who has rob'd, murder'd and been guilty of all the Cat-
> alogue of human crimes is innocent when compared to the one who did such
> a thing knowingly. An adequate punishment may be found perhaps for a

fault, however heinous, that may be committed upon an individual, but is it in the power of man to invent tortures equal to those felt by a whole nation that the aggressor in this case might be properly repay'd? Humanity itself must startle at the thought of making a single object miserable in this respect, even for a short time, but what must be said when we reflect that in present circumstance the misery is not only entaild upon thousands who now live but must of necessity be convey'd to endless generations?

Regrets about the transmission of disease were compounded by crime. The Tongans had an entirely different attitude towards private property and were playfully inveterate thieves. Starting with a stolen hatchet on the first morning in harbor, not a day went by during the three months in which they did not try to steal. They pilfered astronomical equipment, sailing gear, pewter basins and muskets. Even chiefs had light fingers and Lord North's son was caught stealing a cat. (Clerke wrote that the Tongans took "all my Cats, which were very good ones, & as they did not take the Rats with them, of which the ship was full, I felt this proof of their Dexterity very severely.") After Cook flogged a number of chiefs, they responded in a way natural in a strict, hierarchical society: "After this we were not troubled with thieves of rank, their servants and slaves were employed in this dirty work, on which a floging made no more impression than it would have done upon the Main-mast," wrote Cook.

Clerke came up with an ingenious punishment. He shaved the heads of thieves, sending them ashore in a country where a hairless head was a massive embarrassment. Shaved heads for the Tongans became so associated with theft that they looked with suspicion upon the few men on the ship who were bald. Cook responded with less creativity. He flogged his own men when guilty of failing to stop theft. Seventeen times he flogged a crewman in Tonga, an astonishing figure considering that only sixteen floggings had occurred during the previous nine months. Tongan thieves fared worse. Cook put them in irons, bound and ransomed them for pigs, shot at them as they swam ashore, cut off their ears and increased the number of lashes well beyond the navy's legal limit of a dozen. In a spiraling descent in June, Cook seemed to lose control. He flogged one islander three dozen lashes. The next day he gave another three dozen; then four dozen to another offender; six days later he shot and wounded one islander trying to escape with goods; the next day he gave one five dozen lashes for stealing wine glasses. At the end of the month three islanders threw some stones at some men cutting wood. Cook gave one three dozen lashes, another four dozen and the last, an attendant of Paulaho's, six dozen and then cut two deep gashes in his arm.

The mood in Tonga soured into what Ledyard called "one continual broil." Tongans assaulted sailors outside of town. Some sailors lost all their clothes and limped back to the shore camp naked. David Samwell almost killed an islander when he had his pockets picked. William Bligh and John Williamson took some supplies at gunpoint when islanders refused to trade; the islanders knocked them down and stole their muskets. Cook sent all the marines from both ships to guard the shore encampment. "Scarce a day afterwards passed without some of our people being robbed and insulted on shore," wrote Burney. "Instead of asking us into their houses which they had hitherto done whenever we passed by, the doors of their plantations were shut and fastened against us. Most of the Sailing Canoes left the Bay and it was evident they began to think we had staid long enough." One day a drunk Mai squabbled at the tent encampment with a marine on duty. He hit the marine. Ledyard, seeing this, ran over and soon was "pushing him away and threatening to beat him," wrote James Burney. "Omai, who among these islands had always passed for a very great man, was so much incensed at this rebuff that he immediately left the tent, declaring his resolution to return no more to the ship." Once Mai sobered up, Cook sent him a conciliatory message and the affair was forgotten.

Tensions reached a climax when Cook gave away some of his precious livestock. He publicly distributed cows, sheep and horses to Finau, Paulaho and another chief and had Mai lecture the Tongans about the "vast trouble and expence" of bringing them from England. The next day one of the ship's goats and two turkey-cocks went missing. Cook impounded three sailing canoes and stormed ashore in a red-faced rage. He sent Ledyard and other marines to arrest Paulaho and Finau. Sitting in a house together, the two kings calmly drank kava with the marines and promised that the animals would be returned.

Outside the house armed warriors gathered, who, Ledyard wrote, "seemed determined to rescue their prince or perish in the attempt." Women began to weep, and Paulaho's grandson pleaded with the marines.

Cook invited the kings to dine on board the *Resolution*. The crowd surged as the kings walked under guard, with the marines fixing their bayonets and the drummer beating time, towards the boats. Ledyard said, "This was too much, and the terrifying parade and the pompous stile of the guard, and all the flourishes of our operations" made violence seem inevitable. Paulaho regally ordered his warriors back, assuring them that he and Finau were fine. The warriors withdrew, Ledyard noted, "with great reluctance." The kings remained on board the ship until late afternoon before Cook returned them ashore. Soon after, the goat and turkeys were returned and Cook released the canoes. This scenario of Cook storming ashore and kidnapping kings would soon backfire with deadly results.

After eleven weeks the *Resolution* and *Discovery* left Tongatapu, and after a week at 'Eua—where Cook was pleased to eat turnips he had planted on his previous visit—the sailors finally heard the magical command to make sail for Tahiti. "The crews of both ships received their orders with alacrity," wrote John Rickman, "for, though they wanted for nothing, yet they longed to be at Otaheite . . . every other place they touched at was an uncultivated garden in comparison with that little Eden."

It was a month's passage. The men caught an eight-foot shark but did not see a single bird. The wind was finally favorable, except for a storm that tore through the ships one evening at the end of July, ripping two of the *Resolution*'s sails to pieces and snapping the *Discovery*'s maintopmast.

Tahiti, which the *Resolution* sighted on 12 August 1777—exactly thirteen months after leaving Plymouth—was enchanting. The deeply forested ridges and valleys folded upon each other in undulating waves from seven-thousand-foot peaks to the sea. Rivers cataracted and poured into the sea. Coconut trees lined the beaches. Breadfruit, floppy pandanus, drooping casuarinas and hibiscus trees supplied some of the islands intense verdure. For these unwashed men, the island issued an overwhelming sweet perfume of coconut oil, sandalwood and fragrant flowers.

The ships pulled into Vaitepiha Bay on the eastern side of the island. Hundreds of villagers swam and canoed out to greet them. "The shores every where resounded with the name of Cook," wrote Rickman. "Not a child, that could lisp Toote, was silent; their acclamations filled the air." The first news for Cook, who had not been at Tahiti in three years, was that the Spanish had come. The Tahitians took Cook to a house above Vaitepiha Bay and told him an unusual story.

Three times Spanish ships, sailing from Callao, the port near Lima, had come to Tahiti. Domingo de Boenechea captained the first ship, the *Santa Maria Magdalena*, known as *el Aguila* or the Eagle. Boenechea stayed a month in late 1772. Four Tahitians took passage for Peru when the *Aguila* departed; one died in Valparaiso, another in Lima but the last two were with Boenechea when he returned in November 1774 to set up a mission station. The Spanish erected a two-room, prefabricated house, with numbered oak planks on a hillside above the bay. Boenechea died while in harbor, and his officers buried him behind the mission, near a nine-foot wooden cross carved with the name of Charles III, the king of Spain. The *Aguila* sailed home in January 1775, leaving two friars, Geronimo Clota and Narcisco Gonzalez; a servant, Francisco Perez; and a marine, Maximo Rodriguez. The mission was a disaster. The friars rarely left their house and converted no one. Even the two Tahitians who had been baptised in Lima abandoned their new faith. Rodriguez, however, made friends and took a sixteen-day hike around the island. In November 1775 the Spanish returned, collected the hapless monks and their staff and departed.

The fumbling attempt at spreading Catholicism upset Cook, and he resented the intrusion of another European power upon what he considered his private domain. After touring the mission, he angrily ripped up Boenechea's gravemarker and carved on the back the name of King George III and the dates that English ships had visited the island. Moreover, he was nonplussed about the fact that the Spanish had left some goats, dogs, black Iberian pigs, cats that had gone wild and a fine, solitary bull. After all the aggravation of ferrying Noah's Ark halfway around the world, Cook had been trumped by the Spanish.

For Ledyard and the crew the Spanish incursion was a lark. They enjoyed kicking through the remains in the mission house, finding an old gold-laced hat, a claw-footed bathtub and a mahogany chest with some Spanish documents. Mai quickly claimed the house as his home during the ships' stay in the bay. (The house survived until a 1906 tsunami hit the island.) The crew learned that the Spanish had belittled the English, telling the Tahitians that it was a small, worthless nation. The Tahitians had seen the Spanish ships, which were bigger than the Whitby cats, and had watched as the Spanish kept a strict discipline. The officers dressed in uniform and its crew slept on the ships and never allowed Tahitians to board them.

To counteract the Spanish show of power and discipline, Cook's crew set off fireworks and distributed some of the red tomtit feathers they had assiduously collected in Tonga—Tahitians prized red feathers above almost all other objects. When the sailors learned that the Spanish had kept their distance from Tahiti's beguiling women, they eagerly did the opposite. The Tahitians, wrote David Samwell, "all unanimously condemnen'd [the fl]esh-subduing Dons, for that self denial which may [be de]emed meritorious in Cells & Cloisters, but will be always looked upon with Contempt by the lovely & beautiful Nymphs of Otaheite." Wasting no time in their patriotic effort to outdo the Spanish, the sailors leapt onto the beach that first day, waved red feathers and made love with the lovely & beautiful Nymphs of Otaheite. The value of red feathers fell five-fold overnight.

After ten days, Cook sailed around to Matavai Bay, his old anchorage on the north side of the island. With its already famous black sand beach, virescent, plunging gorges and eager women, Matavai Bay was perfect after the tribulations in Tonga. There was little theft. Cook relaxed and flogged just three of his men during the stay. He got a series of massages from a group of women "till they made my bones crack and a perfect Mummy of my flesh." He planted another garden and finally discharged most of his livestock. Although he admitted that the Spanish bull was a fine specimen, he was consoled by the fact that its line would have ended had he not brought his cows. Cook gave away three cows, another bull, a horse, a mare and the rest of the sheep and "found my self lightened of a very heavy burden, the trouble and vexation that attended the bringing of these Animals thus far is hardly to be conceived."

Louis Bougainville, the French captain who visited the island in 1768, had named it La Nouvelle Cythere, the birthplace of Venus, and beyond the curvaceous sweep of the shore was a sailor's paradise. A holiday atmosphere permeated the ships' sojourn. Ledyard spent many idle hours in houses and in the hills, eating and talking with friends. He watched the Tahitians surf, a pastime the Tahitians did with great skill. The Tahitian women were incredibly attractive to the men who hailed from Western countries where pockmarked faces, dirty hair and haggard bodies were the norm. The young women had firm figures, bright white teeth, short hair (Tahitian men wore their hair long) and were fastidiously clean and sweet smelling. They even shaved their armpit hair, something no other Polynesian women did. They were playful and attentive and thoroughly uninhibited. "We wanted no coffee-houses to kill time, no Ranelaghs or Vauxhalls for evening entertainments," Rickman purred. "Ten thousand lamps, combined and ranged in the most advantageous order by the hands of the best artists, appear faint, when compared with the brilliant stars of heaven, that unite their splendor to illuminate the groves, the lawns, the streams of Oparree. In these Elysians fields, immortality alone is wanting." Proof that this was better than Eden was the fact that Tahiti did not have any snakes.

If not immortality, then at least a life-long souvenir of their visit seemed appropriate. *Tattoo* was a Tahitian word. For many centuries, people on all the continents practiced some form of body art, but it had gone into decline in Europe. Roman emperors had banned the practice, both Jews and Muslims forbade it and by the time Wallis landed at Tahiti it was all but absent from Western European society. Polynesians were experts. Using a sharp row of shark's teeth and plant dyes, they created elaborate patterns that symbolically sealed up the life force within the person. Many Tahitian men had their buttocks entirely blackened by tattoos; the women had tattoos on their arms and hands. Many visiting sailors got tattoos, some forming clubs like the "Knights of Otaheite," with membership stars tattooed on their left breast. Others got feathers tattooed on their chests, mottos on their thighs or the date of when they first sighted Tahiti on their arms. Ledyard got his hands tattooed and probably other parts of his body. Tattoos became an expected rite of nautical passage, like a ducking at the equator.

He was probably sober. Most of the men's fun occurred without the lubrication of grog. Early in the visit to Tahiti, Cook gathered the company on the quarterdeck of the *Resolution* and formally told them the purpose of the expedition: to find a northwest passage through the North American continent back to the Atlantic. The voyage might extend for four years, with two summers exploring the north, and the ships' supply of spirits would not last unless they conserved it. He proposed that the men reduce their allowance of grog to just a Saturday evening half-pint glass. With the soft breeze blowing and their new girlfriends beckoning, anything, even the reduction of their grog—"a Seaman in general would as soon part with his life, as his Grog," commented one officer in amazement—was languidly approved.

The only ferment came from talk of war. Tahiti was fighting with Moorea, a neighboring island. Cook declined to get involved, but asked for a demonstration of the Tahitian navy. This review of the sailing canoes, complete with a mock fight, included Ledyard and the marines marching on the beach with their band playing British tunes. One day an islander came to the ship and said four Spanish ships were back at Vaitepiha Bay. Maximo Rodriguez was on board and they intended to attack the English. The Tahitian said he had boarded the ship and had been given clothing by one of the commanders. The shirt and trousers, William Ellis said, "appeared to be perfectly new, which with the many protestations and assurances the man made respecting the truth of the report" sent the ships into a frenzy. Cook ordered the decks cleared for battle, the guns mounted and all women ashore, "which was a task not easily effected," wrote Rickman. Cook sent a boat around to Vaitepiha, but when it returned two days later, the ruse—perhaps a part of an internal Tahitian power struggle—was discovered.

At the end of September, the ships reluctantly weighed anchor. Cook gave the Tahitians a portrait of himself painted by Webber (which survived well into the nineteenth century). Mai exchanged his supply of red feathers for a gorgeous double sailing canoe that he dubbed the *Royal George* and outfitted with a Union Jack ensign. Dozens of other canoes, filled with the girlfriends of sailors, followed in the ships' wake, like camp followers in a medieval crusade.

The first stop on the ships' leisurely tour of the Society Islands was Moorea, an island just off Tahiti that the British had called York Island but never visited. Moorea looked like a smaller replica of Tahiti, with jagged peaks, richly vegetated, curving slopes and streams emptying into the sea.

This paradise turned out to be a sort of hell. When the sailors went ashore they saw evidence of a recent Tahitian raid: all the trees in the bay were stripped of their fruit and a nearby village had been sacked. The local chief begged for two goats. Cook felt, with only four goats left, that he had none to spare. He sent a boat to Tahiti to collect two of the goats he had donated there, enclosing red feathers as payment. Before the goats arrived, one of Cook's original four went missing. Evidently a marine goatherd had stolen some breadfruit and coconuts from a Moorean, and the goat, grazing amongst the smoldering ruins of a village, was taken in revenge. Then a second goat disappeared.

Smarting from his ineffectual measures at Tonga, Cook flew into a splenetic fury. He sent a threatening message to the chief. Soon the islander who stole the first goat returned it to Cook. Cook placed him in irons and forbade his friends from bringing him food or water. The next morning the second goat was still missing. Cook, feeling "as I could not retreat with any tolerable credet," laid waste to Moorea. In a two-pronged attack, he took three dozen armed men on land across the island, while Williamson guided three armed boats to the other side. Through the trees warriors hurled rocks at the men. Cook ordered the marines to fire at them. One warrior was killed. Ledyard and the rest of the crew went into a village and burned houses, killed dogs and hogs and decimated breadfruit plantations and a canoe-shed filled with war canoes. Not satisfied, they went down to the coast and burned some canoes and broke up others, taking the wood back to the ship. Islanders desperately filled two war canoes with stones and sunk them offshore, but Cook ordered that the canoes be raised with ropes and then destroyed.

That evening, the goat was returned to the ships. The Mooreans, showing a surprising amount of forgiveness, released unharmed an officer from the *Discovery* whom the warriors had captured when he was separated from the marauding group.

The damage to Moorea was incalculable. John Rickman, the *Discovery* lieutenant, estimated they destroyed two hundred huts. Mooreans lost their food, their homes and their transportation. Each canoe took months of work, especially the war canoes, which could fit up to a hundred paddlers and were symbols of wealth and power. The men of the *Resolution* and the *Discovery* were aghast at the violence. "When ever Capt Cook met with any Houses or Canoes, that belonged to the party (which he was informed) that had stolen the goat, he ordered them to be burnt and seemed to be very rigid in the performance of His orders, which every one executed with the greatest reluctance except Omai, who was very officious in this business and wanted to fire upon the Natives," wrote George Gilbert, a young midshipman, adding, "and all about such a trifle as a small goat." James King wrote most prophetically about the incident in his journal:

> Not being able to account for Captn Cooks precipitate proceeding in this business, I cannot think it justifiable; less destructive measures might have been adoptd & the end gain^d, whether it was simply to get what was of little value or Consequence back again or in future to deter them from thefts; I doubt whether our Ideas of propriety in punishing so many innocent people for the crimes of a few, will be ever reconcileable to any principle one can form of justice. I much fear that this event will be a very strong motive not only to these Islanders, but to the rest, to give a decided preference to the Spaniards, & that in future they may fear, but never love us.

Ledyard, having been in the guard of marines that faced the angry warriors of Tongatapu during the kidnapping crisis, condemned Cook's behavior in Tonga, calling it "disgustful." He penned a prophetic aphorism: "Perhaps no considerations will excuse the severity which he sometimes used towards the natives on these occasions, and he would perhaps have done better to have considered that the full exertion of extreme power is an argument of extreme weakness." Repulsed by the horror of Moorea three months later, he preferred to keep silent and his journal contained just a single sentence about the two weeks spent at Moorea.

Cook's obsession with livestock, which was at the root of the carnage, had an ironic coda. After the *Resolution* and *Discovery* departed, the Mooreans landed at Tahiti and killed all the animals Cook had left there.

The day after the pillaging of Moorea, the expedition slunk out of the harbor and headed to Huahine. Rats and cockroaches so dominated the holds that once they anchored in Fare Harbor, Ledyard and the men set up planks and a landing stage, hoping in vain that the rodents and bugs would merrily relocate to Huahine.

Although the attempt at volunteer repatriation failed, the *Resolution* disgorged a sizable amount of its contents. Mai decided to settle at Huahine instead of returning to his home island of Raiatea, which had been overrun by Borabora invaders. The ships' carpenters erected a house for Mai near the beach at Fare Harbor. Using local wood and parts of the canoes taken from Moorea, they quickly crafted an eight-by-six-yard house, with a ten-foot ceiling, a loft and a small basement. On a wall they carved a Latin inscription, the name of King George III and the date. The front door had a lock, which was necessary because Mai had an expensive collection of English goods: umbrellas, worsted caps, kersey jackets, linsey drawers, earrings, linen suits, pewter plates, toy models of horses, coaches and wagons, hand-organs, whipsaws, swords, muskets, fowling pieces, pistols, a twenty pound keg of gunpowder, portraits of King George III and Queen Charlotte and a suit of armor made in the Tower of London. Cook gave him most of the remaining livestock: two horses (the mare was pregnant), geese, turkeys, ducks, a boar, rabbits, two cats, a monkey, sows and a goat (also pregnant). They planted an elaborate garden, which included almonds donated by the daughters of a Cape Town officer and grapevines taken from the Spanish mission at Tahiti. After his new estate was completed, Mai hosted numerous dinners where Ledyard and other sailors mowed through Mai's wine cellar, the expedition's band played concerts and Cook sent up fireworks.

The good cheer went on until a Borabora man stole a sextant from the observatory. After Mai caught him, Cook shaved his head, flogged him and cut off one of his ears. The man in turn ravaged Mai's new garden and announced he would kill him once Cook departed. Cook had him seized a second time and put in irons. Again the ship's mood was not synchronized with Cook's, and a week later he escaped. Tom Morris, the marine guarding him, confessed he had fallen asleep and left the keys within reach. Cook, furious, had Morris flogged twelve times for three straight days and disrated William Hervey, the master's mate in charge of the watch, sending him before the mast of the *Discovery*.

Leaving Mai and the two New Zealand boys who were to stay with him (though they had thought they were going with the ship back to England) proved wrenching. Cook ordered a five-gun salute. Te Weherua stood in a canoe, quietly sobbing; Koa twice jumped out of a canoe and swam to the ship before he was restrained; and Mai, staying on board the *Resolution* as long as possible beyond the reef, burst into tears when he said farewell to Cook. He feared he would be killed after Cook left, and so they devised a way for Mai to inform Cook of his situation at the next stop, Raiatea, by sending colored beads—he apparently was not literate enough to write a note.

At Raiatea, Mai's message arrived—two white beads indicating all was well—but he also asked, via his messenger, for more axes and two more goats, since the goat Cook gave him had died in childbirth. Cook agreed to the requests and thereafter nothing more was heard from Mai. There was some ambivalence among the sailors about the effects of the four years the young Raiatean had spent in European society. Ledyard, smarting from the confrontation they had in Tonga, was less than charitable: "Omai had ever since our arrival among these isles been declining not only in our estimation but in the opinions of the natives, among whom he was envied for underserved riches and dispised for his obscure birth and impudent pretentions to rule and command, in short his ignorance and vanity were insupportable. . . . It is certainly to be lamented that Omai will never be of any service to his country from his travels, but perhaps will render them and himself too the more unhappy." Cook appreciated "his great good Nature and docile disposition. . . his gratifull heart." Rickman thought the islanders liked him only because of his "accidental riches." Bayly said many on the *Resolution* cried at the farewell.

The two New Zealanders had won universal approval from the sailors. Koa was, as Gilbert wrote, "always full of mirth and good humour and for his mimicry and other little sportive tricks, was the delight of the whole ships company." David Samwell wrote in his journal after leaving Huahine:

> If ever I felt the full force of an honest Heart Ache it was at that time. . . . [Te Weherua] was a modest sensible young fellow, he always behaved with the greatest Propriety during his Stay with us & was much esteemed by us all. [Koa] was very humorous & lively, by his many Drolleries he used to create no small Diversion on board. He was a favourite with all, & every one of the Jacks took a delight in teaching him something either in Speech or Gesture, at which he himself was eminent, and as the sagacious New Zealander perceived that he was caressed and applauded according to his proficiency in this kind of Learning, he became a diligent Student and in a short time was a perfect adept in Monkey-tricks & the witty Sayings of Wapping & St. Giles.

Through the years that followed, flickers of news about Mai and his Maori companions appeared in Europe. In 1789 Captain Bligh, arriving with the *Bounty*, visited Huahine and found that all three were dead, the house was gone and just a solitary stallion grazed on grass in the paddock. In 1808 the London Missionary Society set up a mission station at Mai's old spot, and children were taught under a shaddock tree planted by Cook. Even in the twentieth century, some of Mai's possessions—a jack-in-the-box, pieces of armour, a cutlass—turned up on the island.

Mai, the story emerged, had become the center of a conflict between Huahine and Raiatea about three years after Cook's departure. Raiatea warriors demolished his house in a skirmish and flung his gunpowder into the sand, and he died soon afterwards of a fever. With the passing of his protector, Te Weherua soon succumbed to illness, and then little Koa, the witty Sayings of Wapping & St. Giles no longer of use, lay down and died.

Desertion in the South Seas was always a problem for early Pacific expeditions. On the first Cook voyage two marines deserted in Tahiti. On this voyage there had been the short desertion in New Zealand, and now, with a long and dangerous trip in the frozen north looming, everyone talked about leaving the ships. Certainly it crossed the mind of Ledyard, who had fled Dartmouth after a year and would eventually run from the British navy. "The Natives were Constantly Inviting us to Stay Amongst them," wrote Alexander Home, the *Discovery*'s quartermaster. "Their promise was a Large Estate and A Handsome Wife and Every thing that was fine and Agreeable. . . It was not to be Wondered at that Such proposals were Listened to by many and some of good Sense too for it was by No Means Visionary Dreams of happyness but absolutely real yet the pleasure of it Seemed So Exquisite that one Could Scarcely Believe its reality."

In Raiatea the pleasure got too exquisite. Late one night John Harrison, a marine on the *Resolution*, disappeared after his guard duty ended. Two days later Cook led two armed boats to the other side of the island and found him in a house, wearing a loincloth and flowers in his hair and sitting between two women, his musket at his feet. He was put in irons and flogged twenty-four lashes. Cook brought Ledyard and the rest of the crew to the quarterdeck and harangued them. The men on the *Discovery*, however, missed the lecture, and a week later a sixteen-year-old midshipman (whose father had sailed with Byron) and a gunner's mate went off in a canoe to an island beyond Borabora. There were other hesitant attempts at desertion, and Cook began to muster the ship's company twice a day to ensure that no one else deserted. With the help of the marines, he took a Raiatean chief and his daughter and son-in-law hostage. Within an hour, Clerke wrote, "we had a most numerous Congregation of Women under the Stern, cutting their Heads with Sharks Teeth and lamenting the Fate of the Prisoners, in so melancholy a howl, as render'd the Ship whilst it lasted, which was 2 or 3 Hours, a most wretched Habitation." After a week of tension, including a failed ambush on Gore and Clerke, the islanders returned the two deserters. Cook flogged the gunner's mate twenty-four lashes and sent the midshipman before the mast.

One final stop, Borabora, was on the agenda before the ships left the South Pacific. Running short of iron, which was used for trade (most commonly for sex), Cook went to Borabora and reluctantly sought a French anchor Bougainville had lost. At Borabora the sailors said farewell to the entourage of sailing canoes filled with their paramours. They had spent ten glorious months in Polynesia, and George Gilbert spoke for the men when he wrote, "We left these Islands with the greatest regret, immaginable; as supposing all the pleasures of the voyage to be now at an end: Having nothing to expect in future but excess of cold, Hunger, and every kind of hardship, distress attending a Sea life in general, and these voyages in particular, the Idea of which render'd us quite dejected."

6

Soothed a Homesick Heart—The Search for the Northwest Passage

SEVENTEEN MONTHS OUT OF PLYMOUTH, John Ledyard finally experienced the essence of a voyage of discovery. There were no maps or charts for what lay ahead. Since 1527 the Spanish had been sailing annually from Mexico to the Philippines and had never once found land. Was it an empty ocean? In the Society Islands, Captain Cook asked islanders—men who had traversed great swathes of the Pacific in their sailing canoes and had populated islands thousands of miles apart—if they knew of any islands or people to the north. They did not.

With a shock, then, the sailors spotted an island two days after crossing the equator. It was Christmas Eve 1777. They anchored off the lee shore. In a boat William Bligh found an opening through the reef, and the sailors took the ships into a little lagoon. Like the year before, Ledyard celebrated Christmas on an uninhabited island. Unlike Kerguelen, however, Christmas Island had no water and officially was an atoll, the world's largest at three hundred thousand acres. Instead of seals, there were sharks and turtles. For sport, some of the men lashed sharks together by their tails or tied boards to their necks. "This is called spritsail yarding," joked James Trevenen, a midshipman on the *Resolution*. Turtling was a more profitable pastime. Ledyard and the crew collected more than three hundred sea turtles in the next few days and wrangled the heavy amphibians onto the ships. Three men, "invited by the mixed melody of the birds in the woods," according to Rickman, got lost on shore during a turtling excursion. The two *Discovery* men sent on the rescue mission got lost themselves and spent the night in a trackless thicket full of biting ants. The next day they reappeared on the shore blistered by the sun, half-naked and so ravaged by thirst that they had drunk turtles' blood. Cook could not resist his agricultural impulse, even on an isolated, humanless island, and planted coconuts, yams and melons.

A greater jolt came two weeks after they left Christmas Island. Thinking the wintry north was approaching, Cook had issued fearnought jackets and trousers to the crew. But on 18 January 1778, a shimmering green peak rose up on the edge of the horizon. It was another archipelago of large and richly vegetated islands filled with people. Cook named them the Sandwich Islands, after the fourth Earl of Sandwich, First Lord of the Admiralty. (He was also the man who, too busy to leave the gaming table, called for a slice of cold roast beef and cuts of bread, thus inventing his namesake food.) The natives called it Hawaii, and in the thousand years since they had reached the islands from Polynesia, they had never seen an outsider.

Off Oahu, many islanders paddled out, shouted and gesticulated at the sailors. Jem Burney handed over a small bag of nails tied to a rope and asked in Tahitian, "What is the name of your island?" Amazingly, the islanders responded in kind, and it turned out that these islands, a forty-day sail from the Society Islands, were populated by a Polynesian race. Ledyard and the other sailors, thrilled to be able to communicate, handed them gifts of trinkets, red cloth and nails. Seeing the strangers were not hostile, the paddlers dropped their supplies of stones into the water and gave them loincloths, fish and pigs in return. "I never saw Indians so much astonished at the entering a ship before," wrote Cook. "Their eyes were continually flying from object to object, the wildness of their looks and actions fully express'd their surprise and astonishment."

Ledyard went ashore at Kauai in one of three armed boats to look for an anchorage. As the men landed, animated islanders tried to lift the boats and carry them onto the beach. Lieutenant Williamson, commanding the party, shot and killed one islander during the commotion; no one told Cook until after they left Hawaii. Sailing around the island, Ledyard and the others saw a "prodigious surf" off the north shore—today a famous surfing spot. At Niihau the churning tumble of waves drove them away from land. Lieutenant Gore led a party of twenty men in a boat over the surf, and the wind and surf were so high that they were forced to spend the next two nights ashore.

Normally this would not be a problem, but, in an effort to prevent the introduction of venereal disease to this virgin land, Cook had deliberately banned women from the ships and ordered his men not to make congress with them. "This created a general murmur among the seamen," reported Rickman, "whose pleasure was centered in that kind of commerce, in the new discovered islands wherever they went." In compensation, Cook restored the daily ration of grog, which had been stopped since arriving at Tahiti half a year before.

The strict orders and the mollifying rum did not work, however, and the murmuring turned into lovemaking. The sailors disguised women as men and brought them on board, and the stranded men on Niihau took advantage of their forty-eight hours ashore. "The women on this island, besides having beautiful figures, were very complaisant, surpassing in these respects those on the other islands of the South Seas," wrote Zimmermann. One woman, according to Samwell, offered "no bar to the Performance of her Devotions at the Temple of Venus, for like the rest of her Countrywomen she scrupled not to grant every favour to our people. Tho' with no mercenary View as she would take nothing from them in return. Indeed we found all the Women of these Islands but little influenced by interested motives in their intercourse with us, as they would almost use violence to force you into their Embrace regardless whether we gave them any thing or not, and in general they were as fine Girls as any we had seen in the south Sea Islands."

The fortnight in Hawaii had been peculiar. Enormous crowds flocked to every beach they approached and prostrated themselves when Cook came ashore. Women offered sex for free. The *Resolution*'s quartermaster, Thomas Roberts, died of dropsy. Samuel Gibson, Ledyard's sergeant, almost drowned when he passed out drunk upon the gangway and fell overboard.

As soon as Europeans reached the North American continent, they began searching for a way through it. Commerce was the issue as much as geography. The merchants of London and Lisbon wanted to reduce the twelve-month journey to the riches of the Orient to a six-week dash. They dreamt of a Northwest Passage.

This will-o-the-wisp was impossible to find. Famous navigators like Sebastian Cabot, Martin Frobisher and Henry Hudson had failed to discover it. So the imagination took over. French cartographers sketched in a Mer d l'Ouest, an inland Mediterranean connected by rivers to the east. The Spanish invented the Straits of Anian, linking the Pacific to the Atlantic. Many armchair geographers argued that a Northwest Passage must exist, if only to balance the Strait of Magellan. In Venice in 1596, an old Greek pilot nicknamed Juan de Fuca told a British traveler about sailing into a huge inlet on the west coast of America. This shadowy story soon became proof of a Northwest Passage. In 1708 a London book claimed that Bartholomew de Fonte, an admiral in New Spain, had in 1640 sailed up a west coast river at 53 degrees latitude and actually bumped into a Boston fur trader.

For Great Britain the Northwest Passage became as important as calculating longitude. In 1745 the House of Commons passed the Northwest Passage Act, offering £20,000 to any British subject who "shall find out and sail through any passage by sea between Hudson's bay and the western and southern ocean of America." In 1775 Parliament revised the Act to say that the passage must lie north of 52 degrees latitude. The next year the admiralty laid down strict instructions for Cook for his third voyage: "You are very carefully to search for, and to explore, such Rivers or Inlets as may appear to be of a considerable extent and pointing towards Hudsons or Baffins Bays; and if from your own Observations, or from any information you may receive from the Natives. . . there shall appear to be a certainity, or even a probability of a Water Passage into the aforementioned Bays, or either of them, you are, in such a case to use your utmost endeavours to pass through with one or both of the Sloops." The admiralty was completely serious about the Northwest Passage. They included in the *Resolution*'s hold two small vessels ready to be assembled if the Passage proved to be too narrow or shallow for the sloops. They also sent Richard Pickersgill, a veteran of Cook's first two voyages, to Newfoundland in 1777 to meet Cook when he sailed through from the Pacific.

The admiralty's instructions were secret, for two other European powers already had colonies on the West Coast of the continent. From the west the Russian Empire had begun to spread across Alaska. Peter the Great sent the Danish captain Vitus Bering on what became two stumbling voyages of discovery. Bering died on the second one in 1741, without ever having stepped on Alaskan soil, but his consort ship briefly landed a crew for water—a German naturalist on the expedition commented that ten years of preparation resulted in ten hours of exploration. The survivors of the journey brought home nine hundred sea-otter pelts that fetched high prices in Canton. In the next decades, Russian fur traders, called *promyshlenniki,* ranged across the Aleutians, mainland Alaska and British Columbia to take advantage of this market. But the West knew little of this, since the scale of the fur-trading was small and Russia kept it confidential. Both Russian maps of the Alaskan coastline that Cook carried were almost willfully inaccurate.

Meanwhile, nervous about rumors of Russian inroads on territory they had claimed since Balboa, Spain looked north from their colony in Mexico. In the 1760s they settled San Diego, Monterey and San Francisco and then began launching expeditions north to learn where the Russians were. In 1774 Juan Perez sailed the *Santiago* into what are today Canadian waters. The next year Bruno de Hezeta took the *Santiago* out for a second voyage, with Juan y Quadra sailing the little thirty-six foot schooner *Sonora* as consort. They got separated; Hezeta found the mouth of the Columbia River and Quadra reached Alaska, but neither saw any sign of Russian inroads.

If the Russians were not considered an immediate priority for the Spanish, the English were, and the ancient rivalry between Spain and Great Britain played out over the west coast of America. News of the Perez voyage reached London in May 1776, and when the admiralty's secret instructions to Cook for his third voyage leaked out two months later, it looked like a blatant riposte. Madrid, instinctively suspicious, ordered her California posts to arrest Cook if he arrived at a port in New Spain and sent out a ship—but only in February 1779—to find him.

Luckily for Cook, when he made landfall on the North American continent, he was just a few miles north of the farthest reaches of New Spain. At daybreak on 7 March 1778, the *Resolution* and *Discovery* sighted land near what is now Coos Bay on the Oregon coast. The officers, short of meat and long on impatience with their rodent passengers—one had just eaten a hole through the *Discovery*'s quarterdeck to get at some yams—celebrated with a "fricassee of rats." The thrill of reaching the coast was tempered when a brutal westerly wind turned it into a lee shore. Cook, constantly tacking in the blow, called the first landmark he saw Cape Foul Weather. Along with Cape Town, Cape Horn and Cape Hatteras, this was one of the four worst headlands in the world, and the *Resolution* and *Discovery* had approached it in winter. The weather worsened and a hard storm with sleet and snow hammered the ships. They lost three degrees of latitude in two days. Weaving in and out of sight of land, they struggled back up the coast. On his first voyage Cook had ignored the Heads of Sydney harbor in Australia, and now again he failed to sail into one of the world's great waterways when he coasted past what he noted as a "small opening in the land" at dusk, which turned out to be the Strait of Juan de Fuca. The ships finally sighted their first serviceable harbor on the morning of 29 March.

The Mowachaht clan of the Nuu-chah-nulth nation called the place Yuquot, meaning "where the wind blows from all directions." For more than four millennia, the Mowachaht had summered at this spot, and like most places the sailors visited, the natives considered it the center of the world. The sailors called it Ship Cove in St. George's Sound on the coast of New Albion. (Perez, leading the 1774 Spanish expedition, had called it Surgidero de San Lorenzo, the Roadstead of St. Lawrence.) In time it would be named Resolution Cove, in Nootka Sound at Vancouver Island in British Columbia, Canada. Nootka was so Brobdingnagian that it was impossible for the sailors to see that it was in fact a tree-studded, fjord-indented island a couple of miles off the coast.

Ledyard knew it was North America and that he was the first American citizen to land on the west coast of the continent. He wrote in his journal that day: "Though more than two thousand miles distant from the nearest part of New-England I felt myself plainly affected: All the affectionate passions incident to natural attachments and early prejudices played round my heart, and indulged them because they were prejudices. It soothed a home-sick heart, and rendered me very tolerably happy." Ledyard immediately found that the Mowachaht reminded him of his Indian classmates at Dartmouth. "I had no sooner beheld these Americans than I set them down for the same kind of people that inhabit the opposite side of the continent."

Even more interesting was their possession of trade goods from the east coast. He noted that their wampum was identical to what was seen in New Hampshire and that their copper bracelets and iron knives probably came "from the Hudson Bay Company." Ledyard guessed that the Mowachaht were at the terminus of a vast continental trading network that extended three thousand miles east to the British and French colonies on the other coast. The Mowachaht knew about and wanted specific European-style items, a fact that could not be explained by Perez's one brief visit in 1774 (Perez, indeed, never even came ashore). In their lust for metal, the Mowachaht eventually depleted the ships' supplies. "Whole suits of cloaths were striped of every button, Bureaus &c of their furniture and Copper kettles, Tin canesters, Candle sticks, &c all went to wreck," wrote Samwell. "These people got a greater middly and variety of things from us than any other people we visited." When a group of new Indians paddled into the Sound, the Mowachaht threatened war to preserve their trading monopoly with the Europeans. John Webber, the expedition's artist, went to a house to sketch some totem poles. The owner "seemingly displeas'd," for these were religious items, screened them off with a mat and asked for payment. Webber, empty pocketed, resorted to ripping a brass button off his coat. "This instantly produced the desir'd effect, for the mat was remov'd and I left at liberty to proceed, as before. Scarcely had I seated myself and make a beginning, but he return'd & renewed his former practice, till I had disposd of my buttons, after which time I found no opposition in my further employment."

The Mowachaht, led by their savvy Chief Maquinna, exhibited real trading acumen. When they learned Cook liked wild garlic—which they did not eat themselves—they ensured a steady supply for him. The sailors were inept at catching fish, so the Indians brought the catch of the day. When a party of sailors went off to cut grass, the Mowachaht stopped them and asked for payment. In all three voyages, never once had a native demanded payment for something that grew wild. Cook heard the commotion and came to pay the owner. Later he encountered more demands from other owners. "There was not a single blad of grass that had not a separate owner," Cook wrote, "so that I very soon emptied my pockets with purchasing." Ledyard, observing this, wrote that as Cook walked away he, "with a smile mixed with admiration exclaimed, 'This is an American indeed.'" The same system would have prevailed with firewood and drinking water, but Cook was not within earshot of either the wooding or the watering parties when the Indians first approached with their demands, and the sailors simply laughed off requests for payment. The Indians tired of asking, yet later "made a Merit on necessity and frequently afterwards told us they had given us Wood and Water out of friendship." Cook eventually started calling the Mowachaht "our Landlords."

The landlords impressed Ledyard. "In their manners they resemble the other aborigines of North-America," he wrote of the Mowachaht. "They are bold and ferocious, sly and reserved, not easily provoked but revengeful. . . . Like all uncivilized men they are hospitable." He admired their hunting equipment, creative uses of whale blubber, comfortable and functional clothing and other evidence of their ability to survive in harsh climates. While observing their whaling techniques, he wrote a paean to which all Americans, with their niggling sense of inferiority to Europe, could relate:

> They have a harpoon made from a mushel shell only, and yet they have so disposed of it as to subdue the great leviathan and tow the unwieldy monster to their shores. Let not man think meanly of himself, but claim that glorious rank his amazing powers so justly entitle him to. If Descartes and Newton from the improvements of age could produce at last the magnificent system of Philosophy that hath immortalized them; why should not these glorious savages, who, without any of those great collateral assistances, without which they [Europeans] could have done nothing, have discovered such astonishing sagacity, be intitled to equal veneration, and the name of Ben Uncus be as great as that of Isaac Newton.

To compare Ben Uncas, the seventeenth-century leader of the Pequot tribe, with Newton might be like mixing apples and oranges, but Ledyard rightly pointed out that no one should feel insecure about their abilities and achievements. Few contemporaries spoke with such sympathy towards non-Europeans.

For Ledyard and the crew, the differences between Nootka Sound and their previous landfall in Hawaii were stark. The ship's thermometer hovered around freezing much of the time, and fog and rain wetted the decks. The Mowachaht spoke an entirely different language. They lived in long communal houses. Their sturdy canoes needed no outriggers. They produced amazing goods. Ledyard and the other sailors, as acquisitive as any tourist, eagerly snapped up wooden seal decoy helmets, bentwood visors, basket hats, bladder harpoons (blown to float once they speared a whale), bentwood spruce root fishing hooks (steamed in beds of kelp seaweed until malleable), stone daggers and tomahawks, whalebone clubs, cedar bark garments, wood rattles filled with pebbles and herring rakes. Even Cook showed enthusiasm for the curiosities and bought three carved masks.

There was little sexual activity, though Cook had not banned it as he thought, noting the commercial connections to the east coast, that venereal diseases were already present across the continent. Among the Mowachaht, only slave women were allowed to prostitute themselves. According to the ever-vigilant Samwell, a few officers paid "a Pewter plate well scoured for one night." Some scrubbed and washed the women as well as the pewter plate, in a "ceremony of the mop and pail" before taking them to their cabin.

One marvelous advantage about Nootka Sound was that there was an abundant supply of fine-quality peltry. The Mowachaht brought the skins of beaver, sea otter, fox, raccoon, wolf, bear, cougar and deer to sell to the sailors. Beaver was the most popular trade item, since beaver hats were the fashionable rage in England: The *Discovery* left with more than three hundred beaver skins on board; the *Resolution* carried more than fifteen hundred. But it was the sea-otter skins that proved to have the most far-reaching effect. In less than ten years European ships would crowd the Sound trading for them, bringing massacres and smallpox and, for the Mowachaht, the end of their way of life. By 1790 all of Europe knew of this little bay off the coast of America and its supply of otter fur, and war nearly broke out between Spain and Great Britain over its sovereignty. For John Ledyard, the furs would become a sort of memento mori, and he spent the rest of his life trying to get back to Nootka Sound.

At the end of April 1778, they bent their sails and left Nootka. The Mowachaht came out to say farewell. As they had done a month before, they sang a song. One man, probably Maquinna, flourished masks and danced on a stage of loose boards erected on a canoe. The natives waved their newly acquired swords, saws and hatchets and said goodbye.

The weather was thickening, and as Ledyard and the crew cleared the Sound, a storm hit them. It lasted for five days and at times the driving winds and turbulent skies grew so strong and dark that Ledyard could not see the length of the ship. When they sighted land again, they had drifted south six degrees of latitude. Even more ominous than the storm and the lost six degrees was a prodigious leak in the fish room. After cursing the men at Deptford for the hundredth time, they started the pumps. There were few days in the next two and a half years in which the *Resolution* did not have discharged water streaming down the sides of its hull.

Ledyard then sailed the longest unmapped coastline in the world. In the month at Nootka, William Bayly had taken almost a hundred astronomical observations in an exhaustive effort to get a good starting point for the longitude and latitude of the Northwest Coast. But knowing those numbers did not help much. Without a map, Ledyard and the sailors began to nervously coast a bewilderingly broken labyrinth of islets, inlets, waterways, sounds, shoals, bays and rivers. Ledyard fought some of the most treacherous conditions of the voyage. Driving spume kicked up into his face, stinging his hands. A cold miasma of mist and rain enveloped him on the deck. His ship was a tiny windblown piece of wood, forever at the mercy of the elements. Although it was summer, Ledyard's journal was filled with entries like "heavy snowstorm," "hard squalls with sleet," and "lost sight of land and had blowing weather with sleet and rain." Coupled with the extraordinary challenge of simply sailing along this sinuous coastline was the hopeless goal of finding the Northwest Passage. The men had to investigate as much as they could. Vague openings had to be traced. Tides had to be measured. The constant call of the leadsman measuring the depths echoed in the wind.

They passed the snow-capped peak of Mount Edgecumbe and then Mount St. Elias, where Vitus Bering had anchored more than thirty years before. They stopped in Prince William Sound to fix the *Resolution*'s leak. Some natives came out in bidarkas or kayaks, which with their tight, waterproof sealskin exterior struck Ledyard as an ingenious method of transportation. Ledyard and some of the other sailors eagerly traded for clothes, finding native outfits better adapted for the climate and conditions. Anxiety about the Passage produced two fruitless searches: an eight-day examination of Prince William Sound, thick with whales and seals and islands and then sixteen days up Cook Inlet, even thicker with rocks. The ships lost anchors. The *Resolution* scraped a shoal. On the way into the inlet, the crews bestowed cheerful names like Cape Hope and Mount Welcome on prominent features they encountered; on the return trip, with the true nature of the search for the Passage more clear, they chose doleful names like Seduction River. The birthday celebration of King George III on 4 June provided the only joyful reprieve.

On 19 June Clerke fired the *Discovery's* guns, not in alarm but to inform Cook of a startling exchange with some natives. Wearing breeches and waistcoats, they had given Clerke a box containing several notes written in a European script on European paper. The words were unintelligible, but one date, 1778, was obvious. Ledyard and the other sailors thought they had stumbled upon that most exotic of their species—the shipwrecked or marooned sailor. Cook was less romantic and pushed onwards. He wanted to gobble up degrees of latitude, not look for castaways. Ledyard and the crew grumbled: tens of thousands of miles and eighteen months away from Cape Town, and their captain insisted on ignoring their first evidence of a fellow European.

Retribution came a week later. Instead of meeting the Europeans and learning about the coastline, Cook ran hard through the shoal-infested waters. One night in the midst of a pea-soup fog, the sailors heard breakers. When the leadsman sounded twenty-four fathoms, the men dropped anchor. "On the 27th the fog cleared up, and we found ourselves embayed with rocks, reefs and an island, all within two cables length," wrote Ledyard. "We were not only amazed to find ourselves in such a frightful situation, but were still more astonished to conceive how we got there, as the least accidental deviation from the course we had steered would have been fatal." Two minutes later and they would have wrecked.

They named the place Providence Island but soon found out from nearby natives that it was called Unalaska. Here the natives also showed they had prior contact with Europeans, but Cook again pushed on. Ledyard and the men coasted through a pass and, temporarily finished with the Aleutians, headed northeast to the Alaska mainland.

The rest of the summer passed in a funereal fog. The *Resolution* lost another anchor in five fathom water until, as Ledyard wrote, "a mad-hardy Tar" dove into the freezing water and recovered it. The weather was awful. He and the men sailed through the fifty-mile-wide Bering Strait, but in the lowering fug of cloud and snow they did not know it. Ice hung from the rigging. It snowed so hard one day that Ledyard spent his four-hour watch shoveling. Fevers and cold afflicted the men. Out of the seventy men on the *Discovery*, only twenty men mustered one day at the capstan to weigh an anchor. William Anderson, the *Resolution*'s surgeon, died of tuberculosis. Ledyard saw few natives and visited just a single village.

On the morning of 17 August, Ledyard could see both the sun rising and the moon setting—a perfect time to make calculations. They were at 70 degrees 33 minutes latitude, 197 degrees 41 minutes longitude, four degrees north of the Arctic Circle. The northern horizon blinked with sunlight, and in the afternoon they came upon the Arctic icepack. "Being then in the latitude of 70 41, not being able to stand any fa[r]ther," Cook wrote with heavy disappointment, "for the ice was quite impenetrable and extend[ed] from WBS to EBN as far as the eye could reach." Not more than one hundred and fifty miles from what is now Barrow, Alaska, the ships were nearly clear of the Alaskan mainland and could possibly have sailed directly east to England if not for the icepack. This was discouraging. Both Hudson in 1607 and Phipps in 1773 had not encountered ice until eighty degrees.

The ships tacked about the pack, looking for openings, but there were none. The ice pack, in fact, was drifting south. Its only benefits were its blue-white beauty and, as Ledyard described the walrus, the "numerous herds of sea-horses who repose themselves" upon it. "The noise they make is a mean betwixt the barking of a dog and the bellowing of an Ox," wrote George Gilbert. Cook, as usual, tried to eat them. The recipe for walrus was labor intensive: hang the carcass for a day to let blood drain; tow it overboard for twelve hours, boil it four hours, cut into steaks and then fry. Cook's palate was famously adventuresome, and he found walrus delicious. Some of the sailors had been to Greenland and considered walrus, even with such elaborate preparations, inedible. Cook cut meat rations again, forcing the hungry sailors to try it. "The people at first murmured, and at last eat it through mere vexation," wrote Ledyard. "The Tars swore they would eat it or any thing else that Cook did, for they were certain that nothing would kill him in the heavens above or the earth beneath or in the waters under the earth."

Retreat from the ice was the only answer, and as they headed south Cook announced that the ships would return to Hawaii for the winter. The *Resolution* sprung a new leak on the starboard side, and Cook brought over all able men from the *Discovery* to help bail. On 2 October 1778, they sighted Unalaska. Cook laid up his ships in Samganoodha Bay (now English Bay) and sent his men out to collect berries and wild purslane. He then sent John Ledyard on a journey.

⟨ ≈ ⟩

He was called a "Jonathan," English slang for an American, but John Ledyard was sui generis. He was an American in the Royal Navy. He was a marine with more deep-sea sailing experience than many of the able seamen. He was one of the few marines not to get into trouble on the voyage. Molesworth Phillips, the lieutenant in charge of the *Resolution*'s marines, fought a duel in Tahiti. Samuel Gibson, his right-hand man as sergeant, got so drunk in Hawaii that he passed out, fell off the ship and almost drowned. A private tried to desert in the Society Islands. In the first three years of the voyage on the *Resolution*, Cook flogged all but four of the fifteen privates. Cook punished them for "neglect of duty," "drunkenness and neglect of duty," "theft," "sleeping at his post," and, the catch-all of eighteenth-century disobedience, "insolence." On the fifteen British ships that sailed around the world in the 1760s and 1770s, an average of 10 percent of those punished were marines. On Cook's third voyage, the marines were so undisciplined that more than half the time Cook flogged someone, it was a marine.

The word Ledyard's mates used to describe him was *intelligent*. He had gone to college and studied for ordination, and he was more well-read than many of the officers. In their writing the crew often linked Ledyard with intelligence. He "was an intelligent man" wrote William Ellis. George Gilbert wrote that he "was a very intelligent man." Cook referred to him in his journal as "Corporal Lediard of the marines, an intelligent man." King wrote that he was "an intelligent decent looking man."

Intelligence was needed for the risky journey Cook had in mind for him: he had to determine if any Europeans actually lived on the Aleutians. Besides the strange note delivered to the ships in June, there was other evidence of foreign influence. The Aleutians asked for tobacco, rum and snuff and sometimes wore blue linen shirts. For a few days the officers of the ships discussed possible plans. They could send an armed group, but it would proceed slowly, and if the men were killed in a battle it would greatly weaken the security of the expedition. On the other hand, one man could go much faster and not threaten the voyage if lost. John Gore recommended his "intimate friend" John Ledyard.

In the spirit of riding a sulky up to Dartmouth or canoeing the Connecticut River to Hartford, Ledyard took another uncommon journey at Unalaska. Cook told him to return in a week. If he did not return, Cook would wait another week and then sail without him. He handed Ledyard a few bottles of rum, wine and porter beer. Ledyard added brandy, tobacco and bread, which were "presents adapted to the taste of the Indians." He went unarmed. For a guide he hired a young native Siberian named Perpheela (Cook called him Derramoushk), who brought two of his servants.

The foursome left Samganoodha in the morning and hiked northwest the entire day. Ledyard estimated they covered fifteen miles. Just before dark, they approached a small Aleutian village. All the villagers came to see the stranger, and the children crowded around Ledyard, touching his clothing and laughing. "Being much fatigued" by the trip and half-anxious about "the apprehension of any insult or injury from the Indians," Ledyard was very relieved at this warm reception. Despite their interest in him, Ledyard saw that they did not show "that extraordinary curiosity" that natives had when encountering Europeans for the first time. Perpheela, who "seemed proud and assidious to serve me," took Ledyard into one of the homes. He gave some gifts to his host family and shared a simple meal of his own bread and brandy and their dried fish. "Ceremony was not invited to the feast," Ledyard wrote, "and nature presided over the entertainment until morning." At dawn Perpheela woke him. Ledyard gave some parting gifts and they headed off. He found that his feet had swelled overnight— he had not hiked that much in a single day since rambling in Cape Town. They headed into rough, hilly country and it began to rain. In midafternoon they climbed down to Unalaska Bay.

Perpheela wordlessly grabbed a lone bidarka, threw in the party's luggage and paddled off across the bay. Ledyard, feeling a bit uneasy, walked with the two attendants on a path skirting the edge of the shore. Two hours later, a bidarka appeared in the mist. Sent by Perpheela, the two paddlers talked briefly with the attendants and motioned for Ledyard to climb into the kayak. Ledyard hesitated. It was a two-man kayak and the only space left was in the hold between the two paddlers. Trusting in the islanders and aware that if the kayak tipped over he would probably drown, Ledyard climbed in, stretched out in the dark, wet hold on his back with his head facing forward, and "submitted thus to be stowed away in bulk."

Into the choppy bay went the kayak with its blind and helpless passenger. After an hour in this awkward position, Ledyard felt the kayak strike a beach. The paddlers got out and carried the kayak, with Ledyard still in it, inland a few hundred yards. They drew him out by the shoulders into a cold night. It was in this inglorious method, squeezed and buffeted, that John Ledyard became the first westerner to meet a Russian fur-trader.

Ledyard's escorts took him to a lighted house. Inside were dozens of people, both Indian and Russian. Ledyard sat on a bench and a servant handed him a change of clothes. "I was much fatigued, wet and cold," he wrote and yet had to give "the same chearfulness" to his hosts that they gave to him. In perhaps his most oft-quoted maxim, he wearily added that "hospitality is a virtue peculiar to man, and the obligation is as great to receive as to confer." Ledyard brought out his gifts, saying they came from Commodore Cook, an Englishman. The Russians took off their hats, and one man kissed Ledyard's hand and told him they were subjects of Empress Catherine II of Russia. Ledyard said that Cook wanted to meet them and the Russians agreed to visit the ships. They sat down to a dinner of boiled whale, fried halibut and broiled salmon. The Russians were not interested in Ledyard's bread, "but they were very fond of the rum, which they drank without any mixture or measure." Seeing Ledyard was tired after "being harrassed" the past two days, they showed him a corner where he could sleep. Ledyard rolled up in some furs, and as he fell off to sleep, he saw in the dim lamplight the Russians and the Indians perform an evening vespers ceremony in the style of the Russian Orthodox Church.

Drained by his journey and relieved at its probable success, Ledyard slept late into the morning. When he awoke, a servant took him to a sweat lodge. Ledyard sat down and began to undress. Before he finished, the "very tight extreemly hot and suffocating" air made him faint and he toppled backwards. He came to under a splash of cold water on his face. He continued to undress and joined a group of Russians on the tiered benches. Indians threw water on him and scrubbed him with soap. When they were finished, Ledyard returned to the house for a breakfast of whale, walrus and bear. "The flavor of our feast as well as its appearance had nearly produced a relapse of my spirits." He quickly slugged down a shot of brandy, but this did not restore his appetite. Despite his fear of appearing ungrateful, he nibbled on some broiled salmon and his own bread.

After breakfast it began to snow and a soft, niveous blanket settled over the tiny village at the edge of the sea. The Russians delayed his departure until the following day. Ledyard spent the time learning and comparing the vocabularies of the natives from the Aleutians and from Siberia. The weather eventually cleared and he explored the settlement. Moored in a cove was an old thirty-ton sloop and a small hut filled with sails, cordage and cannons. A Russian told him it was the ship Bering had sailed on his famous Alaskan voyages. Ledyard obtained a kayak and paddled out to the ship for an hour of poking around the relict. The Russian might have been confused himself or perhaps was pulling Ledyard's leg. While it made a good story, it was all but impossible for either the *St. Gabriel, St. Peter* or *St. Paul*, Bering's three ships, to have ended their days at Unalaska.

The next morning Ledyard, three Russians, and some servants headed back to the ships. They sped across Unalaska Bay in a twelve-oared boat, hiked across the snow-swept hills, spent the night at the same village as before and reached the ships by sundown, five days after Ledyard had departed from the *Resolution*.

These three Russians were the first Europeans the ships had seen in since December 1776, and despite the fact that they did not speak a common language, the next fortnight passed with a relaxed feeling. They ate meals and got drunk together. A number of officers retraced Ledyard's steps and visited the Russian settlement. Gerassim Ismailov, the leader of the settlement, came for dinner. Ismailov, one of the pioneer promyshlenniki, had been in the Aleutians since the mid–1760s. Cook presented a quadrant to him and asked him to forward some letters via his commanders at Petropavlovsk and St. Petersburg to London. (The letters arrived in London in March 1780).

On 26 October 1778, the day before Cook's fiftieth birthday, the *Resolution* and *Discovery* again put to sea. Immediately four days of snow-swept gales hammered them and they lost sight of each other. The *Discovery's* main tack snapped off, killing John MacIntosh, an able seaman, and wounding four others. A few days later a storm shredded the *Resolution's* main topsail. It was with great relief that after a month's passage, the men sighted the cloud-tipped volcanic peak crowning the island of Maui.

It had been a tremendously difficult ten months. The weather had been awful, and the tension of charting a storm-blasted crazy-quilt shoreline had been high. Ledyard and the rest of the crew were back in the Sandwich Islands and looked forward to a couple of months of sex, sleep and sun.

7

Grief on Every Countenance—
Death on the Beach

FEW PERIODS IN THE ANNALS OF EXPLORATION have been as analyzed as much as the *Resolution* and *Discovery*'s next four months. For two centuries afterward, the accounts that Cook's sailors wrote after returning to England were the primary sources for discussion. Until the 1950s, when New Zealand professor J. C. Beaglehole began transcribing and publishing sailors' journals, logs and narratives that lay moldering in the admiralty's archives in London, the following handful of sailors shaped the public's perception of the events in Hawaii: John Rickman (1781), Heinrich Zimmermann (1781), William Ellis (1782), John Ledyard (1783), Captain Cook and James King's official authorized history (1784), David Samwell (1786) and James Burney (1819).

The men who published these narratives (Samwell's was a pamphlet) were, with two exceptions, officers on the voyage. Lieutenants, surgeons and captains of the voyage, these were aristocratic men. King was friends with Edmund Burke, his uncle was speaker in the House of Commons, and he had studied science in Paris and Oxford; Burney came from a famous family, his sister was the novelist and diarist Fanny Burney and his father a musical historian; Ellis had gone to Cambridge; Samwell was a doctor and highly-regarded poet. In composing their accounts, they wrote for a British audience that believed in the Empire, the savagery of the South Seas native and the godlike genius of James Cook.

Just two non-officers from Cook's third voyage published manuscripts: Heinrich Zimmermann and John Ledyard. Zimmermann, an able seaman on the *Discovery*, wrote an account, *Reise um die Welt mit Capitain Cook*. Zimmermann was a German from the Palatine who had, before joining the voyage, credible claims to the working class. He wrote, "Among other occupations I worked for a brazier and gilder in Geneva, for a bell-founder in Lyons, for a sword-maker in Paris and in a sugar refinery in London." His book, however, was extremely rare and was only translated into English in 1926.

When John Ledyard published his account of the voyage in the summer of 1783 in Hartford, he offered a unique perspective. He was the only American writer, and the only one besides Zimmerman who had sailed before the mast. Unlike the other writers, Ledyard did not owe fealty to Great Britain and did not feel obligated to join in the adoration of Cook. To understand the epochal events of November 1778 through March 1779, many missionaries, settlers, historians and journalists read Ledyard's account. As the only writer to declare that Cook was in part to blame for the killings and destruction that punctuated the visit, his book became the sole source for an alternate view on the interactions between the Europeans and the islanders. Only recently has Beaglehole's publications brought forth a flood—memoirs, journals, letters, even marginalia—showing that many of Cook's men shared Ledyard's attitudes as well as contradicted him at times. But for nearly two hundred years, Ledyard stood alone.

Upon returning to Hawaii, Cook decided not to land for seven weeks. Instead he tacked on and off the coast of Maui and then the big island of Hawaii. The same problems that plagued the ships when they had first encountered the islands at the beginning of the year—pounding surf, rough winter winds and lack of an ideal harbor—again pushed them out to sea. But the ships could have anchored, as they had before, and attempted to get ashore.

During the seven-week interregnum, the sailors grew intensely frustrated. Old sails, unfurled in anticipation of easy summer sailing, were shredded in hammering storms. The *Resolution* and *Discovery* got separated for thirteen tense days. When the skies cleared, Ledyard and the crew gazed longingly at the white beaches and lush gardens along the shore. But Cook would not land, "to the great mortification of almost all in both ships," wrote James King. "We were jaded & very heartily tired."

Cook, ever keen to substitute local products for the ships' provisions, ordered the brewing of sugar cane into a liquor, something he called "a very palatable and wholesome beer." The plan backfired. "Not one of my Mutinous crew would even so much as taste it and demanded their grog," wrote Cook. He stopped their grog rations completely. The men, as a midshipman wrote, "remonstrated with yᵉ Captⁿ by Letter, at the same time mentioning the scanty Allowance of Provisions servᵈ them, which they thought might be increase's where there was such Plenty & that bought for mere trifles." Cook summoned all hands to the quarterdeck. After the bimonthly reading of the Articles of War—the cheerless recital of punishable offences at sea—he admitted he had somehow been unaware of their short food allowance since leaving Alaska, and he agreed to restore full fare. But he "look'd upon their Letter as a very mutinous Procceding" and announced that if they did not drink the sugar cane they would only get water. The next day he discovered William Griffiths, the cooper, had deliberately opened the cask of sugar-cane beer in order to spoil it, and gave him twelve lashes.

Women provided little succor. Cook ordered that no Hawaiian women be admitted to the ship and that no man infected with "the Venereal disease" sleep with native women. A list of tainted sailors was kept on the quarterdeck "in order to prevent as much as possible the communicating of this fatal disease to a set of innocent people." The proscription of sex was rendered meaningless as soon as the first islanders came on board off Maui. They, as King wrote, "apllyd to us, for help in their great distress: they had a Clap, their Penis was much swell'd, & inflamed." The fifteen-day visit at the beginning of the year had been enough, and venereal diseases had now spread throughout the archipelago. A few women did sneak on board during the seven-week cruise, but many of them got seasick in the winter storms.

Christmas 1778 was passed on board, with each man given a pint of brandy. For Ledyard, the cold of Kerguelen or the heat of Christmas Island was better than this painful purgatory. Even the beasts of the deep seemed to mock him and the other sailors. One evening a whale played so near the *Resolution* that it spouted water into the faces of the watching men.

The published accounts of the voyage elided this period. Rickman wrote that "it was with the kindest treatment from their officers that the men could be kept to their duty," and after Christmas "not a murmur was heard." However, for Ledyard this was a case of Cook's obsessive need to survey and chart his new discoveries: "This conduct of the commander in chief was highly reprobated and at last remonstrated against by the people on board both ships, as it appeared very manifest that Cook's conduct was wholly influenced by motives of interest, to which he was evidently sacrificing not only the ships, but the health and happiness of the brave men, who were weaving the laurel that was hereafter to adorn his brows."

After circling much of Hawaii, Ledyard and the men came upon a fine bay. On 17 January 1779, the *Resolution* and the *Discovery* anchored a quarter mile offshore in Kealakekua Bay. The reception was electric. Thousands of people—estimates ranged as high as fifteen thousand, and all agreed it was the most natives seen at one spot on any of the voyages—appeared in the bay. Hundreds swam around the ships for hours, without tiring, "like shoals of fish," wrote Cook. The bay filled with countless canoes. Cook allowed women aboard and dozens flung themselves at the sailors, "remarkably anxious to engage themselves to our people," wrote William Ellis. So many islanders climbed aboard the *Discovery* that it almost tipped over. "The crouds on shore were still more numerous," Ledyard wrote. "The beach, the surrounding rocks, the tops of houses, the branches of trees and the adjacent hills were all covered, and the shouts of joy, and admiration proceeding from the sonorous voices of the men confused with the shriller exclamations of the women dancing and clapping their hands, the oversetting of canoes, cries of the children, goods on float, and hogs that were brought to market squealing formed one of the most tumultuous and the most curious prospects that can be imagined."

When Cook came ashore, it got even stranger. As he passed along the beach, all the islanders except the priests fell to the ground and covered their faces with their hands. The seriousness of their prostration was almost laughable, according to Ledyard. After Cook walked past them, they rose and followed him. "But if Cook happened to turn his head or look behind him they were down again in an instant, and up again as soon, whenever his face was reverted to some other quarter, this punctilious performance of respect in so vast a throng being regulated solely by the accidental turn of one mans head." Later that day Ledyard, in full uniform, led the marines to a walled, half-acre sweet potato field near a stone temple (which the Hawaiians called a *heiau,* and the sailors, using Tahitian, called a *morai*). With the permission of the Hawaiian priests, the marines set up the tents and observatories, and Ledyard posted sentries before sunset. James King was in charge of the tents, accompanied by the astronomer, William Bayly, some sailmakers and carpenters and a gaggle of young midshipmen. The priests, with King's agreement, decreed the camp taboo. They forbade canoes to land near it, islanders to approach it and Europeans to leave it after dark. They even marked the taboo territory by placing white rods on the stone walls.

The slippery slope towards violence, as only Ledyard noted, started at the tent encampment. The sailors there were very glad to be out of their hammocks and have the quiet and stability of the camp as opposed to the noisy tumult of the heeling *Resolution* and *Discovery*. "We enjoyd a tranquility about our Dwellings that was the very reverse" of the ships, wrote King. But the taboos on women entering the camp or the men leaving the camp at night prevented them from meeting with their mistresses. Ledyard discussed the matter with the priests but they could not come to a solution. A few of the midshipmen, "mortified," according to Samwell, at the proscription of women visitors, "offered a large Bribe to the Priest to let a Girl or two come in the Night, but he was proof against the Temptation," and said no. The midshipmen then began sneaking out at night. In the light of the moon (which was full on the first of February) it was obvious what was going on. The sentries started to emulate the officers, and soon the sailors and marines, in a farcical sexual roundelay, tripped over each other in the shadows under the trees. "It was impossible for a number of men upon a half an acre of ground to go out and return all upon the same business and not have some reencounter that would lead to a discovery," wrote Ledyard. He joined in these "sacrifices to Venus," as he said, and again, like in Tonga, came down with venereal disease requiring a second treatment by the ship's surgeon.

The priests soon stopped the hypocrisy by lifting the taboo and removing the white rods. Many islanders started to spend their days there, watching the marines, learning how to wrestle and box English style and even how to use muskets, and the nighttime visitors came and went with less secrecy. "We live now in the greatest Luxury," wrote Samwell, "and as to the Choice & number of fine women there is hardly one among us that may not vie with the grand Turk himself." Still, this violation of the priests' taboo on the camp was the start of the cycle of troubles. "They knew it was a breach of covenant," wrote Ledyard. "This might be esteemed trivial on our part and indeed it was, but it was the beginning of our subsequent misfortunes."

The next two weeks passed without too many problems. One morning King invited Ledyard to attend an hour-long ceremony involving Cook at a local shrine. Ledyard was quite impressed, especially by the priests who were "vociferating with a strong sonorus voice a kind of amen" during an oration. Ledyard watched the islanders dance, play games and surf the legendary waves of Hawaii. As one of the few sailors who knew how to swim, he even saved one older woman from drowning. This feat and his general interest in the islanders made him, as he boasted, "well known in the town." Hawaiians called him the "Kakakoalahi," which meant chief warrior at the tents, and gave him a nickname, Ourero, which possibly was a transliteration of his surname. He attended the funeral of William Watman, the old gunner's mate who died of a stroke. The Hawaiians buried him at their temple amid elaborate rituals that for Ledyard showed "the purest spirit of philanthropy. It is an example that will put seven eights of Christendom to the blush." With his keen eye for detail, Ledyard noted the occurrence of homosexuality among the chiefs of the island, their magnificent feathered hats and the fact that Hawaiians dogs did not bark.

Emigration puzzled him. He wondered about "the extraordinary fact" that "throughout this extended and almost boundless world of waters," in the Pacific, the language, culture, food and even domesticated animals were the same. This humbled him: "It is a subject only fit for a philosopher; and he must be a very good one too. But I am no philosopher: However as a traveler and friend to mankind I shall most freely relate any matter of curious fact to be improved by them." Ledyard laid out the arguments for both Asia and America being the original home of the Polynesians. Despite being a lot closer to the Americas, Polynesia has "but a faint analogy" in culture to South America, but the proximity of the Americas and the wind patterns made it just as probable as Asia." (This theory would reappear under the romantic guise of Thor Heyerdahl and the *Kon-Tiki*.)

The highlight of Ledyard's stay in Hawaii was his attempt to climb Mauna Loa, a thirteen-thousand-foot snow-tipped volcano. Ledyard led a party that included George Vancouver, a midshipman on the *Discovery*; David Nelson, the expedition's botanist; Robert Anderson, the *Resolution's* gunner; William Ellis, the *Resolution's* surgeon's second mate; and Simeon Woodruff, a fellow American and gunner's mate on the *Discovery*. The sextet, escorted by three natives, carried woolen blankets and bottles of brandy. They headed inland and stopped to examine extensive sweet potato and sugar cane farms and breadfruit orchards. At the foothills of Mauna Loa, they spent the night at a little house. Before supper they sat on the stoop, taking in the view. "It was exquisitely entertaining," wrote Ledyard, to look down to the sun-flecked waves in the bay; one of the ships was even visible. The family who lived there, after initially being afraid at the appearance of a half-dozen strangers, roasted a pig and gave them fresh water, which "was a kind of nectar to us" after the brackish water at the bay.

After a chilly night's sleep, the next morning they found an "excessive miry and rough" footpath leading towards the summit. They hiked fifteen miles up lava fields and plunging, umbrageous woods until they found a suitable campsite for the night. Nelson went botanizing, others hunted and Ledyard set about gathering bark and branches for a makeshift shelter under some fallen trees.

Ledyard led them for the summit on the third day, but the trail veered to the south away from the peak. They decided to bushwhack straight up the mountain. After four miles, it was clear that the "impenetrable thickets" made it impossible to go further. They retreated to their campsite, shot some birds for dinner and the following afternoon returned to the bay.

One of the drawbacks of Kealakekua Bay, besides the brackish water, was that it lacked firewood. With their Alaskan supply running short, the cooks needed more fuel for their kitchen stoves. There were, as Ledyard discovered on the hike, very few trees within five miles of the bay. One day Cook came to the tent encampment to ask the priests if he could take the fence around the temple. He offered them two hatchets in return. Ledyard recalled the scene: "The chiefs were astonished not only at the inadequate price, but at the proposal and refused him. Cook was as much chagrined as they were suprized" and ordered his men to take the fence anyway. During the dismantling, Cook again offered the two hatchets "only to evade the imputation of taking their property without payment." The priests again declined. Cook added a third hatchet, shoved them at the priests and left. Some sailors, during the fracas, grabbed the temple's carved idols as curios, while a group of angry natives "hove the wood and images back as we threw them down." According to Ledyard, this was a moment of sacrilege.

The next day there was more trouble when a crew of sailors tried to take the *Resolution*'s recently repaired rudder back to the ship. The master's mate asked some islanders watching the operation to help, and soon fifty people were at the job. But for them it was a joke. In Ledyard's words, they "pretended to pull and labor very hard, though at the same time they were in fact doing all they could to retard the business, to ridicule and make their pastime of the people." The mate struck a couple of the jesters and argued with a chief. The islanders threw stones, the sailors beat some of them and a general scuffle ensued. Ledyard rushed back to the camp and brought King to talk to the islanders, but they pelted him with stones. Eventually tempers cooled. The islanders left and the sailors were able to get the rudder into the launch.

Clearly it was time to go. On 4 February 1779, the *Resolution* and *Discovery* unmoored and departed. As so often seemed to happen when they left a harbor, the weather turned foul. Women on board the ship got seasick and canoes alongside capsized. After a rough night the sailors discovered that the foremast was badly damaged. They had to do extensive repairs and, with no good harbor in sight, Cook reluctantly ordered a return to Kealakekua Bay. He had signed his own death warrant.

For Hawaiians, the appearance of the pale-skinned sky-breakers had not been the shock that it was for natives at other places of first contact. They had predicted it.

Central to Hawaiian theology were two antagonistic gods, Lono and Ku. Each November beginning with the rising of the Pleiades at sunset, Lono, the ancestor god of peace and fertility, returned for a four-month reign of peace and productivity, while Ku, the god of war, went into seclusion. Makahiki, as it was called, was a carnival-like period of ceremonies, parties and sacrifices. Lono—symbolized with a sheet of white cloth mounted on a stick and crosspiece—made a clockwise circuit of the island of Hawaii. At the end of the Makahiki festival, Lono departed, his priests tore down his shrines and Ku reemerged.

The Europeans' arrival was not a coincidence in the eyes of the Hawaiians. At the right time of year, Cook had rounded Hawaii clockwise in an object dotted with white sails on yards and had anchored exactly in front of Lono's temple at Kealakekua Bay. The Hawaiians, who had a nuanced approach to divinity and humanity, took Cook to be an incarnation of Lono, and Ledyard and the rest of the crew as slightly divine. That was why there was such jubilation at their arrival, not one of the many thousand revelers carried a weapon, and the sexual appetites of the island's women were never satisfied.

The Europeans' sojourn at Kealakekua Bay was unprecedented, but the Hawaiians incorporated it into their cosmology. When the ships returned a week after their departure, however, the Hawaiians could not rationalize it. The Makahiki was over. Ku was back in power, and Lono, his opposite god, was figuratively—and now literally in the form of Captain Cook—supposed to be gone.

A month before, ten thousand people had greeted the sailors. Now only ten Hawaiians came out to say hello. Ledyard and the men unloaded the *Resolution*'s mast at the old tent site. Prices for hogs and yams were much higher. Ku was in power and the islanders craved iron daggers, which the armourers dutifully made using the French anchor collected at Borabora. Ledyard had no inkling of his role in the Hawaiian religious calendar and tried to explain the change in atmosphere in terms he understood: "They had been oppressed and were weary of our prostituted alliance. Our former friendship was at an end, and that we had nothing to do but to hasten our departure to some different island where our vices were not known, and where our extrinsic virtues might gain us another short space of being wondered at, and doing as we pleased, or as our tars expressed it of being happy by the month."

Happy by the weekend was not even possible. On Saturday, 13 February, two days after they had returned, the situation broke into open hostility.

Islanders harassed a watering party. A Hawaiian stole an armourers' tongs from the *Discovery's* forge. He was caught, and Clerke gave him forty lashes and kept him tied to the shrouds until the tongs were returned. A few hours later a second man filched the same tongs and some iron chisels. He leapt off the ship and swam to an escape canoe that sped towards the shore. Thomas Edgar and George Vancouver, both officers on the *Discovery*, gave chase. The thief fled into the hills, leaving behind the stolen equipment, and Edgar and Vancouver, still angry at the thief's audacity, impounded his canoe. Palea, a high chief and the main go-between for the sailors, intervened. They tussled and Edgar smacked Palea on the head with a paddle. Palea snapped the paddle in two. A crowd, watching the fight, hurled stones at the unarmed sailors and one man snatched Vancouver's hat. Unable to swim, Edgar and Vancouver waded through the shallows to a rock in the bay where they were pelted with stones and breadfruit and thrashed with broken paddles. Palea nobly stopped the attack and allowed the sailors to row back to their ship.

Cook, meanwhile, was ashore at the tent encampment, examining the *Resolution's* mast. Seeing the commotion and an islander dashing into the hills, he and a couple of marines set off after him. They ran through some villages—where natives taunted and laughed at them—and "came off just at sun-set," Ledyard said, "highly displeased and not a little concerned at the bad appearance of things." Two weeks earlier Hawaiians had prostrated themselves before Cook; now they jeered at him.

The night was tense. An intruder crept onto the wall surrounding the camp, and a nervous sentry fired at him but missed. "Shrill and melancholy sounds" came from nearby villages, which "struck the sentinels with unusual awe and terror," wrote Ledyard. It was to be the last night he or any other sailor slept on land for three months.

Dawn rose clear and warm that Sunday morning, 14 February 1779, at Kealakekua Bay. A marine on the *Discovery* noticed that the six-oared cutter was missing. The sailors had moored it to the anchor's bower buoy and deliberately sunk it to the level of the water to prevent the planks from splitting in the hot sun. With phenomenal stealth and purpose, some islanders, seeking revenge for the melee with Palea, had managed without detection to cut the line, bail the boat and pull it ashore. The sentry informed Clerke, who delivered the news to the *Resolution*.

This was not a catastrophe. The cutter was the *Discovery*'s largest boat, but the ship still had a pinnace and other launches; furthermore, as the cutter never was returned, the *Discovery* borrowed a four-oared cutter from the *Resolution* and the voyage lasted for another twenty months without repercussion. It was more the principle of the matter. King, commanding the tent encampment, came out to the *Resolution* for his daily morning briefing and "found them all arming themselves & the Captn loading his double Barreld piece; on my going to acquaint him with the last nights adventure, he interruptd me & said we are not arming for the last nights affairs, they have stolen the Discoverys cutter, & it is for that we are making preparations." Cook sent boats to the ends of the bay to prevent any islanders from escaping by sea and then left with three armed boats for the chiefs' village of Kaawaloa, a mile north of the temple and the ships' camp.

Until the 1960s, it was assumed that John Ledyard had been a part of the detachment accompanying Cook ashore and thus had been the only eyewitness to publish an account of the events that followed. His vivid writing suggested it, and in 1819, forty years after the event, James Burney included Ledyard in a list of marines who went with Cook. However, with the publishing of the sailors' journals from the admiralty's archives, it became clear that Ledyard was not with Cook but rather in his usual spot at the old camp by the temple. Ledyard pretended he was there—he never said it outright and actually described the events in the third person—because did not want his book to lack a good description of one of the biggest stories of the century.

From Ledyard's actual perspective, the next hour at the tent encampment was eerily quiet. It was seven o'clock, so the usual throng of hangers-on, mistresses and traders had not yet materialized at the camp. Upon returning from the *Resolution*, King was so unconcerned about Cook's errand that, as he later wrote, he was "for some time in the Observatory preparing to take equal Altitudes." Ledyard heard gunfire from one of the boats cordoning the bay. A mile up the beach at Kaawaloa he could see two of the armed boats bobbing offshore and a third disgorging Cook and ten marines onto the beach. They marched through town and a while later came back into sight, surrounded by what Ledyard called "an immense Mob compose'd of at least 2 or 3 thousand people." The mob heaved like one massive monster. There was the sound of gunfire. Marines scrambled to the boats. Then more shooting and a mad frenzy in the shallows. The pinnace came close, its men firing. The boats pulled away and returned to the *Resolution*. The *Resolution* brought its starboard guns to bear and fired two shots into the crowd.

As this was happening, the *Discovery* fired its guns towards the camp. King sent a boat to the ships to explain that everything was peaceful at the camp. The boat did not return. Instead boats flew back and forth between the *Resolution* and the *Discovery*, as King wrote, "& we for about 10 minutes or a quarter of an hour, were under the most torturing suspence & anxiety that can be conceive'd; I never before felt such agitation as on seeing at last our Cutter coming on shore, with Mr Bligh, he called out before he reachd the Shore, to strike the Observatorys as quick as possible, & before he announcd to us the Shocking news that Captn Cook was kill'd we saw it in his & the Sailors looks."

King and Ledyard looked around in fear. There were just six marines and a couple of carpenters to protect the *Resolution*'s mast. A small group of islanders, wrote Ledyard, "resolutely attacked us and endeavored to mount the walls of the Morai [stone temple], where they were lowest, but being opposed with our skill in such modes of attack and the great superiority of our arms they were even repulsed with loss and at length retreated, which affording a good opportunity to retreat to our boats we embraced it and got off all well." In two hours they dismantled the camp and ferried the *Resolution*'s mast back to the ship.

Back on board his ship, Ledyard found a mournful, shocked silence. Captain Cook and four marines were dead. George Gilbert wrote that it was "appearing to us something like Dream that we could not reconcile ourselves to for some time. Greif was visible in evry Countenance; some expressing it in tears and others by a kind of gloomy dejection." As the afternoon wore on, the men discussed what had happened on the shore. There seemed to be no consensus. Alexander Home, the master's mate on the *Discovery*, wrote in his logbook his version of the death of Cook and then added: "I was not present in this Fray being Sick So this Account is Entirely from the Mouths of others Who were present. But these Differed greatly in their Relation of the same Matters So that what I have here said I do not Aver to be the Real truth in Every particul . . . they were so Exceedingly perplexed in their Accounts that it was a hard Matter to Colect Certainty, in particular cases or indeed to write any Account at all."

It seemed that Cook had attempted to repeat the pattern at Tonga and Raiatea of holding the king hostage. He went to the compound of Kalani'opu'u, the king of the island and the living representative of the Hawaiian god of war, Ku. Cook persuaded Kalani'opu'u, who knew nothing about the stolen cutter, to come to the ship. Before he could board the boat, one of his wives protested and Kalani'opu'u sat down on the beach. News came that a chief had been killed by one of the ships' cutters blocking the bay. The mob pressed upon Cook and his party. A man threatened with a dagger. Cook fired his musket. The warriors attacked with stones and daggers. "The business was now a most miserable scene of confusion," wrote Molesworth Phillips. "All my People I observ'd were totally vanquish'd and endeavouring to save their lives by getting to the Boats." Four marines were killed. Phillips, stabbed in the shoulder, managed to climb into a boat and then spilled out to rescue John Jackson, thrashing in the water with a deep wound to his eyes. The men in the boats began firing. Cook retreated into the water but, unable to swim, could not go farther. He was surrounded by warriors and clubbed from behind. Facing the sea, Cook dropped his musket, fell to the water and was stabbed repeatedly with the iron daggers that he had just traded to the Hawaiians.

Once the shock wore off, the ships returned to a state of normalcy. Charles Clerke became the captain of the *Resolution* and John Gore the captain of the *Discovery*. As was customary, they auctioned off Cook's clothes, with the money going to his widow; Ledyard spent five shillings. They tried to recover the bodies of Cook and the four marines, but received none of the marines and only parts of Cook's body—a horrifying package of burnt bones, thighs, calves, skull with one ear attached, arms, and hands—were brought to the ship. Noting the deaths in the ship's muster book, Clerke wrote under the column "Whither or for what Reason:" "Killed by the Indians of Hawyee." At ten minutes before six in the evening of 21 February, with Ledyard and the crew at attention, the *Resolution* flew her colors at half-mast, crossed her yards, fired ten guns at the half-minute and committed the remains of Captain James Cook to the deep.

Anger burned through the ship. Ledyard had lost a fellow corporal and his friend Theophilus Hinks, who also came from the twenty-fourth company at Plymouth. Three other marines were wounded. Revenge was necessary, said some men who begged to go ashore and lay waste like they had in Moorea. Clerke held them off for two days, arguing that more than two dozen Hawaiians had been killed already. But one islander came out in a canoe and, wearing Cook's hat, smacked his buttocks in derision. Clerke fired the *Resolution*'s guns at a crowd watching the show on the beach. The next day a crew, including Ledyard, went to fetch water near the old camp. When they landed, they came under attack from warriors throwing, Ledyard wrote, "whole clouds of stones" and rolling rocks down from nearby cliffs.

The sailors reacted disproportionately. They rampaged through the village, burning houses and bayoneting and shooting islanders. They, wrote Ledyard, "pursued many of them into the flames of their own houses, where if they were not instantly killed they were burnt to death." They loaded their boats with spoils. They decapitated two people and stuck the skulls on poles, tying one pole to the bow of the cutter. Ledyard estimated that the crew killed nearly one hundred Hawaiians and burnt a thousand houses. "Thus ended this day's business," Ledyard wrote coldly, apparently believing the revenge was justified and no longer feeling, as he did earlier in the trip, that exerting extreme power exhibited extreme weakness. King, on the other hand, recognized the inhumanity of the actions: "Our people in this days transactions did many reprehensible things; in excuse of which it can only be said that their minds were strongly agitat'd . . . A common sailor with such a disposition, & sufferd to have its full operation, would soon equal the Cruelty of the most savage Indian."

On the evening of 22 February the carpenters finished refitting the mast on the *Resolution* and the ships again unmoored, leaving Kealakekua Bay astern. As when they left the Society Islands, George Gilbert sounded a feeling of despair at the prospect of heading north. "We sailed from hence with great dissatisfaction, on account of the Death of our unfortunate Commander which still lay heavy upon our minds, as being truly sensible of our loss; this together with the thoughts of the approaching season to the North. The hardships of the last being still recent in our memory— and will never be effaced from mine—rendered us quite dispirited." They spent three more gloomy weeks in the Hawaiian archipelago. They killed a man after a thieving incident. They learned in Kauai that the goats Cook had left there a year before had been the subject of a civil war and been killed, further evidence that his grand Noah's Ark scheme had been a failure. On 15 March Clerke set sail for the north. Unlike Furneaux after the Grass Cove incident at Queen Charlotte's Sound on the second voyage, he was not going to race home, but would follow through with Cook's plan for a second summer exploring the Alaskan coast in search for the Northwest Passage.

8

Not Short of Mutiny— Coming Home

FOR LEDYARD AND THE CREW, nearly a third of the voyage remained. Tropical paradises, with their pleasures and their problems, were left behind, and some of the most challenging and revelatory events of the expedition lay ahead.

At first the going was good. The weather was warm, the breezes steady. The men caught bonito with Tongan fishing lures. Ledyard asked Charles Clerke, the new captain, if he could become the official historian of the expedition. He handed Clerke a paper he had written "which described the manners of the Society islanders and the kind of life led by our people whilst among them," remembered James Burney. Clerke declined, remembering the admiralty's keenness to have a professional writer assemble the journals and logs, and knowing, Burney added, "how many candidates he would have to contend with . . . every one in the two ships who kept journals." Ledyard's suggestion led to each ship composing a weekly newspaper, which they good-naturedly exchanged with each other. Ledyard, as editor of the *Resolution*'s gazette, was a worthy writer, but he "had a passion for lofty sentiment and description," wrote Burney, and "his ideas were thought too sentimental and his language too florid."

In April Ledyard's gazette reported monotony and discouragement. Food was a problem. They went on half rations for bread. In Hawaii pigs had been so plentiful that the quartermasters had preserved sixty puncheons of salted pork, but now it was pork and sweet potatoes ad nauseam. "Our food was the same on monday morning and sunday evening—pork and yams begun, and pork and yams ended all our bills of fare," wrote Ledyard, "and we had besides but half an allowance of the latter of those articles and when pealed, and the rotten and decayed parts defalcated the remainder was, oh ye epecures, but scanty I ass ure ye!"

Storms blew through, tearing the sails, producing new leaks in the *Resolution*, breaking the hatch covering the coalhole and stoving two precious casks of French brandy in the *Discovery*. The crew pumped and bailed for twenty continuous days. "During this we were greatly alarmed at our situation," wrote George Gilbert, "as being at least three week's sail from the nearest land; and even that was the coast of Japan where we could not hope for the smallest assistance, but might rather expect to be cut off or made slaves by those people." On the first of April the thermometer read 83; nineteen days later it was under 30 and snowing. The men, having traded much of their clothing with their Hawaiian girlfriends, shivered in the frost and thanked Cook for having impounded their flannel fearnoughts after leaving Unalaska. Very few had shoes. Clerke was bound to his cabin, sick with tuberculosis that he had caught at the King's Bench.

Ledyard sighted the Siberian coast on 23 April 1779. Two days later the ships lost each other, only to find one another in Avacha Bay at the port of Petropavlovsk (the Harbor of St. Peter and St. Paul) on May Day. Until the discovery of Hawaii, Cook had planned to winter over at Petropavlovsk. Ledyard shivered at the thought. Avacha Bay was still ice bound. The Kamchatkan peninsula looked barren under its coat of snow. The Russians in Unalaska had described the town as a large, prosperous fort, but instead it had only two cannons, six small log cabins and a tiny, scurvy-ridden, smallpox-decimated detachment who would have gladly traded places with the sailors. The reception afforded the two ships was as cold as the air. The governor of the region was out of town, at Bolsheretsk across the peninsula on the Sea of Okhotsk. Petropavlovsk was still reeling from a notorious April

1771 revolt. A Polish exile, Maurice Benyowsky, had murdered the local Russian commander, seized a ship and escaped back to Europe. (Benyowsky, a colorful figure, later proclaimed himself king of Madagascar.) Eight years later, the beleaguered garrison was in no mood to wrangle with two mysterious and imposing foreign ships.

Hospitality soon arrived in the person of the governor, Major Magnus von Behm. James King, John Webber and John Gore went by sledge overland to Bolsheretsk to find Behm, and two weeks later they returned with the governor in tow. Behm had been expecting the ships. Catherine II, the Empress of Russia, had told him about the Cook voyage, and on 20 April he had received a letter from Ismailov at Unalaska. Ismailov's letter was accompanied by a note from a northern fur-trading outpost reporting that relations between the Russians and native Alaskans had improved after the *Resolution* and *Discovery* had passed through; the natives had assumed Cook was Russian, and his unusually humane actions had changed their attitudes toward the Russian Empire.

When Behm arrived at Petropavlovsk, Clerke gave him a gold watch, two fowling pieces, some silver-mounted pistols and one hundred gallons of brandy. In return, out of his own pocket, Behm showered the crew with the necessary and the luxurious: sixty-four leather bags; one hundred sail needles; two hundred and forty fathoms of rope; nine thousand weight of rye meal; cattle; ducks, geese and other poultry; and most wonderfully, four hundred pounds of tobacco. (The ships had run out of tobacco rations while in Hawaii, and on the way north lucky hoarders had sold it at the price of silver.) Behm might have been glad to trade tobacco for brandy, but he was even more pleased at meeting the *Discovery*'s German seamen, Heinrich Zimmermann and Bartholomew Lohmann. Behm was German, from Livonia, and for once the admiralty's oversight of not sending a single Russian speaker on a voyage scheduled to touch upon Russian shores was obviated. Behm had not seen a fellow German in seventeen years.

Spring came to Siberia in late May, and Clerke, in imitation of Cook, sent his men out to fish and gather wild onions and garlic that sprung up once the snow melted. Ledyard and the rest of the crew sold some of their Nootka Sound skins. They got thirty to sixty rubles for sea otter and fifteen rubles for beaver, which were considered fantastic prices. On 4 June the ships celebrated King George III's birthday with a band, streamers and a double allowance of meat. In town Ledyard discovered a Greek priest in charge of the Russian Orthodox Church, and "several gentlemen who had been exiled hither from the court of Russia, particularly a certain Count, who it is said had carried his amours with her Imperial Majesty so far, that to conceal the matter it was necessary her gallant should spend the remainder of his days in the forests of Siberia." The count was Petr Ivashkin. A Russian nobleman, he had been exiled in 1742, not for the colorful crime of intimacy with the empress, but for plotting to kill her. He spoke French and German and played a very good fiddle. Without shame, he bore split, mutilated nostrils, "the customary mark of disgrace," according to William Ellis, for an exile. Later, after nearly sixty years of exile, Ivashkin was pardoned but had grown so accustomed to his life in Kamchatka that he did not go home.

Behm, about to leave for St. Petersburg, agreed to carry Cook's journal, charts and reports to pass along to the admiralty. It was this package, relayed by the British ambassador in St. Petersburg, that was opened in early January 1780 in London. On 11 January 1780, the *London Gazette* announced to the world that Cook had been killed "at the island of O'Why'he, one of a group of new discovered Islands in the 22nd Degree of North Latitude, in an affray with a numerous and tumultuous Body of the Natives."

On 18 June 1779, as the *Resolution* and *Discovery* left Petropavlovsk, the volcanic peak Avachinskaya erupted. "It became almost as dark as night," wrote Ledyard, "and the face of heaven looked very wild." So much lightning ripped through the sky, he said, that "the atmosphere was one continued sheet of flame." Lava, mud and ashes, smelling like rotten eggs, fell onto the ships and coated the decks with several inches of the muck, which "looked very much like a new fallen snow."

With that opening gambit, the Arctic played its cold, harsh game a second time. Clerke followed the Kamchatkan coast and passed through Bering Strait on 6 July. Again the dreaded drifting ice pack checkmated the ships. For two weeks they tried to push beyond it on the Asian side but eventually stopped on 19 July at 70 degrees 33 minutes north latitude, just a couple of miles short of the previous summer's apogee. This summer's cruise was burdened by the absence of Cook and the lack of hope for a Northwest Passage. Still, they were not tracing the impossible coast

1. With his light blond hair, dreamy eyes and fashionable clothes, John Ledyard cut a romantic figure. The only known likeness of him was a portrait painted in 1788 and subsequently lost in Sweden. In 1905 a keen Ledyard enthusiast and Dartmouth alum commissioned a Boston artist to produce a conjectured portrait of Ledyard. The resulting etching provides one possible if slightly subdued image of the great adventurer.

2. In 1757 Robert Hempstead, Ledyard's grandfather, built this house in Southold, New York (top). A young John Ledyard lived there from 1762-65 when his widowed mother moved back home from Groton, Connecticut. The house was torn down in October 1986.

3. During the American Revolution, Ledyard's mother ran a tavern and boardinghouse in the old salt box (below) in Southold. Ledyard stayed there when he deserted from the British Navy in 1782.

4. "That you may flourish in immortal green," wrote Ledyard, giving Dartmouth its iconic color. In May 1773 he wrote a rambling seven-page letter to the president of Dartmouth, explaining why he had suddenly abandoned the college after his freshman year. When his excuses fell flat, he resorted to effusive praise for his young alma mater "whose fruit I was so happy to taste but now no more."

5. Maquinna, the Mowachaht chief, was probably the man who, with red ochre, rattles and soaring song, greeted Ledyard and the other sailors on the Cook voyage when they landed at Nootka Sound of present-day Vancouver Island in March 1778. A Spanish sailor made this portrait of the resolute leader in 1792.

6. John James Audubon painted this excellent oil of the sea otter, which Ledyard first encountered at Nootka. The otter's thick, lustrous coat and the promise of great profits in China spurred Ledyard's ten-year obsession with the fur trade.

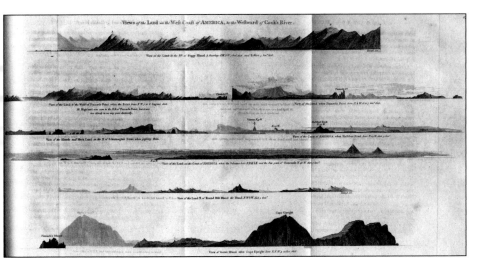

7 & 8. Ledyard was the first U.S. citizen to see the west coast of North America, and the views from the *Resolution* as he inched his way up the Alaskan coast awed him. "I felt myself plainly affected," he wrote in his journal. "It soothed a home-sick heart, and rendered me very tolerably happy."

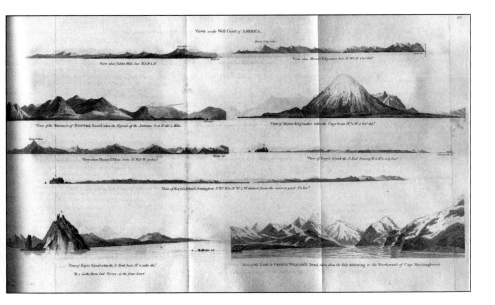

CANOES of OONALASHKA.

9 & 10. On the Aleutian island of Unalaska, Ledyard left the ship and hiked for two days' adventure to find Russian fur traders. At one point, two Aleutians transported him in a kayak with Ledyard lying in the hold "stowed away in bulk." Along the way he slept in native Aleutian-style houses like this one pictured by John Webber, the official Cook expedition artist.

The INSIDE of a HOUSE, in OONALASHKA.

11 & 12. "The emblem of innocent uninstructed beauty," wrote Ledyard about one Hawaiian woman, and John Webber's portrait offered a wistful glimpse into the future of these native islanders. Ledyard was present at one of the most infamous incidents in the history of exploration, the February 1779 death of Captain Cook on the beach at Kealakekua Bay in Hawaii.

A View of KARAKAKOOA, in OWYHEE.

A
J O U R N A L
OF
Captain C O O K's
LAST
V O Y A G E
TO THE
Pacific Ocean,
AND IN QUEST OF A
North-Weſt Paſſage,
BETWEEN
A S I A & A M E R I C A;

Performed in the Years 1776, 1777, 1778, and 1779.

Illuſtrated with a C H A R T, ſhewing the Tracts of the Ships employed in this Expedition.

Faithfully narrated from the original MS. of Mr. *JOHN LEDYARD.*

H A R T F O R D:
Printed and ſold by NATHANIEL PATTEN, a few Rods North of the Court-Houſe,
M.DCC.LXXXIII.

13 & 14. Published in the summer of 1783, Ledyard's memoir of the Cook voyage was a bestseller and the catalyst for American copyright legislation, but for him it was mostly a part of a desperate campaign to return to Nootka Sound. Below is John Webber's sketch of Nootka, with the *Resolution*, Ledyard's home for over four years, in the foreground. Nootka was the key stop on Ledyard's proposed adventure of walking around the world

of Alaska and the weather was slightly less rough, though the *Resolution* was as leaky as ever. The men shot polar bears, which proved to be more palatable than the previous summer's walrus. On 30 July they again passed the Bering Strait and less than a month later were back in Petropavlovsk.

For the second time, however, Ledyard and the crew sailed into Avacha Bay under a new captain. Charles Clerke succumbed to tuberculosis two days before they landed and was buried in a willow grove above the bay. John Gore took over the *Resolution* and James King the *Discovery*. Ledyard and the men stayed seven weeks at Petropavlovsk. They caught hundreds of fish, collected a summer's harvest of wild raspberries, hurtleberries and cranberries, went hunting for wild ducks and bear and danced on the decks to Russian music. They celebrated the day of King George III's coronation and the name day for Catherine II. The *Discovery*'s young marine drummer, Jeremiah Holloway, perhaps having missed his opportunity in the South Seas, unsuccessfully tried to desert with a Kamchatkan woman.

Summer turned to fall. Snow fell on distant peaks and on 10 October the two ships sailed for the south. Gore, in consultation with his officers, chose a southwest course. They missed the Kuriles but glimpsed the eastern coast of Japan and a snow-covered Mount Fiji. They passed Iwo Jima and then Formosa in a "continual gale of wind with very high Severe Squalls, Thunder, Lightning and Rain and an extraordinary high sea," George Gilbert wrote. On 24 November Ledyard and the crew saw a total eclipse of the moon, which, Samwell wrote, "rendered the Air as dark as pitch." That night William Bloom, a young able seaman on the *Discovery*, fell overboard. A good swimmer, Bloom managed to grab a rope hanging off the side of the ship and save himself.

At the beginning of December, Gore and King gathered their crews and ordered them "to deliver up to them their Journals, charts, drawings and remarks of all kinds relative to the Voyage and a diligent search was likewise made amongst the sailors." The order was to prevent any unauthorized versions of the voyage appearing before the official admiralty edition. In the official 1784 account of the voyage, King wrote that "It is with the greatest satisfaction I can relate, that my proposals met with the approbation, and the cheerful compliance both of the officers and men; and I am persuaded, that every scrap of paper, containing any transactions relating to the voyage, were given up." The sailors were cheerful for they expected such an impounding, as it was de rigueur on all around-the-world voyages. Ledyard turned his journal in, probably secreting away a few pages of notes. Other men, including Rickman, Zimmermann, Burney and Ellis, planned ahead and handed in one journal while hiding a second, clandestine copy.

The coast of China hove into view. The two ships paid a pilot thirty-five dollars to escort them to an anchorage in Macao Roads, the outer harbor of the Portuguese colony at the mouth of the Chu Kiang, or Pearl River. On 4 December, almost three years to the day since they left Cape Town, a few officers went ashore to the East India Company warehouse and returned with London newspapers from 1776, 1777 and 1778.

As if returning home after a long holiday to the usual mixture of good and bad news, Ledyard and the other sailors were elated and depressed at what they read. They were astounded to read that the war with the American colonies was still in progress and that the French had joined in the fray. Fearing an attack by American or French ships, Gore ordered a total revamping of the *Resolution* and *Discovery*. The carpenters strengthened the ships' stanchions and railings, converted wood cabins to canvas and erected musket-proof parapets on the decks.

Gore wanted more cannons and planned to sail upriver to Canton to fetch them—like Philadelphia on the Delaware, the trading entrepot of Canton was a hundred miles upriver from the sea. Some old China hands with the East India Company told Gore the Chinese would be greatly offended if he went to Canton, as they had been in 1742 and 1743 when Anson had sailed upriver. Gore agreed and sent King, Phillips and an eleven-man crew in an EIC boat to trade in Canton. They left on 18 December and returned on 8 January with a cannon and ammunition. In the meantime, Gore got nervous and exchanged a spare anchor for six cannons with Portuguese vessels in the harbor.

Even with the added firepower, the *Resolution* and *Discovery* did not feel secure. Every day strangers came on board, eager to meet the men on the famous Cook expedition. The officers told Ledyard and the rest of the crew not to say where they were going. Two Parisians visited and a rumor spread that they were spies. Two sailors, who had previously been in the French navy, claimed to know them, and Gore kicked the Frenchmen off the ship. A pair of Spanish galleons, hailing from Manila, sailed into Macao. The gossip was that they carried millions of Spanish dollars in their holds. Burney, worried the little Whitby cats would be seized and the official journal and logs taken away, spent a month feverishly copying the papers in microscopic print on thin Chinese paper.

His fifty-page manuscript, however, was never needed. When King returned from Canton, he brought the good news of immunity. On 10 March 1779, Benjamin Franklin, the minister plenipotentiary in France, had issued an order to all U.S. ships that the *Resolution* and the *Discovery*, "now expected to be soon in the European seas on her return," were exempt from the rules of war: "You would not consider her as an enemy, not suffer any plunder to be made of the effects contained in her, nor obstruct her immediate return to England." Cook and his men, Franklin said, were "common friends to mankind" on "an undertaking truly laudable." Nine days later the secretary of the French navy sent out a similar decree, ordering French ships to treat Cook as a neutral.

Compared to Kerguelen, Christmas Island and Hawaii, Ledyard's fourth Christmas at sea was easily the most exciting. He was able, with the addition of brightly colored Chinese silks, to fully refurbish his clothing. Ledyard and the men celebrated the holiday as usual and never stopped— so many sailors were drinking arrack, the local brew, that all work ceased on the ships. They caroused on shore, smelling opium smoke, tasting hot tea and hearing the click of mah-jongg tiles. Just before New Year, a few sailors ashore quarreled with some Chinese men. A brawl ensued and Jem Burney, trying to break it up, received a dagger wound in his left arm.

Despite the violence and drinking, the seamen sobered up and emptied their sea chests of the curiosities they had collected over the course of the voyage. The tchotchkes from Tahiti and Hawaii barely raised a flicker of interest, but the sea-otter furs they had casually bought at Nootka Sound and Unalaska and sold for a respectable profit at Kamchatka were worth more than gold. Mandarin tastes, it turned out, prized the sea otter more than any other fur-bearing animal.

The largest member of the weasel family, the sea otter (*Enhydra lutris*) is also the smallest marine mammal. It feeds on sea urchins, mollusks, crabs, seaweed and starfish. It has no insulating layer of body fat for swimming in the cold north Pacific currents, so its jet-black, glossy hide is a marvel of thickness. In each square inch are squeezed sixty thousand hairs. The sea-otter pelt, first introduced by the Russian promyshlenniki a half century earlier, was now the imperial fur. In the bloodless equations of the times, one slave was worth two sea-otter pelts. Ledyard and the crew, however, received not humans but cold, hard cash on the barrelhead for their sea-otter skins. A small, lice-ridden skin already cut as clothing got £15, and a well-cleaned and preserved skin went for £30. One seaman sold his own stock for £200 ($32,000 in 2005). There were some circuitous currency calculations: William Bligh bought a hatchet in England for a shilling, sold it in Tahiti for thirty green beads, fifteen of which he exchanged for six sea-otter skins in Nootka which in turn brought him more than £90 in Macao—a profit of 1,800 percent.

The astronomical prices enlivened the exhausted men, and they turned their London-seeking eyes back to Alaska. "The rage with which our seamen were possessed to return to Cook's River, and, by another cargo of skins, to make their fortunes, at one time, was not far short of mutiny," admitted King in the official account of the voyage. One night two men from the *Resolution*, John Cave, the quartermaster, and Robert Spencer, an able seaman, stole the six-oared cutter and fled the ship in order to sail to Nootka. They succeeded in deserting but never managed to return to Nootka. Five days after King returned from Canton, Gore hastily weighed anchor.

"We had nothing now but a beaten track to pass in our way to our long-wished for native country," wrote John Rickman, but the beaten track had its own surprises. Ledyard and the crew sailed through the South China Sea and then tiptoed past Indonesia, spending a week at Pulo Condor. The officers went hunting. Gore bought seven buffalos for four dollars. The carpenters felled cedar trees. They stopped at Pulau Bangka and came to the coast of Sumatra. Seeing two ships off Java, Gore and King hoisted English colors and prepared for action, but they turned out to be neutral Dutch ships. They passed the Strait of Sunda and sailed with a quartering southeast wind into the Indian Ocean.

A five-day storm during their second week in the Indian Ocean weakened the *Resolution's* rudder, and in early April 1780 it almost twisted off completely. The carpenters jerry-rigged a temporary solution, but when they came to Cape Town they could not steer around Cape Point and had to limp into False Bay on the Indian Ocean side. The governor came on board, delivering letters that had been waiting for them for a year and a half and asking questions concerning the death of Cook.

They spent a pleasant month in Cape Town. It was autumn and the white, gale-spun sand of Muizenburg beach was still invitingly warm. Some of the men went hunting again or wandered in the foothills on the backside of Table Mountain. Gore was so worried about the state of the *Resolution* that he sent a copy of the ship's logs with Nathaniel Portlock, a master's mate, on the *Sybil*, a British frigate also leaving for England. Unable to resist replicating Cook's actions at the Cape, Gore embarked one hundred and twenty sheep on each ship, as well as other livestock.

Into the Atlantic the *Resolution* and *Discovery* went on their final leg. The *Sybil* had taken just ten weeks to get from London to Cape Town, and Ledyard and the men hoped for such fair winds. In June the *Discovery* had a couple of minor crises. While "excercising the great guns," one man "had his arm shattered in a shocking manner," wrote Rickman, when some wadding had been left in from a previous discharge. Then the *Discovery* sprung her maintopmast.

Ledyard and the crew crossed the equator for the fourth time in mid-July, and in early August reached the English Channel. Gore had read in China about an American captain named John Paul Jones who was wreaking havoc on ships in the English Channel, and he deemed it safer to sail around the British Isles. In a giant sweep, he took the *Resolution* and the *Discovery* west past Ireland and landed on 22 August at Stromness in the Orkney Islands, twenty miles north of the Scottish mainland. For a month the wind was unfavorable, blowing from the southeast, and the ships swung at anchor.

It was a frustrating coda to the voyage. They had been at sea for more than four years, the longest circumnavigation in history. Now they were in British territory but unable to get home. "We cou'd get no more intiligence concerning our Friends than if we had been at Otaheite," George Gilbert wrote. King, Bayly and Webber rowed to the mainland and took a coach down to London to report to the admiralty. Samuel Gibson managed to get word to his girlfriend, Jane Oaks, who came to the Orkneys to see him. Gore married them aboard the *Resolution*, but their honeymoon was permanently postponed when Gibson died of malaria on 23 September. He was just days away from completing his third trip around the world.

They finally left Stromness and wound down the east coast of England in the company of the *Fly* and *Alderney*, two ships of the line. They lay at anchor at Yarmouth for three days and on 4 October came into the Thames. Two days later the men lashed the *Discovery* to the shore at Woolwich and the *Resolution* continued up to Deptford. On 7 October 1780, after four years, two months, and twenty-four days, the *Resolution* reached London and the greatest voyage in the age of sail was over.

9

Crooked Billet—
Chasing the Fur Trade

CHAOTIC AND CACOPHONOUS, the arrival back in England startled Ledyard and the other men after fifteen hundred days at sea. Hordes of people crowded the ships. Newspaper reporters asked for interviews. Merchants bargained for curiosities. The officers packed off crates of dried plants to the home of renowned botanist Joseph Banks. Delegations from the ships twice met with British Museum officials to donate dozens of artifacts. Joining the men at the disembarking was one animal remaining from Cook's Noah's Ark scheme, a single half-starved monkey.

On 24 October 1780, the admiralty paid off the men in the offices of the Navy Board at Somerset House. For Ledyard, his visit to Somerset House, the stunning new palace rising from the Thames that housed many government agencies and learned societies, was a heady day. In five years he had gone from a lowly private rusticating in the Plymouth garrison to a sergeant (promoted after Samuel Gibson's death in September) who had sailed around the world. Little did he know that by the end of the decade his portrait would be hanging in Somerset House.

However, walking out of Somerset House in October 1780 was depressing. For his four years of service, Ledyard received £27 pounds 16 shillings and 2 $^1/_2$ pence (the purchasing power of about $5,000 in 2005). Unlike other marines, Ledyard had been extravagant on the *Resolution*. He had purchased a large number of clothes from the navy and smoked more than anyone in the group, spending almost £2 on tobacco. The admiralty paid privates £39, as opposed to Ledyard's gross pay of £52, yet some privates from the *Resolution* had net wages nearly equal to Ledyard. Compounding the low pay was Ledyard's inability to retain it. He invested the money in stocks at the London Stock Exchange and it soon disappeared.

The navy sent Ledyard back to Plymouth. He wanted to return to America, but it would be all but impossible for him to desert from the navy and find passage across the Atlantic, and the penalty if he got caught was death by hanging. Back in Plymouth, the tedium of a soldier in barracks replaced the excitement of a voyage of discovery. He was now a sergeant, but he smarted over all the promotions the expedition's officers received: all the midshipmen became lieutenants, Molesworth Phillips became a captain and John Gore and James King became post-captains. In June 1781, after waiting eight months, he sent a letter to the Earl of Sandwich, the First Lord of the Admiralty. To ensure the safe passage of his letter, Ledyard sent it care of Gore, who was then in retirement at Cook's old sinecure at Greenwich Hospital. Gore added his own preface to Ledyard's letter: "Serjeant Ledyard is a Young active Man who hath done Good service on our late Circumnavigating Voyage, and Is one who from Education and abilities is (I think) Properly Qualified and justly merits a higher Rank Than That which he holds at present. My wish is to recommend him to your Lordships notice In hopes That by your means a Good Officer may not be Lost by being continued the Serjeant." Ledyard's own letter to Sandwich could not be more fawning:

> I had the honour to sail with Captain Cook on his last Voyage upon Discoveries and though in quite a private station it is well known I merited much of his esteem and more than once have been entrusted with very honorable commands as will appear from his own Journals, nor was my conduct less acceptable to Capt. Clerke who succeeded him, and I am also happy to say that Capt. Gore who succeeded them both is equally disposed to represent [me]

to Your Lordship as a deserving Soldier . . . May it please your Lordship, I understand that I am already on the list of those offered to your lordships consideration for promotion, but as yet nothing in my favour has transpired. . . . I am a native of North America, of a good Family and once had considerable connections there, until the rupture with England in 1775 when I abandoned all and entered the Army.

Sandwich employed a pocket veto and no promotion came—perhaps the earl was loath to advance an American. Eighteen months later when Ledyard was back in America, he changed his story and claimed in a public letter to the Connecticut assembly that he had "solicited the Earl of Sandwich in vain for his discharge from the service." The reason for Ledyard's volte-face was that in 1783 in Connecticut he could be branded a traitor for having spent the Revolution in the British marines. Privately, though, Ledyard admitted in a 1782 letter to his cousin that his initial focus upon the end of the voyage was on his military career, and he blamed the absence of Cook, "my friend and consquently my interest at the levee of a certain great Lord" for his failure to gain promotion.

Ledyard had abandoned his good family and considerable connections in 1775, he wrote, but fate brought him home. In October 1781 the admiralty ordered his company onto a cruising frigate heading to North America. That winter they docked at Huntington Bay, the British-fortified port on the north coast of Long Island. Stymied in his hopes of rising in the navy and faced with the unappetizing prospect of fighting against his own countrymen, Ledyard spent many months contemplating his next move. If he stayed in the marines, he could be permanently exiled from America, but if he deserted he would lose a year's accumulated pay and, if caught, would face the death penalty. In January 1782 he managed to smuggle out a letter via two intermediaries to his cousin Isaac Ledyard. After greeting Isaac with his usual effusions—"My heart I send you, my whole heart"— Ledyard told his cousin about his voyage with Cook and of his hopes to return for that elusive domestic bliss "with a pig, a plain wife and land to do as myself is pleased."

In the letter he addressed Isaac as "Monecca," a childhood nickname perhaps referring to Isaac's monkish personality, and signed his name as "Josephus." It was a very telling choice for a nom de plume. Flavius Josephus was an important first-century Jewish historian whom Ledyard liked for his seminal books and prophetic statements—he coined the word "theocracy." But he might have found consanguinity with Josephus for a number of less obvious reasons. Josephus was a digressive writer like Ledyard. He was also adventurous: as a teenager Josephus spent three years in the desert living with a hermit, and he survived a shipwreck off the coast of Italy. Most interestingly, Josephus had switched sides during the Jewish revolt against Roman rule in AD 66, becoming an interpreter for emperors and enjoying Rome's patronage. For an American who had joined the imperial forces of Great Britain while it was putting down a rebellion in his native land, the name Josephus was fitting.

In November 1782 Ledyard's commanding officer signed a permit for seven day's leave. With a copy of Sterne's *Tristam Shandy* as his only possession, Ledyard left Huntington Bay and retraced the path of his 1773 tour of Long Island, the college dropout looking for a parish on his old mare Rosinante. When he didn't return, his officer marked an R next to Ledyard's name, for "run."

John Ledyard, in a playful, Shandian mood, came into Southold on a winter day. He stopped at the local boardinghouse, Moore's Tavern, and, pretending to be a British officer, took a room. Coming down for dinner, he went into the bar and sat by a spitting fire. The owner, Abigail Moore, stared at him and, coming closer, said that he bore a strange resemblance to her son. Ending his charade, Ledyard sprung from his chair and embraced his mother. It had been eight years since they had seen each other.

Ledyard might have pulled this stunt to hide his awkwardness about his responsibility for the parlous state of his family. While the oldest son gallivanted around the world, his mother, brothers and sisters suffered significant war-time depredations. His mother's husband died in January 1776. Forty-seven years old with six children in the house, including three young ones, she resorted to boarding travelers at her home, a rambling old house on the eastern end of town.

Many of her guests were not invited. The British occupied Long Island in December 1776, and in April of the following year they took over Southold. Ten ships sailed into the tiny harbor. The British confiscated all the cut hay in the area, ransacked orchards, used the local church as a depot and commandeered rooms in local houses, including Moore's. "They seized the best room in brother's house," wrote John Hempstead in a letter to his brother Robert, Ledyard's grandfather, "& was more than ordinary prophaine in their speech & behaviour." The only battle fought in Southold occurred at her house a few years later, when a group of local men ambushed the British soldiers staying at her house and killed eleven. Moore often harbored deserters from the British army. One evening a brace of soldiers stormed into her house with swords drawn, demanding she reveal any deserters. She stood them down and they left empty handed. Her son Thomas led a group of men who attacked the informer and drove him to a British ship. In September 1781 marauding British troops robbed and beat a number of neighbors and threatened to set fire to Moore's house, but she again brushed them aside.

Moore did not have much family to comfort her. Her stepdaughter, Jerusha Moore, had become pregnant with the child of Richard Mann, a captain of a local British frigate, the *Swan*. Much in the same way Moore had eloped with Captain John Ledyard, Jerusha stole from the house one night with her intended. Seeing the empty bed, Moore tracked the girl to the *Swan*. She boarded the ship and demanded an immediate wedding for Jerusha on the quarterdeck. Jerusha then sailed off with Mann. Ledyard's brother George sailed to New Orleans and lived in Natchez, Mississippi before surviving a shipwreck off the coast of South America. His sister Fanny, the occupation ruining her millinery shop, fled for Groton in April 1781. Ledyard's grandfather Robert Hempstead, the Southold patriarch, died in 1779. In a letter to her sister about the death of their father, Moore added a poignant line: "I have no news from my son John nor from my son George. All my comfort is that my God is everywhear."

Nervous that the British troops staying in his mother's home would discover he was a deserter, Ledyard left town after a few days, just as his furlough officially ended. He felt "tenderly as the leading descendent of a broken & distressed Family," he wrote a few months later. "Above all, [I] hope to have it in my power to administer to the wants of a beloved Parent & others who languish & fade in obscurity." Somehow, his relationship with his mother survived his lack of support—or even presence—and they continued to correspond for the rest of his life.

As he had so many times as a child, Ledyard crossed the Long Island Sound to Groton. It was a bittersweet reunion, for his hometown was reeling from the battle of Fort Griswold. A vicious end to the seven years of fighting in New England, the battle was more of a massacre. In the summer of 1781 the incessant sniping of New London's powerful privateers had culminated in the capture of the *Hannah,* a rich British merchant ship. On 6 September 1781, Benedict Arnold, now on the British side, brought soldiers (mostly New Jersey loyalists) to the Thames to seek revenge. They routed New London's Fort Trumbull and then pillaged the town, burning more than a hundred houses, dozens of boats, a church and the *Hannah,* still loaded with stores.

Across the river, Arnold's troops assaulted Fort Griswold. Under the command of Ledyard's Uncle William, the earthworks fort withstood the British for a couple of hours but eventually fell. During the battle there was confusion when the fort's flag disappeared, as if the Americans were surrendering. It had only been shot down and the colonialists fought on until finally surrendering. When the leader of the British, Major Bromfield, entered the fort and asked who commanded the fort, William Ledyard gallantly handed his sword to Bromfield and said, "I did, sir, but you do now." The major, believing the Americans had violated a rule of war in a false capitulation, took the sword and plunged it through William, killing him instantly. The British granted no quarter and killed the other Americans. Eighty-one died, most after the surrender.

The British burned almost all of the barns, shops and homes in Groton, including Ledyard's childhood home and schoolhouse. More than twenty-eight Ledyards were killed or wounded that day. The number was so high because many Ledyards were in town for a family wedding: In late August Mary Ledyard, William's daughter, had married Captain Thomas Seymour, her Hartford first cousin. William Ledyard left a widow and seven children, including a son born just ten days before the battle. Youngs Ledyard, Jr., John Ledyard's first cousin, was killed, leaving his wife with three children and twins who would be born eleven days after the battle. Ledyard's uncle Thomas Seymour survived with thirteen bayonet wounds, while his cousin Billy Seymour had a leg amputated at the knee. Fanny Ledyard ministered to the wounded after the battle, earning the nickname Angel of Groton.

After a few harrowing weeks, Ledyard moved on and by Christmas-time he was in Hartford, resettled amongst his Ledyard and Seymour relatives at the old Arch Street home. "You will be surprized to hear of my being at Hartford—I am surprized myself," wrote Ledyard to his cousin Isaac on 5 January 1783. After telling of his escape from Huntington, he explained his present situation: "I am now at Mr. Seymours, and as happy as a Bee. I have a little Cash, Three pairs of Breeches, Three Waistcoats, Six pairs of Stockings, Two Coats, and half a dozen ruffled shirts. . . . I eat & drink when I am asked, and visit when I am invited: and in short generally do as I am bid. All I want of my Friends is Frienship; and Possessed of that I am happy."

Happy as a bumblebee, Ledyard was at peace for the first time in a decade. His cousins, aunts and uncles swarmed over the house, including his Uncle Thomas, soon to be mayor of Hartford; his cousin Tom, known as the Beau Sabreur of Saratoga for escorting British General John Burgoyne to captivity in Boston; and his cousin Mary Juliana, just fourteen but well on her way to becoming one of the most celebrated beauties in America. At Arch Street Ledyard was in the center of a swirl of practical jokes and rambunctious, high-velocity repartee.

Nestled in his family, the future lay open to him. With the Ledyard name, his grandfather's training and his own experience in the West Indies trade, he could have become a merchant. Perhaps the field of law would have made sense, with his quick-witted ripostes and his uncle's reputation. But Ledyard eschewed ordinary professions. He pined for the life of adventure.

The first step, as he saw it, was to ask for a position as a government-paid explorer. On 6 January 1783, he wrote a public memorial (or formal letter) to the governor of Connecticut and the Connecticut General Assembly asking for money and a job: "Your Memorialist, having lost his pecuniary assistance by his abrupt departure from the British is thereby incapacitated to move in a circle he could wish without the Assistance of his friends & the patronage & recommendations of the Government. . . . He therefore proposes. . . that he may be introduced into some immediate employment wherein he may as well be usefull to his country as to himself during the War." No appointment as official state traveler ensued, but Ledyard did secure an audience with John Trumbull, the governor of the state and a colleague of his grandfather's. Trumbull in turn introduced him to Nathaniel Patten.

A young Scottish bookbinder, Patten ran a prosperous bookstore near the Hartford courthouse. In 1780 he started publishing books and almanacs to augment his income. When a Connecticut sailor blew into town fresh from one of the epic adventures of the age, he saw a chance to make a profit. Patten paid Ledyard twenty guineas, a sum almost equal to Ledyard's take-home pay from the voyage itself, for the rights to his story.

Writing an account of the voyage was always one of Ledyard's goals. Midvoyage he had asked Captain Clerke for an appointment as official historian of the expedition. Now, with Patten's backing, he could become an unofficial chronicler. He spent the winter and spring of 1783 scratching away in Uncle Thomas's law offices and produced his only book published in his lifetime, *A Journal of Captain Cook's Last Voyage.*

Patten was a diligent printer. With paper, type and ink scarce after the long war, he still managed to produce an elegant book. He printed the book in two parts, the first half in June and the rest in July. Later in the year he produced a single edition, a leather-bound duodecimo two-hundred-and-eight-page volume measuring four by seven and one-half inches. A "Chart shewing the Track's of the Ships" around the globe, made by an anonymous etcher, faced the title page. Patten tinkered with the letterpress, correcting misspellings and typographical errors for later editions. How well it sold was unclear, for in 1783 there was no bestseller list, but the *Journal,* one of the first published in America on Great Britain's exploratory voyages to the Pacific, was bound to be popular. In early August booksellers in Philadelphia offered the book in local newspapers, and soon it was being sold across the country. In 1821 a researcher for Jared Sparks, Ledyard's first biographer, interviewed Patten, who reported that he no longer owned a single copy of the book. "I have understood," the researcher told Sparks, "the work was very popular at the time, & that Mr. P. made no inconsiderable sum from the Publication." It found its way into dozens of public libraries and hundreds of private homes.

Assisting Patten in the sale of the book was the new idea of copyright. In his January 1783 memorial to the Connecticut assembly, Ledyard asked for "the exclusive right of publishing this said Journal or history in this State for such a term as shall be thot fit." Ledyard's petition to protect his proposed memoir led to a remarkably broad and quick response. The assembly formed a committee that reported days later "that in their Opinion a publication of the Memorialists Journal in his voyage round the Globe may be beneficial to these United States & to the world, & it appears reasonable & Just that the Memorialist should have an exclusive right to publish the same for a Reasonable Term." The Connecticut assembly accepted the committee report and at the end of January 1783 issued an "Act for the encouragment of Literature and Genius," declaring a resident of the United States had sole power to publish a book for fourteen years and had the right to apply for a second term of another fourteen years. In March 1783 Massachusetts passed a similar act, in April Maryland did likewise and by April 1786 all thirteen states had a copyright law. In 1787 the new U.S. constitution declared in its first article that congress had the power to pass copyright legislation, and in May 1790 at its second session Congress passed the first national law protecting copyright. Thus *A Journal of Captain Cook's Last Voyage*, although it did not contain a notice of Connecticut's copyright in its front matter, had the noted distinction of being the catalyst for American copyright protection.

A fluid if prolix and sometimes grandiloquent writer, Ledyard produced a fascinating narrative. As a scaffolding for the text he wrote in diary form, but he rarely gave the reader a sense of his daily duties or routines. Unlike most other round-the-world accounts, he sidestepped the issues of navigation and seamanship that confronted the voyagers. Instead he regularly halted the chronological momentum for absorbing digressions about the physical and human landscape of the places he encountered. He gave over sixteen pages to a description of Tonga, twelve pages to Tahiti and eight pages to Nootka. The heart of the book was Hawaii. Ledyard wrote sixty-nine pages on the archipelago, about his experiences, his hike up Mauna Loa and the island's lively culture. The death of Cook was the dramatic denouement for the book. Ledyard's description vibrated with energy and foreshadowing and was a serious, honest attempt to see Cook's death from the Hawaiians' point of view.

Part of the pleasure of his book, indeed, was Ledyard's fascination with native peoples. He wrote about their religions, social customs, clothing, diet and governments. He pondered migration patterns and twice listed vocabulary words in an effort to discern common origins. He reported about homosexuality and cannibalism, two titillating subjects for his audience, but discreetly passed over the predominant activity for the sailor ashore, sexual liaisons with island women. Unlike other published sailors from the Cook voyages, Ledyard did not issue too many broad generalizations but rather gave the natives the benefit of the doubt. He often admitted his knowledge was imperfect. When discussing Tahitian religious beliefs, he wrote: "Much has been said about them by former voyagers, and in truth too much, especially about their religion which they are not fond of discovering, and therefore when urged on the matter have often rather than displease those who made the enquiry told not only different accounts, but such as were utterly inconsistent with what we knew to be true from occular demonstration." Ledyard appreciated the fact that no matter how well he acquired a language or how much time he spent talking and observing the natives, he could never rectify the innate imbalance of his relationship to the islanders. Writing to Thomas Jefferson in February 1786, Ledyard said, "I had frequently observed that when a European queried a savage about a circumstance that perhaps he was totaly ignorant of, that he was nevertheless unwilling that the European should know it or even think that he was ignorant and to divert his suspicions would make use of the most wily arts and rather than appear to be less informed of the common affairs of his country than the European would say any thing to make the European think favourably of him."

Extricating himself completely from eighteenth-century European norms was impossible. He described Tongans as "wild untutored creatures." Tasmanians were "inactive, indolent, and unaffected with the least appearance of curiosity." The Siberian natives, he wrote, "are indolent, ignorant, superstitious, jealous, cowardly, and more filthy and dirty than the imagination can conceive." Yet, Ledyard repeatedly praised the people he met, finding them refreshingly bold and contented. His enlightened attitude was most clear when he articulated the disparity in the voyage-long fulcrum that swung between the sailors and natives: theft. He condemned Cook's harsh treatment of thieves with his prophetic statement that "the full exertion of extreme power is an argument of extreme weakness." When describing how even Finau, the Tongan chief, stole from the ships, he argued that two radically different approaches to property were in conflict, with the Europeans coming off worse:

How often Phewnow [Finau], have I felt for thee, the embarrassments of these involuntary offences against a people thou didst as well love and wouldst as soon have befriended when thou wast accused and stood condemned as when not and at that instant would most willingly have shared with thee those distresses which resulted only from imputed guilt and a theory of moral virtue thou couldst be no farther acquainted with, than from the dictates of uncultivated nature or imagine from the countenances of strangers—more savage themselves with all their improvements than thou wert without a single one of them.

Ledyard's respect of native cultures went so far that he promulgated a new theory. Reversing the usual concept of progress, he argued that civilization was the original state for all societies and that these islanders had only moved farther away from it than Europeans.

The most revolutionary part of the book was the most subtle. As the first American citizen to see and touch the west coast of the North American continent, Ledyard did more than simply report on the people and the landscape. Ever since Columbus told Europe about the New World, everyone wondered how big it was. Many imagined that the continent was small, that the west coast was close to the Mississippi. On page sixty-nine, Ledyard cleared up the mystery. He said that both Oregon and Nootka Sound were at 233 east longitude, revealing that the North American continent was much bigger than most people had supposed.

Ledyard produced the fifty-four-thousand-word memoir in just four months and it contained errors. There were lapses in grammar, punctuation, syntax and fact. The biggest error was straight plagiarism. In 1822 Ledyard's Uncle Thomas said that his nephew wrote the book "principally, from memory." But that was not true. On his desk was a copy of John Hawkesworth's three-volume *An Account of the Voyages Undertaken by the Order of His Present Majesty for Making Discoveries in the Southern Hemisphere*, published in London in 1773. Hawkesworth mixed many of the officer's logs, including the journals of Cook and Joseph Banks, to distill the admiralty-sanctioned version of the Bryon, Wallis, Carteret and first Cook expedition. Ledyard also probably had a copy of the official version of the second expedition, written by Cook and published in 1777, as well as unsanctioned versions from the first and second voyages. Two books on the third voyage surreptitiously appeared in London, one published anonymously in the summer of 1781 and William Ellis's two-volume edition in 1782. Ledyard left England before Ellis's book appeared and probably did not see it before his own book was published. Ledyard certainly obtained a copy of the anonymous 1781 edition before he sailed for America.

There are traces of the other books in Ledyard's narrative. For his Tahiti section, he borrowed Hawkesworth's vocabulary list, some phrasing and ideas and occasionally a verbatim sentence. But with the anonymous 1781 edition, he did not borrow but rather stole. Ledyard used the 1781 book for details—dates, longitude and latitude measurements, bearings—that otherwise he would not have been able to remember without notes. He reproduced a number of anecdotes and historical material and even made a fair facsimile of the 1781 chart for the frontispiece. Most egregiously, though, was the fact that he took the final thirty-eight pages of his book—the voyage from Kamchatka in June 1779 to London in October 1780—directly verbatim from the anonymous edition.

The appalling theft of eleven thousand words was noticeable within months of Ledyard's publication date. In the fall of 1783 Robert Bell, a Philadelphia publisher, issued a version of the 1781 anonymous journal. (Although, to confuse matters more, Bell used the title page and some footnotes from William Ellis' book.) With both Ledyard's and the 1781 anonymous book circulating, readers soon discovered that Ledyard had plagiarized. It was never clear whether Ledyard or Patten was at fault. "Being in haste to pursue his adventures, as soon as he had indulged his eager wishes to see his friends," wrote Ledyard's cousin Philip Freneau by way of explanation, "he allowed himself no time to compile and arrange the Papers, but left them with some person of that place in a loose and disordered State, of course they went into an incorrect, as well as inelegant Edition." Ledyard, on his way out of Hartford, might have flung the 1781 book at Patten and asked him to use it to fill out the rest of the story; or Patten, frustrated by a manuscript that ended sixteen months before the voyage did and an author no longer in town, might have done the borrowing himself. Either way, Ledyard deserved the blame. Because of his appropriations, historians well into the twentieth century pegged Ledyard as the author of the 1781 anonymous edition. It is ironic that Ledyard's 1783 *Journal*, the book that established copyright protection in the United States, was so blatantly in violation of the copyright ethos.

The soft, black gold of the sea-otter pelt was the cause of the plagiarism. John Ledyard was sick with fur fever. Bitten by the bug in Kamchatka, it had developed into a full-blown, body-wracking, hallucinatory illness at Macao. The ease of collecting sea-otter furs on the west coast of North America and selling them on the east coast of China was preposterous. The supply and demand seemed endless. Ledyard and the other sailors had seriously considered mutiny when that picture became crystal clear at Macao and two men from the *Resolution* deserted in hopes of returning to Nootka. Frustratingly, Ledyard glimpsed the promised land of milk and honey, and then he had to turn away and sail for home.

For Ledyard, a prime purpose of *A Journal of Captain Cook's Last Voyage* was to promote his plan of returning to Nootka and Macao. In his memorial to the Connecticut assembly, Ledyard promised that his book "may be essentially usefull to America in general but particularly to the northern States by opening a most valuable trade across the north pacific Ocean to China & the east Indies." In his description of Nootka Sound, he listed the varieties of animals, "the richness of their furr" and the prices they sold for in Kamschatka and Macao. Ledyard wrote ruefully, "it afterwards happened that skins which did not cost the purchaser sixpence sterling sold in China for 100 dollars. Neither did we purchase a quarter part of the beaver and other furrskins we might have done, and most certainly should have done had we known of meeting the opportunity of disposing of them to such an astonishing profit." Ledyard now wanted to meet the opportunity again. Setting up a triangular trade route, he hoped to take a ship around Cape Horn, collect furs at Nootka, sell them at Macao, winter in Hawaii and then return via Cape Town. As the only American to have been to all these places, he was perfect for the job.

Hartford was no place to make it happen. Ledyard had dedicated the book to John Trumbull, but the governor had no means to implement his scheme. He would have to go to Philadelphia. In April 1783 news reached Connecticut that Great Britain had formally declared a ceasefire. Ledyard, as a British navy deserter, now felt more secure in moving around the country. After two years wasted in barracks and ships and four months holed up in a law office writing a book manuscript, Ledyard was free to pursue his latest dream. He left Hartford in May 1783, more than a month before his book was published. On his way to Philadelphia, he visited his beloved cousins Isaac and Ben in New Jersey and flirted with Ben's sister-in-law, Eleanor Forman.

The City of Brotherly Love's forty thousand residents made up, after London, the largest English-speaking metropolis in the world. It was America's wealthiest city, busiest port (a ship under full sail was in the city's official seal) and the cosmopolitan center of the new nation. Unlike Boston, with its narrow warren of streets, Philadelphia was laid out in an orderly grid. Most streets had redbrick sidewalks and working gutters and were lit at night, except during a full moon, by whale-oil lamps. Philadelphia had more newspapers than London and more industry than the rest of the colonies combined. Yet it was still quaintly rural. Walking west from the Delaware, one reached open farmland by Eleventh Street. Pigs rooted amongst the giant piles of horse manure and garbage in the cobblestoned streets. In this Quaker city the majority were non-Quakers, none more obvious than the German-speaking farmers who wheeled their produce-laden wagons down High Street on Philadelphia's market days, which were every day in the summer.

Ledyard went, quite possibly on purpose, to the Crooked Billet, an old inn on Water Street that had been the scene of a classic American rags-to-riches story:. In October 1733 a seventeen-year-old boy from Boston spent his first night in Philadelphia at the Crooked Billet. He had arrived that morning, fallen asleep at a Quaker meeting service and spent almost the last of his money on three breadrolls, two of which he gave away. That afternoon he took a room at the Crooked Billet. "Here I got a Dinner," he later recalled. "And while I was eating it, several sly Questions were ask'd me, as it seem'd to be suspected from my youth & Appearance, that I might be some Runaway." The boy was Benjamin Franklin.

Another New Englander seeking his fortune sixty years later, John Ledyard reenacted Franklin's inauspicious beginnings. After taking a room and eating breakfast, Ledyard went out for an exploratory walk around the docks. It was a dispiriting sight. In May 1783, after eight years of war including two years under British occupation, Philadelphia was exhausted.

The economy was in a deep depression. The maritime industry was particularly hard hit. The British had lifted the blockade on the Delaware only in April 1783, but had simultaneously closed their ports to American ships. Americans could not sell their cod in the West Indies or their lumber in England. Even British ships were not allowed to carry American goods. Nor were the former colonies producing much: a shortage of slave labor had devastated southern plantations, and cotton, tobacco, rice and indigo production were all below prewar levels. Most American ships had been lost, burned or captured during the war, yet the shipyards stood empty as no one had money to pay for new boats. The only masts in the harbor were foreign ones, bringing goods that flooded the local markets. "I first went to Mr. Clanagans [Blair McClenachan]: he had no navigation," wrote Ledyard in a letter to Isaac. "To two other houses to no purpose: I then went among the shipping, and examined them thoroughly: I doubt that I should even be put to it to get to Sea before the mast: The most of the shipping here are foreigners. Sixteen Sail of Seven different maritime powers arrived here a few days ago. Fourteen Sailors went out to the Northward [to Boston] the morning I arrived for want of Employ: and numbers are Strolling the Docks of the City on the Same Account. There is at present little home navigation."

After four disheartening hours, Ledyard returned to the Crooked Billet. In the quiet of his room he emptied his pockets and "counted my cash—and turned it over—& looked at it, shook it—my hand—recounted it & found two French Crowns, half a Crown, one fourth of a Dollar, one eighth of a dollar, and lastly twelve Coppers. Shall I visit H—'s? I looked at my Stockings—my Breeches: they will do—my shoes—If I look that way—my Two Crowns & I shall part. We did part—I put my new pumps on, washed, shaved, and walked to H—'s where I had determined not to go." Swallowing his pride, Ledyard walked in his new shoes to the home of Anne and Andrew Hodge, Jr. The youngest of Squire John Ledyard's fifteen children, Anne Ledyard had married Hodge in Philadelphia on 6 September 1781, the same day that so much of their family was killed at the battle of Fort Griswold. With the bitterness of his grandfather's will still fresh in his mind, Ledyard was unwilling to lean upon his step-aunt.

But with such a pitiful amount of currency (though of typical variety, as the dollar did not become the official U.S. monetary unit until 1785), he had no choice. He found his uncle Andrew Hodge on his way out the door, heading to Princeton. Ledyard quickly scribbled a note to Isaac for Hodge to carry. After recounting his first day in Philadelphia, Ledyard ended his note to Isaac with a hesitating request: "I am at a loss whether to say anything about money here: or depend upon this Letter meeting you at Prince Town—wait the return of Mr. H— the chance he has of seeing you or—I don't know what to do.—I have determined—Send me Either by Mr. H.— or the first Conveyance some Cash." How Ledyard managed to hemorrhage money was a mystery. Unless he had enormous debts in Hartford, possibly from more stock market failures, he should have had some of the twenty guineas advance Patten gave him for his book.

In June 1783 Ledyard secured an interview with Robert Morris, the one person who could finance his fur-trade scheme. Morris had emigrated as a teenager from Liverpool and worked his way up in a merchant house firm in Philadelphia until he became a partner. Morris served in Congress, signed the Declaration of Independence, and chaired the Secret Committee of Commerce. In 1781 with the collapse of public credit, Congress appointed him superintendent of finance. He started the first national bank, collected taxes from the states, settled war debt with Great Britain and employed private contractors to provision the army. Mixing profit and patriotism, Morris was known as the financier of the revolution, and he was the most powerful and wealthiest businessman in the country. Ledyard never said how he finagled his way into his offices, but with the Ledyard family's merchant connections his name was probably enough.

Morris took a liking to Ledyard. They assuredly talked about the West Indies trade—Morris had once been attacked by French privateers off of Cuba, a circumstance Ledyard knew well from his father's tales. Ledyard's idea for buying furs in Nootka and selling them in China beguiled the dewlapped Liverpudlian. "I have been so often the sport of Fortune, I dare scarcely credit the Present dawn of the most luxuriant prospects," Ledyard told his cousin. "But it is a fact that the Hon'l Robert Morris is disposed to give me a Ship to go into the N. Pacific Ocean. I have had two interviews with him at the Finance Office, and tomorrow I expect a conclusive one. Ye beneficient! What a noble hold he instantaneously took of the Enterprise!"

Morris called in Gouverneur Morris, a lawyer and former member of Congress who assisted at the finance office, and the three men talked over the proposition. Because the British controlled the trade routes to India and China and because of the great expense involved with sending a ship around the world, there had been barely any thought previously of directly trading with Asia. Ledyard's timing was perfect. The war had just ended. The United States, with all its former markets closed to it, needed new places to buy and sell goods. Robert Morris, having just announced his resignation from his post (which did not come into effect until 1784), felt free to use his sizable fortune and business network on new private ventures. Both Morris and Ledyard drew up business plans. Ledyard calculated for two straight days and came up with "a minute detail of a Plan and estimate of the outfits" that cost £2,000 less than Morris's plan. The only hitch, Ledyard thought, was that both Morrises wanted to use American sailors.

Starting with these initial meetings in Philadelphia, John Ledyard plunged into a tangled web of thieving partners and powerful, hidden interests. The project went through various permutations and always, on the fringe, dangled the innocent Ledyard. Although his force of personality and keen determination meant much, he was no match for the ensnaring Machiavellian machinations of American merchants.

Robert Morris assigned Daniel Parker to manage the project. A Bostonian, Parker was a former artillery officer who had developed an extensive procurement business in the latter days of the war. Through Morris, his company held contracts to supply the Continental army in New York, New Jersey and all of New England, as well as to provision George Washington's retinue and to evacuate the British from New York. Because of this early version of outsourcing, Parker was at the center of American economic activity.

In July in New York, Parker met with Ledyard and introduced him to his New York partner, William Duer, an Eton-educated entrepreneur married to Lady Kitty, the daughter of the infamous brigadier general Lord Stirling. Duer had more experience in the China trade than anyone else, having worked for the East India Company in Bengal. The financial arrangement, worked out between Ledyard, Parker and Duer, was that Morris would put up one-third of the expenses, Parker and Duer another third and Boston merchants the rest. On 19 July Parker and Ledyard traveled up to Boston to find ships and investors. The two men were a formidable team: Parker had the financial connections to obtain a ship, crew and cargo, and Ledyard had his usual brio, his glib-talking enthusiasm and the spectacularly unique fact that he was the only man on the continent who had seen all three points in the plan's trading triangle.

Parker placed an order for a ship to be built in Boston by John Peck, America's first great naval architect. The news of the Peck-built ship, to be called the *Empress of China*, hit the papers on 21 August 1783, when the *Salem Gazette* reported: "We hear that a ship is fitting at Boston for an intended voyage to China; that her cargo out, in money and goods, will amount in value to £150,000; and that she will sail the ensuing Fall. Many eminent merchants, in different parts of the continent, are said to be interested in this first adventure from the New World to the Old. We have, at an earlier period than the most sanguine Whig could have expected, or even hoped, or than the most inveterate Tory feared, very pleasing prospects of a very extensive commerce with the most distant parts of the globe."

Guy Carleton, the British commander-in-chief in the United States, followed the progress of the project with great interest, since the China trade was an extremely lucrative part of the British economy. At the end of August Carleton reported to Lord North in London that the *Empress* was bound on the first of October "for a voyage of Discovery, to Examine the Coast of California, and in what manner a trade may be established in the South Seas and with India." After sailing around Cape Horn, the ship was to cruise the coast of South and North America up to 62 degrees latitude, collect furs and sail for Canton. The ship was to carry eighteen cannons and be manned by eighty seamen and four or five of her officers who had been in India; the "Pilot [Ledyard] was with Captain Cook in his last Voyage." A second ship, named the *Deane*, Carleton added, was to take a cargo of dollars in ginseng and go via Cape Town to Canton.

As autumn came to the eastern seaboard, convoluted issues delayed any departures. Parker placed orders for ten thousand pounds of ginseng. (Besides furs, the only known medium of trade at Canton was the dried root of *Panax quinquefolius*, which grew wild in the Appalachian mountains.) Parker reorganized his partnership by adding a Philadelphia associate of Morris, John Holker. An English-born Frenchman, Holker had arrived in America in 1778 as an agent for the French navy and had partnered with Morris on many projects. Ledyard, his fundraising venture in Boston an apparent success, went to New London to look at three ships Parker had purchased, the *Columbia*, *Comte d'Artois* and *Bourbon*. He met with the two men refitting the ships, Parker's brother Benjamin and John Deshon, the nephew of the captain Ledyard had sailed with in 1774.

Despite being back on familiar ground, Ledyard did not feel comfortable. In a September 1783 letter to his young sisters in Southold, Ledyard told of a "series of perplexities & even distresses which have alternatly & conjunctivly persecuted me with the most extreme severity. My affairs at present wear a more promising appearance, but they are now not such as I could wish they were, without being extravagant in my desires: a few weeks will alter them so much as almost entirely to determine my future prosperity in point of Interest & consequently my chief happiness." To his mother in the same month, he painted an equally plaintive picture: "These different engagments have led me into different situations: sometimes I have been elated with hope: sometimes depressed with disappointment & distress. My prospects at present are a Voyage to the East Indies & eventually round the World: It will be of about 2 or 3 years duration."

Obstreperously unreliable men, Parker, Duer and Holker maneuvered behind each other's backs. They bickered over which ships to take, which routes they would sail, who would captain them, who would serve as the supercargo—their representative on the ship who would handle the trading in Canton—and what percentage of the profits the supercargo would receive. Duer, the original supercargo, complained of the supercargo's terms, Parker's unreliability and the route. "I must decline going," Duer wrote when he gave up the supercargo post, "for the State of my Affairs and that of a Young Family will not justify me in adding a dangerous Experiment in Navigation to one of Commerce." Major Samuel Shaw, a former aide-de-camp to General Henry Knox, was another possible candidate as supercargo, but in November he backed out too. "I don't go to China," he wrote to a friend. "Parturiunt montes, nasutus mus—the intended voyage has been so altered that it scarcely retains an original feature."

"The mountains are giving birth to a mouse," wrote Major Shaw, but it was really a dysfunctional family of morally myopic mice squabbling over cheese. In October James Swan, leader of the Boston consortium, pulled out of the partnership, forcing Morris and Holker to front half the money and Parker and Duer the other half. Parker seemed congenitally incapable of actually producing any cash. Speculating on currency exchange rates and pocketed payments, he shifted invoices to Holker and Duer.

Delay followed delay. In October Carleton reported to London that two ships would leave in November, with "a Mr. Ldard, who sailed with Capt. Cook" on board one.

Still no ship departed. In November Duer confessed to Holker that he no longer trusted Parker: "The Fact is, my Freind it is Time to wake from a Reverie of beleiving men much sincerer and honester than I find them. I have for these two Years been Surrendering my own Judgment to my Cost, and making Sacrafices to one Man at least that I know does not deserve them: his Duplicity to me I can never forgive, and I must confess that I am afraid of a Concern under his sole Direction." In the last weeks of the year, matters came to a head. Scaling back their ambitious plans, the partnership decided to send the new *Empress of China* directly to Canton, bypassing the Nootka leg. The total cost for the *Empress*'s voyage was $119,000, an astronomical sum—$2.2 million in 2005—that would have bought twenty-four thousand acres of prime land in America. They simply could not afford a second one, especially as it involved the unknown variable of Nootka Sound. Ledyard was not invited to join the Canton-bound *Empress*, and his fur scheme was abandoned.

Ledyard was left in the dark for months, as Parker did not tell him the truth. Comfort Sands, one member of the cartel, later recalled that through the winter Ledyard was "anxiously waiting the Event, & was without Money or Friends." Morris gave him a retainer fee, his cousin Isaac lent him $50 and Sands "advanced him from time to time the Money that he wanted." He rambled around Connecticut, visiting friends and contacts like Ezra Stiles, the president of Yale. When he finally learned the facts, it was too late to protest. He later said that Morris "shrunk ingloriously behind a trifling obstruction," but in reality he knew it was not just Morris but the whole conniving group of them, as he wrote to his cousin in November 1784: "The flame of Enterprize that I excited in America terminated in a flash, that equally bespoke the inebriety of head & pusilanimity of heart of my patrons. Perserverance was an effort of the understanding that Twelve rich Merchants were incapable of making."

On Sunday, 22 February 1784, the *Empress of China* sailed out of New York harbor. The country was reeling from the longest and fiercest winter in recorded history. A tremendous New Year's Eve storm and a January thaw had led to serious flooding, and the next month set a still unsurpassed record as the region's coldest February ever. On eight consecutive mornings in Hartford, the mercury did not get above minus twelve. Just days before the ice in New York harbor had melted enough for the ship to sail. As it left the harbor, the *Empress* saluted the Sandy Hook battery with a federal thirteen-gun blast, to which the battery replied with twelve guns. "The morning being pleasant drew a large party of gentlemen to the battery, congratulating each other on the pleasing prospect," reported a New York newspaper. As the Sandy Hook battery was near his cousin Ben's house, it was possible that Ledyard was among the party of onlookers, watching the black hull of the *Empress* cut through the ice-chocked waters, his dream sailing away.

The *Empress of China* was loaded with eleven pipes of brandy and wine, eight barrels of tar and turpentine, two million dried ginseng roots and $20,000 in silver specie to buy Chinese products. In January Major Samuel Shaw, who had in the end agreed to go as supercargo, had inspected the seven leather cases of specie and found that it added up to $17,700. He confronted Parker, who promised to supply the missing bullion. When Shaw opened the cases in Macao, he discovered the missing specie had not been returned.

By then the game was up. Four days after the *Empress* sailed, Morris sent a statement to Holker to settle some accounts. Holker vigorously protested and within weeks they rancorously dissolved their partnership. Meanwhile, Parker desperately tried to stave off bankruptcy. He sent the other ships, originally bought for the China trade, out on more traditional voyages: the *Columbia* went to Amsterdam via Charleston with tobacco; the *Comte d'Artois* sailed to France where she was sold; and the *Bourbon* departed to Cadiz with a cargo of masts and ships' timber. In July 1784 Parker dissolved his company and fled the country, having embezzled more than $200,000 from his various creditors. Almost everyone involved in the scheme filed lawsuits, with some dragging on for more than thirty years. Duer later became the first assistant secretary of the treasury and, after causing a tremendously ruinous financial scandal due to his rampant and illegal speculation, ended up living the last seven years of his life in debtor's prison. Morris, too, ended up in jail. He served as a senator from Pennsylvania and then, in a catastrophic fall from grace, the former richest man in America lost all his money in land speculation and spent three years in debtor's prison.

The forgotten casualty of the *Empress of China* saga was John Ledyard. On the first of June 1784, he wrote a letter to his mother: "Since I saw you last, I have passed through a great many difficulties and disappointments, which my most intimate friends are, and must be for the present, at least, unacquainted with, as it will answer no good purpose to break their repose, or add to my cares, by reflecting on what is past, and thence anticipating evil. You have no doubt heard of my very great disappointment at New York. For a moment, all the fortitude, that ten years' misfortune had taught me, could hardly support me." He told his mother that he was sailing for Spain. Three weeks later he boarded the *Bourbon* in New London and sailed out of the harbor of his childhood. "If I succeed in my wishes," he told his mother, "it may be two or three years before I return."

He was wrong. He would travel on three different continents, dine with the most famous men of the age, see great cities, cross legendary rivers and walk thousands of miles, but it was the last time he touched American soil.

10

Bought for a Bagatelle—
An American in Paris

WHEN JOHN LEDYARD ARRIVED IN EUROPE in the summer of 1784, he became a harlequin. Not unlike the shape-shifting shamans who greeted him at Nootka Sound, Ledyard in the last five years of his life was a liquid person, constantly changing his masks.

Physically, he was ordinary except for his unique aura that blazed around him. He was of average height, certainly nothing like the six-foot-three George Washington. He was thickly set, broad-chested and broad-shouldered, but lithe in the legs. His aquiline nose gave him a formal tone and his cornflower blue eyes gave a faraway look to his appearance. "Though scarcely exceeding the middle size," Henry Beaufoy, a London friend, wrote that Ledyard "was remarkably expressive of activity and strength." His flowing blond hair was so light it was almost white; a lock of it in the 1820s resembled flax. "In person he was middle in stature," wrote Samuel Forman, a brother-in-law of his cousin Ben, "pretty stock, very light complexion, light blue eyes—white hair & eye brows—when talking if standing he was very erect, looking right into his friends eyes."

He was a good listener, yet his effervescent personality and buoyant intellect bubbled up so brightly that he did more of the talking. Nathaniel Cutting, a Boston merchant, called him "an eccentric genius." Andrew Kippis, Captain Cook's first biographer and a friend of John Adams and Thomas Jefferson, wrote that "This corporal Lediard is an extraordinary man." The Virginia coterie in Paris nicknamed him Oliver Cromwell, for he seemed fated to great fame and great failure. Thomas Barclay, the American consul in France, told Ledyard he had never seen such a medley of traits in one person. Henry Beaufoy agreed, but thought a harmony underpinned it all:

> His manners, though unpolished, were neither uncivil nor unpleasing. Little attentive to difference of rank, he seemed to consider all men as his equals, and as such he respected them. His genius, though uncultivated and irregular, was original and comprehensive. Ardent in his wishes, yet calm in his deliberations; daring in his purposes, but guarded in his measures; impatient of controul, yet capable of strong endurance; adventurous beyond the conception of ordinary men, yet wary and considerate, and attentive to all precautions, he appeared to be formed by Nature for atchievements of hardihood and peril.

As an intellectual, he stunned his friends with the power and originality of his ideas. Thomas Paine spoke about the reaction people had when first reading Ledyard's *Journal of Captain Cook's Last Voyage*: "His manner of writing had surprised them as they at first conceived him a bold but illiterate adventurer. That man, said Sir Joseph [Banks] one day to me, 'was all Mind.'" Thomas Jefferson said he had "a talent for useful & interesting observation" and called him "a man of genius." From men like Banks and Jefferson, who were at the epicenter of Western science, these were rare compliments. The geniuses thought Ledyard was a genius.

Ledyard reveled in physical activity. With the greyhound as the family symbol, he was naturally restless, fluid and quick moving. He walked twenty-four miles in a morning in France. "I am constantly thinking about Hills," he wrote in his diary, and whether a rocky outcropping outside Hanover, New Hampshire, or Mauna Loa in Hawaii, Ledyard wanted to stand on top of it. "I am too much alive to care and Ambitious to sit still," he wrote. Illness, "a stalking ugly ghost of a thing," as he called it, rarely approached his door. He occasionally had a cold or a slight fever and once mentioned "a slight debility and some of Cooks rheumatism in my bones." But usually when he was feeling ill, he would "hold my head up, laugh & jog on the way with a careless impudent assurance, & if by chance she flings a cold or a headache at me which is seldom the case I esteem it a prelude to an attack & without more ceremony knock her down as I would another assassin." He endured diabolical traveling conditions and though often exposed to smallpox, tuberculosis and malaria, he never came down with anything worse than venereal disease.

Alternating bouts of mania and depression were Ledyard's modus operandi. He promiscuously dispensed opinions and facts. "I seize the evanescent incidents and state them as they rise obedient to the instant impulse," he told his cousin Isaac. He spoke of "a kind of foolish good-natured delirium" that sometimes stuck him, of "a mind diseased" and of "the very cave of moping melancholy—the bursting of the heart strings—the dark abyss of despair itself." Arguing that his flights of fancy were not harmful, he aphorized that "to be foolishly happy is still happiness and to be wisely so is no more." Often he seemed just on the edge of reason. His Dartmouth classmate, James Wheelock, mentioned how Ledyard was often lost in "intense thought." Jefferson wrote that "he is a person of ingenuity and information. Unfortunately he has too much imagination." Beaufoy noted the "inquietude of his eye." In Spain "a fit of uncommon melancholy" confined him to bed for four days. In Hartford he described his mood swings: "shut up, bolted, barred, debarred, excluded & eternally locked out & beyond restoration, precluded from any rank, claim or pretension to Sociability & lost within the pale of frozen Maidenism—height of the highest stage of Phrenzy, depth of the lowest deep of chagrin, envy, incapacitated concupisence, anticipated misery."

Ledyard had a deeply bifurcated personality. He loved clothes. In his letters home he would detail his wardrobe before his circumstances or plans. In Philadelphia in the spring of 1783, he felt compelled to spend his remaining money on a new pair of shoes and felt equally driven to tell this to his cousin Isaac. Yet he was extremely tough. Brimming with self-abnegation, he willingly committed himself to poverty and hardship. He repeatedly threw himself into dangerous circumstances, flaying himself with days of hunger, lice-ridden bedding and unwashed clothing. Many days began without Ledyard knowing when he would sleep that night.

Fame was his goal. In 1783 he began referring to himself as "John Ledyard the Traveler." Deliberately crafting his own persona, Ledyard felt it necessary to add a dollop of what Jefferson called his "singularity of character." Besides the exotic and obvious tattoos he got in Tahiti, he dressed with uncommon clothes and styles. He kept an open collar, even in winter and wore unusual Turkish breeches. His personality made it difficult for him to blend into the crowd and his dreams made it impossible. He proudly stood on the margins of society, in a class of himself: "It seems decreed by some that I, John Ledyard, shall hop, skip & jump about on this World of ours in such an untraversable way, that it can hardly be asserted whether he moveth in the General Circle, in his own Circle, or whether in any Circle at all." In a letter to Isaac, he proudly said that others thought of him as "the mad, romantic, dreaming Ledyard." It was a cunning ploy. He excelled at making a name for himself. He befriended the most famous men of his generation. Despite, or because of, his eccentricity, they readily found him eminently persuasive and agreed to back him on the most outlandish projects. He did not hold a job for the last six years of his life, but it was no matter, since he had an unusual ability to separate money from the billfolds of rich men. For instance, he convinced Sir Joseph Banks, one of the leading intellectuals of the era, to give him large sums of cash for not one but two expeditions.

Since there had never been a historical figure quite like him before, his mentors came from literature. He read Shakespeare, Confucius, Addison, Virgil and Milton, as well as the Bible. He loved Laurence Sterne's freewheeling stories of Tristram Shandy and imbibed Swift's *Gulliver's Travels* with gusto, but his true polestar was Don Quixote of the Mancha. He had read Cervantes' novel as a young man, and in 1773 when he toured Long Island looking for a parish he nicknamed his horse Rosinante after Quixote's poor nag. Like Quixote, he traveled with an eye towards mocking shenanigans. Ledyard's college career seemed a figment of Cervantes' imagination: he drove a sulky to Hanover, he blew the conch shell with exaggerated enthusiasm, he staged a mid-winter camping trip—could it not have waited until the snow melted?—and he jumped into a canoe without a map. The stunt at the British garrison at Gibraltar was Ledyard's way to send up the military's demand for discipline. There, in the serried, red-coated rows of marching men, was a grinning, insouciant imposter. When he reached his mother in Southold after his seven years' absence, he toyed with the usual clichéd return of the prodigal son by pretending to be a British officer. At Hartford during a farcical fight over a letter from Isaac Ledyard, he mock-attacked his aunt with a hat for a shield and a handful of corn as ammunition.

Ledyard's response to the physical trials of traveling matched Quixote's. Thomas Jefferson said Ledyard was a man "of fearless courage and enterprise." The bruises, the sleeplessness, the dirty-fingernail poverty, the greasy hair, the sweat and mud-soaked clothes were real. Yet, it was as if his sufferings were happening to another person. Staggeringly buoyant, he brushed aside his past pains and talked of trying again. He would leave on a moment's notice. He would promise a new destination, despite the lack of money, clothes, prospects or good sleep. His imagination remained unassailable. Quixote "who fancies that everything is done by enchantment," wrote Cervantes, was an "ambassador of the imagination." If so, John Ledyard was minister plenipotentiary.

In August 1784 under the captaincy of Samuel Smith, the *Bourbon* sailed into Cadiz, the Andulasian port city. Ledyard, despite the contributions of his erstwhile fur colleagues, was again indigent. He carried just three French crowns in his pocket and a single trunk as luggage. But he also carried a packet of hope. After a year of working on Ledyard's project, Robert Morris, the Philadelphia financier, had not completely abandoned him. Morris had written him letters of introduction, and Ledyard tiptoed his way into the small British colony of expatriates.

Having been to Spain before, Ledyard quickly grasped the nuances of Iberian life. He took naps during the hot afternoons and ate dinner late in the evening. He devoted a long letter to Isaac about the European opinions of the new United States. He dined regularly with the British consul, Sir James Duff, a Virginian merchant named Harrison and a large number of affable Irish expatriates. His most interesting friend was General Count Alexander O'Reilly. An Irish soldier of fortune, O'Reilly had fought succesively for the Spanish, the French and the Austrians. His height of fame came in 1769 when as the Spanish governor of New Orleans he quelled a rebellion, but six years later he bottomed out when he led a disastrously unsuccessful attack on Algiers. At present he was the governor of two southwestern Spanish provinces. One afternoon O'Reilly took Ledyard in his carriage "clumsy and Gothic as the Devil, dragged by five jaded mules with a hempen harness" to a bullfight. Ledyard thought the men on horseback displayed more courage and skill than the matador and pronounced the whole sport "a barbarous amusement."

Amidst the swirl of dinners and outings, Ledyard felt slightly out of place. After telling his cousin about many elaborate dinners, he asked, "but what I am doing among these gentry with only half a Dollar and four Rials in my Pocket." Screwing up his courage, he tried to revive his fur-trading scheme. He originally thought of abandoning the *Bourbon* and going to Marseilles or Bordeaux to find backers. He then met a British official in Cadiz on route to Morocco and persuaded him to back his proposal. "I have him mounted and he is now somewhere in the Town as busy in the affair as a dozen such heads as mine could be," Ledyard reported. When that partnership fell through, he stayed with the *Bourbon*. In September Captain Smith, unable to sell his cargo of sixty-two masts, forty thousand and seven hundred staves and thirty-eight cords of wood, left Cadiz to try the French navy at Brest. "It is a cloudy day with me," Ledyard wrote Isaac of his fur-trade scheme, with his first stop proving unsuccessful. "However my Hobby tells me I shall have fair weather tomorrow: and I believe it because I wish it."

The *Bourbon* sailed north and landed at Brest on the coast of Brittany. Captain Smith was again unable to sell the masts and spars or even the ship itself. Ledyard, unimpressed with Brest, said farewell to Smith and the *Bourbon* and left town. Escorted by "a d—d Holland Consul," Ledyard spent forty-five livres riding overland through Quimper to Lorient. It was an interesting trip. Ledyard noted that the French dialect in Brittany closely resembled Gaelic and Welsh and that Great Britain and Brittany "are more alike than any two states in America." He wanted to stop and visit Kerguelen, the French navigator who lived near Quimper, but the Dutch official would not deviate from their itinerary.

At the end of September 1784, Ledyard reached Lorient and instantly needed "a sort of Fortitude [to] accompany the turns of my Fortune." His fur-trading scheme was back in business and more promising than ever. In two weeks he formed a company of Lorient merchants, led by a trader named Berard, and obtained a four-hundred-ton brig to sail for Nootka. It was almost too good to be true, and in October Ledyard wrote Isaac with a gimlet eye on the proceedings. "I have been so much the Sport of accidents. I have, it is true, in my LOrient Negociations guarded every avenue to future disappointment, with such Wonderful Skill, that I think the devil himself could not surprize me: but this head I wear is so much a dupe to my heart—and as other times my heart is so bedeviled by my head that I have not much confidence in matters of businees in either." After telling his cousin his exciting news, he continued: "But here comes a but—pray Heaven they may not butt the modicum of brain out of my head which Morris hath left there—the but is this: I have arrived so late in the Season in this Country, that the Merchants have procrastinated the Equipment untill next Summer and requested me to stay here untill then: allowing me genteely for that purpose. And was I but certain that no vile misfortune would enventually happen, I should be quite happy." Ledyard was too late in the season.

Wintering out in Lorient was decidedly pleasant. He learned French. He sampled local delicacies like oysters, goat cheese and cider wine. He walked around Lorient's immense natural harbor. He started outfitting his ship. Through his letters of recommendation from Robert Morris, he befriended Thomas Barclay, a merchant who had just become the U.S. Consul in France. Barclay introduced him to the leading figures in Lorient. "I keep the grandest company in L'orient & am universally respected," Ledyard smugly told his brothers. With an English friend, he took a midwinter trip to Normandy. They stayed in the village of Conflans Sainte Honorine, the home of the Marshal de Conflans who had commanded the French fleet in the battle of Quiberon Bay in November 1759. The Marshal's son, now lord of the manor, had ignored their arrival in the village even though, Ledyard wrote, they rode "in a superb manner" with the Englishman's coach and servants "in a most elegant Stile." Staying at a local tavern, Ledyard went into the kitchen to cook dinner for himself and his companion. The staff saw the tattoos on his hands and asked the Englishman's servants about them. When told that Ledyard had sailed around the world with Cook, they hurried to tell Conflans that these were no ordinary visitors. Conflans sent a note asking if they would come to his estate. "It was too late," wrote Ledyard. "The Englishman & I had begun pell mell upon a joint of roast. If Jove himself had sent a Card by Blanchard inviting us it would have been the same." They finished their meal and went to Conflans in the evening.

Despite the light-hearted winter, there were inklings that something would go wrong. Tension between France and Austria threatened to explode into war. The Lorient merchants applied to King Louis XVI for a royal commission for the voyage, permission to visit China and letters of recommendation, but Versailles never replied. Ledyard heard rumors that other nations were sending ships to Nootka. In Cadiz an Englishman told him that in early 1784 a seven-hundred-ton ship commissioned by Empress Catherine II of Russia had left London with a Russian captain and three officers who had sailed on the third Cook voyage. In Lorient Ledyard met a St. Petersburger who claimed that not one but two Russian ships had cleared for Nootka Sound. In a British newspaper in November 1784, he read that an English ship had gone to Nootka and already returned to London. None of the rumors were true, but they made Ledyard jittery, for he clearly was not the only one with a fur-trading scheme.

In the end, Ledyard's timing could not be worse. In 1785 the French launched the La Perouse expedition. Having grown exceedingly jealous of the British and their illustrious Cook expeditions, King Louis XVI organized two naval frigates at Brest, *L'Astrolabe* and *La Boussole*, under the command of Jean de la Perouse, to sail on a voyage of discovery in the Pacific. The La Perouse expedition, which sailed in August, was modeled in many ways after Cook's: the ships carried an astronomer, a physicist, three naturalists, three draughtsmen and a mathematician—the only addition was a priest. An enormous undertaking, the La Perouse expedition sucked up all available French resources for voyages to the Pacific, and Ledyard had to admit defeat. In a dispirited letter to Isaac, Ledyard was typically philosophical about the latest disappointment: "My envious fate hath again unhorsed me and while in full pursuit of glory, left me the jest, and riddle, of the drama. . . . My L. Orient negotiations, with one eye on Bob Morris and one on Berard—the devil's in it, said I, if this negotiation falls through and yet it did fall thru as easy as a needle would pass through the eye of a camel, so very easy, that notwithstanding my general credulity I could hardly believe it for a month after—the devil is in it, said I, if it fails—never once dreaming that it was as possible for the devil to be in it as out of it."

After what he called "this enormous thrust from Bliss," Paris seemed his only choice. He knew no one there. He had just three louis d'or in cash. But Lorient was finished, and he had twice left New London with less money. "Thus Vasca de Gama & Columbus mounted, flying from a positive evil, to a possible good," wrote Ledyard. "Some might imagine I joged on heavily, and in melancholy guise: no. The velocity of my journey exceeded the violence of the storm which preceded it." It took the mail four days to go from Lorient to Paris; in forty-eight hours John Ledyard was standing in front of the Louvre, hands in his empty pockets, a trunk at his feet, an American in Paris.

Until 1750 Paris was not the capital of France. There was no article on Paris in Diderot's *Encyclopedia*, and nearly 60 percent of the contributors to the epic book lived outside the city. Most cities developed as entrepots for the sea trade. Paris, a hundred miles inland, had barely any commerce.

But in the past few decades, Paris had become the Paris of nightlife, food, sex and fashion. The City of Lights appeared when streetlights were installed in 1745. Restaurants, a particularly public way of eating, were invented in Paris in the 1760s. In a population of half a million there were an estimated twenty thousand prostitutes—about 13 percent of the female population, or about a quarter of all women ages fifteen to thirty-five. *Les filles publiques* worked mostly on the Right Bank, though large numbers gathered near Place Maubert and in the Grenelle plain. For those less aggressive, the glimpse of garter on the legs of ballet dancers at the Opera would have to do. Paris was the epicenter of the new fashions in clothing, hairstyles and jewelry. Every morning thousands of barbers carried their instruments of torture and pounds of flour to the homes of aristocrats. Women applied such wide swathes of rouge to their cheeks that one greeted a woman by kissing her on the neck, and they piled their hair a foot high, holding it with a heavy spray of starch.

Spectacularly modern in the waning days of the ancien régime, Paris was reinventing itself. City officials painted street signs on tin plaques and in 1779 started numbering houses, with white numbers on a red background for streets parallel to the Seine and white on black for perpendicular streets. Real estate boomed, and noblemen turned their old estates into housing developments. New public structures surprised visitors: the Halle aux Bleds, the municipal grain market with the largest dome in France, bridges like the Pont de Neuilly and Neuf and theaters like the neoclassical Odeon. The City of Lights now had phosphorous matches and cylinder lamps. The famous *boue de Paris*, the black, viscous street mung that rotted cotton and leather, slowly ebbed—in 1780 the city outlawed the archaic practice of emptying chamber pots out windows into the streets. Fads swept through the city, breaking up formal class distinctions in a jostling fever of shared interests. In 1784 dukes and peasants rushed to the Comedie-Francaise to see the *Marriage of Figaro*, Caron de Beaumarchais' new play in which the nobility's pretensions were skewered. Thousands participated in hypnotic séances led by the Austrian healer Friedrich Mesmer that seemed to prove his theory of animal magnetism. More than a hundred thousand Parisians came to Versailles in 1783 to watch an eight-minute balloon flight of a sheep, a duck and a rooster. Soon cafes had balloon teams, balloon hairdos became au courant and no garden party was complete without the launching of a miniature hydrogen-filled replica.

At the heart of the Paris pageant was the Palais-Royal. Created by Philippe, the duc d'Orleans and cousin of the King, the Palais-Royal was located near the Louvre and Tuileries. The duke transformed his gardens into a lengthy series of wooden stalls that resembled a shopping mall. High and low society mixed in an exhilarating manner. Because it was private property, it was safe from the police. Chiffonniers (ragpickers), milliners, whores, stationers, puppeteers, mimes, coconut sellers, professional rhymers, tisane hawkers, wigmakers, pickpockets, booksellers and professional idlers made money off the thousands of people who congregated at the Palais-Royal's cafes, boutiques, theatres, lending libraries, clubs and bordellos. For a few sous you could peek at a four-hundred pound German or watch as the Café Mecanique served its customers with dumb-waiters. You could join the chess club above the Café de Foy, watch magic-lantern shows, play billiards or simply stroll the promenades in one of the world's first deliberately designed spaces for people watching.

Paris was the most intellectual city in the world. Literacy rates were high and in some sections of town, like Montmarte or rue Saint-Denis where artisans tended to live, more than three-quarters of its citizens could read. Vendors hawked books from stands on bridges and along the quais, at cafes and even in the lobbies of theaters and the Opera. There were pamphlets and the daily newspaper, the *Mercure de France*, and every morning bill stickers pasted the city's walls with notices and placards giving the news. For the aristocrats there were the famous salons, the weekly gatherings for discussion, readings and a touch of gossip that kept a tight schedule: Mondays at Madame Geoffrin, Wednesdays at Madame Helvetius and Fridays at Madame Necker. Some of the cerebral punch of the city had been lost with the deaths of Voltaire and Rousseau in 1778 and Diderot in 1784, but many younger intellectuals had eagerly taken their place.

Paris in the summer of 1785, despite the looming Revolution, was at a good moment. It had a touch of the nouveau riche, a garish opulence, a sense of optimism, a vibrant mixture of high and low and an acute focus on satisfying every whim. London was a thousand years old. Paris was new. The aphorism was true: London was a riddle, Paris an explanation.

A lone traveler like Ledyard was unusual for Paris. There were more foreign residents in the city than there were annual visitors, as Paris was not yet considered a must-see for tourists. (About five thousand English-speaking expatriates lived in Paris.) The few transients and French commercial travelers usually lodged themselves at hotels des voyageurs in the Right Bank near the Palais-Royal. Ledyard found his way to such a hotel, probably on rue de Richelieu near Voltaire's birthplace.

With three louis d'or in his pocket, Ledyard suffered a case of déjà vu. Exactly two years ago, he had arrived in another capital city and, pitifully counting up his coins in his hotel room, had concluded he needed help. In Philadelphia he went to his aunt's house. In Paris, after staring at his small change, he again left his hotel. Thomas Barclay, the American consul in Lorient, had suggested Ledyard visit a U.S. government official in Paris who might lend assistance. Ledyard took a letter of reference into the crowded, bustling, manure-covered streets of Paris. He walked across rue Saint-Honore, the Right Bank's main shopping thoroughfare, with its fancy shops and speeding, one-horse cabriolets. He went past the Theatre des Italiens into today's ninth arrondissement. In a little dead-end street off the Chausee d'Antin he came to the Hotel de Landron at number five cul-de-sac Taitbout. He knocked on the door. A servant answered and brought Marc, the maitre d'hotel, to speak with Ledyard. Marc escorted him into a courtyard with a pleasant garden, then up steps and through a second, more elaborate doorway into the house. He went into a drawing room where a fire crackled and admired the paintings on the wall—especially Salome holding John the Baptist's head on a platter—the neoclassical furniture, silk damask curtains, coffee-urns, busts, piano, papers and stacks of books. He then met their owner, the man of the house, the person who would change his life: Thomas Jefferson.

On the surface they were a mismatched pair. Jefferson was the U.S. minister plenipotentiary to France. He mourned for his wife, who had died three years before, and cared for his two surviving daughters. Ledyard was fancy-free, with no family encumbrances. Jefferson was notably reticent, a laconic sphinx with a patrician air. Ledyard was garrulous and far from reserved. Jefferson hated the damp chill of the European winter and kept a fire going from September to June. Ledyard went camping in midwinter. Jefferson was twenty-three before he first left Virginia, and until he left for his job as minister in France, he had never seen two-thirds of the American states or been farther from home than Philadelphia. The blond Connecticut traveler came from a family of merchants and sea captains and had sailed around the world. The redheaded Virginian Jefferson, hailing from landed gentry, hated the sea. With its impressments, piracy and battles, the ocean brought problems to his new country. In his *Notes on Virginia* he wrote "To remove as much as possible the occasions of making war, it might be better for us to abandon the ocean altogether, that being the element whereon we shall be principally exposed to jostle with other nations; to leave to others to bring what we shall want, and to carry what we can spare. This would make us invulnerable to Europe, by offering none of our property to their prize, and would turn all our citizens to the cultivation of the earth; and, I repeat it again, cultivators of the earth are the most virtuous and independent citizens." Jefferson suffered from severe hydrophobia. His uncle had died at sea and he sometimes panicked on ferryboats or ships. The only time water was friendly, it seemed, was in his morning cold-water foot baths that, he claimed, prevented colds.

Still, Jefferson and Ledyard acted like long-lost brothers. They discovered common ground in their biographies: they both came from prominent families in their respective colonies, had lost their fathers while still

young—Ledyard when he was ten, Jefferson when he fourteen. The life of
the mind was extremely important to both men. They discussed the science
of the compass. They shared a passion for using language as a means for
tracing historical migrations, and Ledyard gave to Jefferson a long memorandum comparing English with the vocabularies of the Chippewa, Nad-
owessioux and Nootka Indians of North America. They regularly prowled
through literary Paris, visiting dealers in the Palais-Royal and Rue Saint-
Honore and along Quai des Grands Augustins. (When Jefferson returned
to Monticello in 1789 he had to build two hundred and fifty feet of running shelves to accommodate all his new books.) The two men bonded over
more than books and ideas. Both epicureans—Jefferson bought seven pairs
of women's gloves on the Fourth of July 1776—they indulged together in
food, wine and clothes. Combining their love of walking and clothes was
a common occurrence. "Our minister who is a Brother to me, & sometimes
I go buy a fine pair of pumps to walk in," wrote Ledyard to his cousin Isaac.

With his characteristic hospitality, Jefferson welcomed Ledyard into his
circle. A number of fellow Americans lived at cul-de-sac Taitbout: Charles
Williamos, Swiss by birth and so perpetually without direction that he was
rumored to be a spy; William Short, a young Virginian protégé who
worked as Jefferson's private secretary; and Colonel David Humphreys, a
former aide-de-camp to General Washington who was secretary for the
American delegation to France. Humphreys had grown up in Hartford and
was a childhood friend of Isaac and Ben Ledyard. At Jefferson's *petit soupers*,
his simple late afternoon meals at cul-de-sac Taitbout, Ledyard met a daz-
zling array of characters that orbited around the magnetic Jefferson. "We
find at our Ambassador's table between fifteen and twenty Americans in-
clusive of two or three ladies," wrote Ledyard. "We are very generally a Set
of poor dogs; I am not worth a Sol myself and yet am not the poorest of
my brethren. We as generally want the easy elegance of the European manners, tho we do not want those among us who are determined to be possessed of it. There are Some instances of an equal poverty of
understanding—but rare and the brightest Side of our general character is
Solid erudtion and good Sense. It is remarkable that we are neither despised
nor envied for our love of Liberty, but very often caressed." Besides Jefferson's housemates, regular dining guests included Thomas Barclay; D'Han-
carville, an elderly Greek scholar who had been in debtor's prison and had

been expelled from Italy for publishing pornography; "that lump of universality" David Franks, a friend of Ben Ledyard's who was en route to Morocco on a mission to the Barbary States; and the Fitzhugh brothers, Daniel and Theodorick, two Virginian tobacco magnates. Some afternoons at chez Jefferson involved odd visitors. "You see what a day brings forth," wrote Ledyard to his cousin Isaac in September 1785:

> I took tea with our minister this morning and while chatting who should be announced at the door but John Lamb esquire, in propria persona with one black eye and a leg broke in a gale of winds off the Isle of Wight, with a pair of tarnished black stockings hanging about his heels like Monsieur Souffrein, a thick greasy pair of buck skin gloves, a long beard, hair uncombed, coat, waistcoat and Breeches full of dirt and rumpled all in a heap, one part of the flap of his breeches unbuttoned and a greasy coarse hat in his hands, well pinched up in the front cock—and Credentials in his hand from Congress as Plenipotentiary from the States of America to the Dey of Algiers and the Emperor of Morocco!

Lamb and Ledyard went out carousing and, with Lamb "drunk as a lord," they stumbled home late at night.

Certainly the good food, rich conversation and interesting companionship were attractions at Jefferson's meals, but there was also the chance to save money. "Such a Set of moniless rascals have never appeared since the epoch of that happy villian Falstaff," wrote Ledyard after one dinner. "I have but 5 french crowns in the world, Franks has not a Sol, the Fitzhughes can't get their Tobacco money and the Consul tho' worth in reality 20000 £ Sterling dines here to save half a Crown." Jefferson did more than feed the penniless American expatriate community. He often gave them large sums of money, and Ledyard wasted no time in availing himself of Jefferson's renowned financial espousals. On 1 June 1785, Jefferson noted in his daily account book that he paid his servants wages of 226 francs, paid a craftsman 369 francs for repairing his prized phaeton carriage and "Gave Ledyard of Connecticut 120f." This was the equivalent of a thousand dollars in 2005, no small sum for someone Jefferson had just met.

Through the scene at cul-de-sac Taitbout, Ledyard slid effortlessly into the swirls of expatriate life in Paris. Within days of arriving in Paris, he managed to meet the legendary Benjamin Franklin. "Poor Richard" had wowed Paris ever since he arrived in December 1776. His jowly face appeared on teacups and spoons, and women wore wigs in the shape of his trademark soft marten fur cap. For the French, he was a symbol of good Quaker simplicity, though he was neither Quaker nor an advocate of simple living— when he departed from Paris in July 1785, a barge loaded with one hundred and twenty-eight crates of belongings followed him down the Seine.

One afternoon Ledyard dined at Franklin's home, an elaborate rural chateau outfitted with terraced gardens, octagonal ponds and one of his lightning rods. "I think it will be difficult for any subsequent Plentpotentiary to have as much personal influence in France as Doct'r Franklin," Ledyard wrote admiringly.

It will at least be so untill the cause that created that venerable patriot shall become less recent in the minds of these people, & in truth a very few years are sufficient to effect that in this country & distinguished virtue & distinguished vice are equally disagreeable after a certain period of duration.... Though under constant pain from the Gravel in the Bladder and bent down with age, that excellent old man exhibited all the Symptons of good cheer, of health, the gay philosopher and friendly countryman—I am now reading Some of his miscellaneous writings and my bosom glows with admiration and pride.

After comparing notes about the Crooked Billet, Franklin carried a packet of Ledyard's letters back to America.

A more frequent dinner companion was Gilbert, the Marquis de Lafayette. The six-foot-one redheaded marquis was six years younger than Ledyard. When his mother died at age twelve, he came into the largest fortune in France. Seven years later, not speaking a word of English, he went without leave from his French military academy to America, ready to lead troops. He survived numerous battles and returned in January 1785 a hero to two countries. His mansion at 183 rue de Bourbon on the Left Bank was a shrine to the Revolution, with a portrait of George Washington above the fireplace mantle, a stars and stripes flag on the wall, and a gold-lettered copy of the Declaration of Independence in his study, the half-filled frame awaiting its French counterpart. Ledyard and other Americans constantly flowed in and out of the rue de Bourbon, attending Lafayette's Monday afternoon American dinners which often included the singing of American war anthems. Two young Native Americans, Kayenlaha, a Onondaga, and Peter Otsiquette, the young son of a Frenchman and an Oneida woman, worked as servants for the household, as did Ezra Bates, "a careful man of Connecticut" according to Jefferson. John Caldwell, a fourteen-year-old orphan of a U.S. army chaplain and George Greene, the son of the late General Nathaniel Greene, also lived in the house. Ledyard and Lafayette became good friends. Years later Lafayette referred to Ledyard as "the good & extraordinary Man" and added, "Mr. Jefferson & myself, I am proud to say, had indeed a great share in his affections." Ledyard often wrote favorably about the marquis in his letters. "I esteem him and even love him, and so we all do except some few who worship him." He wrote prophetically of Lafayette that "he has planted a tree in America and sits under it at Versailles."

Through such renowned friends, Ledyard managed to meet most of Paris's elite. He mentioned Count d'Estaing, Count d'Artois and duc de la Rochefoucauld among his acquaintances. He even glimpsed the royal couple. In September 1785 Ledyard visited the royal pleasure ground at Marly, watching fireworks near Queen Marie Antoinette: "It was a mere rural revel and never before did I see Majesty and tag rag and bobtail so philosophically blended—a few country fiddlers scraping and Kate of the mill tripping it with dick of the vineyard. Indeed, Spouse of Lewis thou will never be humiliated with the Idea of that Indistinction which awaits thee." Another afternoon Ledyard spotted King Louis XVI while "he was shooting partridges in the fields without Paris. He was dressed in a pair of common Musqueto Trowsers, a short linen frock and an old laced hat without a Cockade: he had an easy, gentlemanly appearance but a few Attendants had he none I should have taken him for a Captain of a Merchant Ship amusing himself in the fields. He had the lounging Swaggering Salt-water gait in the greatest perfection though I susppose he never saw Salt-water in his Life."

Ledyard sampled all of Parisian life. He went to the theatre. He viewed the duc de Chartres' paintings and found that a Rubens reminded him of his old flirt Eleanor Forman. He went twice to the Louvre for the 1785 Salon, where David's "The Oath of the Horatii" was the headliner. "I am not only pleased with all the great & lovely passions they inspire me with but am also rendered happy by the proofs they give me of the greatness of the human mind which seems capable of infinite improvement." He talked politics and scorned the English newspapers whose articles on America "are so extremely illiberal and false in their accounts." He viewed "the little muddy, shallow, meandering river seine" from the Church of Notre Dame. He toured the various gardens in the city, deciding that the Tuilleries offered "the most consummate display of artificial elegance and grandeur." Ledyard found Parisians to be polite: "So fascinating are the charms of address, that they are happy to deceive and be deceived, at the expense of their understandings, and perhaps I am a fool to be disgusted with it." Ledyard visited the palace at Versailles with Barclay and Franks but they were refused entry to the galleries because they were wearing muddy boots.

The Palais-Royal was a natural attraction. He sometimes took tea there with an English lieutenant friend. Many of his friends were having affairs: William Short was deeply in love with the wife of the duc de la Rochefoucauld, and Lafayette had a beloved mistress in Madame de Hunolstein. Ledyard might have joined in the Parisian parlor game of amorous intrigues and found a woman to bestow his fantastical energies upon, but in the Palais-Royal he exhibited an uncharacteristic prudish side: It "is a vile cinque of pulution & contaminated not only by bawds, pimps, & procuresses, & not only by such of those who by the glare of dress, equipage or assumed titles hide their worst deformities but by three live strumpets, coarse common street whores. The very appartments of this superb, rich elegant building are inhabited by coarse-bred, impudent, abandoned digusting bawds, women, whores & impoverished young debauches without pretension to family, fortune or education." Disgusted or not, Ledyard found time to talk with the prostitutes. One afternoon, after dining with Franks, Barclay and the Fitzhughes, Ledyard led them into the Palais-Royal. He took a chair and talked with a married couple who knew his name. "The lady who called to me had her little old four feet 5 inches husband with her—& a true parisian husband is he—an inch more in his stature, a year less in his age, or a scruple more of virtue or understanding in him would have dis*qua*lified him." Ledyard, lampooning the usual wooings of a prostitute, "made use of the words superierment, superb, manfique, charmant, beau, belle infinement &c." Then he seized the hand of the woman and the husband withdrew "while I had entertained his Lady with a thousand and one appointments made by his lady & sealed with a thousand rapturous kisses & protestations of eager desire and eternal passion."

Other sides of Paris interested Ledyard. He visited the Bicetre prison, the less famous but more sinister counterpart to the Bastille, and found hundreds of prisoners confined in dank underground cells, some in chains. Two mornings in a row he went to the place where city officials brought dead bodies found in the streets; Ledyard estimated that the Parisian murder rate was more than one per day. He went to a foundling hospital and the adjoining Hospital de Dieu for pregnant women. Eighteen abandoned infants were brought into the hospital the day he visited, adding to the three hundred already there. Poor women, unable to feed their own babies, had abandoned them on church steps; the "dear little Innocents. . . happily insensible of your Situations" were then sent out from the hospital to rural wet nurses where the mortality rate for foundlings was fifty percent. The custom for visitors was to give a few sols and quickly depart, but Ledyard, horrified by the fate of these babies, flung down six livres. He went next door to the women's hospital where the majority of patients suffered from venereal disease. Ledyard, a man who had twice contracted venereal disease, walked thoughtfully through the halls. He spotted a woman lying in a bed motionless. She looked dead. Thinking he might be wrong, he seized her arm and felt her pulse, but it had stopped. He motioned to an attendant, and soon a group of nuns surrounded the bed. Pretending she was not yet dead, they gave her the last sacrament and then flung a sheet over her face.

In the autumn, with the chestnut trees turning buttery yellow, Ledyard grew tired of the hypocrisy, bustle and extravagance. "Paris is the only place," Thomas Jefferson wrote to William Short in 1815, "where a man who is not obliged to do anything will always find something amusing to do." Ledyard, with no real direction in his life, felt a bit overwhelmed by the choices. As in Cadiz, he thought himself an imposter. He was desperately poor. He was embarrassed about his rooms, a "Gloomy garret" in his Right Bank hotel. He was "curiously wretched," he wrote, "without any thing but a clean shirt" and unlike most of his American friends he bore no impressive-sounding titles or commissions. He felt dissipated and scorned for "the vilanous, unprofitable life I have led." He also was a bit lonely. "I see a great deal and think a great deal but derive very little happiness from either because I am forced into both and am alone in both." He began to retreat to his rooms for a quiet evening. He smoked a pipe, drank Burgundy wine and, with his "sharp spandly new pen" he bought at the Palais-Royal, he wrote letters home. Instructing his cousin Isaac on how to read his letters, Ledyard wrote: "Treat it as you would a friend who pops in with an [ad]dress to take Coffee with you."

Miraculously, his letters to Isaac Ledyard soon carried news of renewed life for the old fur-trading scheme. Early in his sojourn in Paris, Ledyard befriended John Paul Jones. After Robert Morris and his cynical band and then the dissembling Lorient merchants, Ledyard thought that a third attempt might prove the charm. Jones was another bright star in the Parisian firmament. He was the son of a Scottish gardener, a visionary adventurer and a hero to America and France after his *Bonhomme Richard* captured the *Serapis* off the coast of England in September 1779. He was also unpredictable, vain, ambitious and paranoid and, for all his ability and access to power, a risky partner for Ledyard. Forming a company, Jones & Ledyard drew up a business plan written in French. It said they would take a two-hundred-and-fifty-ton ship, manned by forty-five French sailors, around Cape Horn to Hawaii and on to Nootka Sound. After collecting furs, they would sell them either in Japan or Macao and then return via Cape Town. Ledyard would go as supercargo and "take upon himself the charge of making all the necessary arrangements, with the greatest dispatch." The sea-otter skins were easy, the plan averred: "such precious furs might be bought for a bagatelle." (Ledyard claimed he had all the necessary sailing charts, except for Cape Horn.) The estimated costs were £1,250 for the ship, £1,250 for equipment, £500 for provisions, £500 for cargo and £250 for wages for the crew; in return Jones & Ledyard calculated that three thousand furs would sell at ten louis d'or a piece in China and that they could buy Chinese products and make a "modest profit" of £10,000 back in France. Thus, they reckoned the total profit from the eighteen-month voyage would be more than 1,000 percent, £36,750—$5 million in 2005.

In the summer the plan evolved. They boosted the proposal to two ships. Ledyard planned to stay at Nootka for three or four years. "My affairs stand exactly thus," Ledyard wrote to his cousin in the summer of 1785:

> The celebrated Captain Paul Jones has embarked with me in my expedition: he advances all the outfits himself except the two ships, one or both of which he is now at L'orient endeavouring to procure as lent or chartered by the King of france: he tells me he thinks he shall succeed, & his character is to speak & act with great caution: if he should not succeed, he has with the same caution intimated to me that he will reduce the outfits within the limits of his own private fortune & make the whole independently: two or three weeks will determine the matter & I will inform you. Whatever depends upon Jones's stability, perserverance & wishes may be firmly relied upon. He has gone so far as to desire me to procure my Cargoe, send to London for goods &c & advanced me necessary Cash. If we succeed our plan is enlarged, we do not risk all on a single voyage but shall establish a factory upon the Coast—under the grave must I command of—Sir your honor—& under American colours. The first 6 months after our arival we collect our fur, purchase the sovereignity of some little spot—most probably on [Vancouver] Island, & build a small stockade which sufficiently keep in safety my self, a surgeon, my assistant in business & twenty soldiers: one of the ships at the expiration of the sixt months proceeds to China; and when she returns she stays 6 months longer & then both ships leave me & my factory, proceed to China & thence by way Cape good hope proceed to New York where I wish you may see my friend paul Jones & read my Letters—and perhaps the history of Ben Uncas.

The tabloids in England got hold of the story. In August 1785 the *London Chronicle* reported that Jones was in Lorient outfitting three ships for an expedition to Kamchatka to collect furs. More factual news reached Ledyard's doorstep by then as well: The *Empress of China* had sailed into New York harbor in May 1785. After the sale of her hyson tea and nankeen cloth, the profit was $37,000—not extraordinary for a $120,000 investment, but quite positive considering the flagitious partners. American merchants planned more expeditions, and within a year five U.S. ships sailed for Canton, including the *Empress* again. From England, the news was worse.

British merchants were following Ledyard's three-cornered trading scheme. In August 1785 two ships bound for Nootka Sound sailed from London, the *King George* commanded by George Dixon and the *Queen Charlotte* by Nathaniel Portlock; Dixon and Portlock had sailed with Ledyard on the Cook voyage. Ledyard lambasted the British—"I wish to be on the coast before them for they are the worst people in the world to follow in commerce or colonization among an uncivilized people"—in a tone that showed his frustration at not being the first to get back to Nootka.

But he still hoped to go. In September Ledyard wrote to his cousin, "I am hourly waiting with an anxiety not philosophical for the arrival of Commodore paul jones from L'orient—too much depends on it to leave me very tranquil, but let to morrow produce its evils." He then got a letter from Jones who was in Nantes. "He sent me a bill to supply me with some cash & told me to be happy," reported Ledyard. But as autumn progressed, it looked less likely. Ledyard's proposed starting date of the first of October slipped past, and again it was too late to sail around Cape Horn. Jones found prices quoted for ships astronomical, with one merchant asking eighty thousand livres, or three times Ledyard's estimate. Jones asked Edward Bancroft for advice. Bancroft, an American doctor spying for the British government, reported the Ledyard & Jones scheme to his handlers in London. As they were not keen to allow another country, especially America, elbow into their new market, they had Bancroft tell Jones that dozens of English merchants were jumping into the trade. Jones was equally rebuffed by Spain. He wrote to Charles Carmichael in Madrid to find out King Charles III's attitude. It was severely negative, as Spain still considered the Northwest Coast a part of New Spain. The Jones & Ledyard plan died.

Having suffered a third strike against him, Ledyard finally gave up on the fur-trade scheme. His idea, however, blossomed into the first great goldmine for the new United States and a battleground in global politics. In September 1787 John Kendrick in the *Columbia Rediviva* and Robert Gray in the *Lady Washington*, left Boston for Nootka Sound. When the *Columbia* returned to Boston in August 1790, carrying a cargo of China tea and a Hawaiian Islander, she became the first American ship to circumnavigate the world. In the next twenty years, nearly a hundred American ships came to the Northwest Coast to trade, and Nootka Sound was jokingly referred to as a suburb of Boston. In 1790 war almost broke out between Great Britain and Spain over its sovereignty. The fur trade was so enormous that Thomas Jefferson instructed the Lewis & Clark expedition to return from the Pacific via a passing American fur-trading ship rather than retracing their steps. In 1841 the last fur-trading ship departed from Nootka. By then the west was in American hands, a four thousand year-old nation had been shattered, many had made fortunes and the sea otter, the slippery mammal with the thick fur coat, was close to extinction.

11

More Shirts than Shillings—
Walking the World

"Paris is like a strong whirlpool," wrote John Ledyard. "It collects a parcel of light rubbish within its vortex which very seldom returns by the way it entered to the surface of the stream of life, & If I ever do it will not be according to the general course of things I assure you for I bid defiance to them when I left America & even bribed the utmost malice of fortune." As his seven-year fever about furs finally subsided, Ledyard's life eddied into a new stream.

Ledyard made a new plan. It originated with his idea of landing at Nootka Sound, but it had the attractive aspect of having nothing to do with commerce and everything to do with traveling, with adventure, with the biggest dream possible. He would walk from Europe through Asia and then cross North America.

When he first touched the west coast of North America in the spring of 1778, Ledyard was inspired. Having now seen both ends of the continent, he wanted to traverse it. The method came to him immediately. He saw bracelets and knives that had clearly come from the east coast. In seeing trade goods that had crossed a continent, he knew that a person could too. He thought he could cross North America by passing from tribe to tribe—like a knife.

Throughout the discouraging years of fur-trading machinations, Ledyard had clung to the idea of exploring North America. A part of his plan with John Paul Jones included wintering over at Nootka Sound, possibly for three or four years; no doubt some of that time would be spent wandering into the interior. Moreover, commerce clearly was not Ledyard's forte. An unlucky combination of bad timing and mendacious partners had contributed to the failure of his fur-trading idea, but part of the blame lay with Ledyard. His partners must have sensed his footloose ways. He was addicted to that rush of adrenalin when a journey got underway, when a town slipped behind out of view and the open road lay before him. "Ledyard had the most romantic enthusiasm for adventure perhaps of any man in his time," wrote James Burney, an officer on the Cook voyage. He was not a businessman. Bound by the conventional and the ordinary, he would revolt. He deserted from college, divinity studies and the British navy. He was too scattered in interests, too wild in spirit, too undependable in action. He had little enthusiasm for the quotidian details and mind-numbing work of a merchant toting up figures on bills of lading. He was meant to wander. Jefferson said that Ledyard had "an unrivaled intrepidity. . . and of a roaming, restless character." Released from his fur-trade obsession, John Ledyard was going to roam again.

In the winter of 1786 Ledyard told Jefferson about his hopes of traveling across the continent and found a willing listener. Jefferson had long contemplated the world beyond the Blue Ridge Mountains. As a child he had met Indians from the west, including a Cherokee chief, Outacity, who visited his family plantation. Jefferson gave names to some of the western lands: Cherronesus for northern Michigan; Metropotamia for Michigan and northern Ohio; and Polypotamia for Illinois, Indiana and Kentucky. In December 1783 he approached General Rogers Clark about a rumor that the British were organizing an expedition to explore the west. Saying, "some of us have been talking here in a feeble way of making the attempt to search that country," Jefferson asked if Clark might lead a team to "tour to the west and Northwest of the Continent." Three months later Clark replied that he would go if Congress authorized and paid for the expedition, but he thought that "large parties will never answer the purpose. They will allarm the Indian Nations they pass through. Three or four young Men well qualified for the Task might perhaps compleat your wishes."

Nothing came of the Jefferson and Clark plan, but here in Paris was an American who had actually been to the west coast and wanted to go back. In October 1785 Jefferson moved to Hotel de Langeac, a villa at the end of the Champs d'Elysees near one of the new Paris tollhouses. Built for a mistress of a duke, Hotel de Langeac was a much grander establishment than the cul-de-sac Taitbout. It had three stories, an oval salon with a rising sun ceiling and polished floor, newfangled water closets—*lieux a l'anglaise*—stables, carriage houses, servant's quarters, a greenhouse, a porter's lodge and a vegetable garden where Jefferson patiently coaxed sweet potatoes and American corn. Ledyard came frequently to Hotel de Langeac, so often that people posted him letters addressed there.

Amidst the corn on the cob and the running-water toilets, Ledyard and Jefferson hatched an audacious plan. Ledyard, the man who had already gone around the world by sea, would now go around the world by land. Each man phrased its genesis in his own style. "Being of a roaming disposition, he was now panting for some new enterprise," Jefferson wrote in 1813. "I then proposed to him to go by land to Kamschatka, cross in some of the Russian vessels to Nootka Sound, fall down into the latitude of the Missouri, and penetrate to, and through that to the United States. He eagerly seized the idea." For Jefferson, Ledyard was destined to travel. At one of Jefferson's *petit souper*s, Ledyard had kidded David Humphrey about his poetry, and Humphrey pulled out some Hartford scuttlebutt about Ledyard's 1773 canoe trip down the Connecticut. "Our Minister laughed heartily," Ledyard wrote, "observing that it was no unworthy prelude to my subsequent voyages & that I had observed a great consistancy of character from that moment to this—which is something more than some of my friends would have said." For Ledyard, the jump from fur trader to traveler was consistent with his future-looking character. Referring to the fur-trading scheme donkey that he rode for years, he succinctly said: "Farewell old Ass & welcome new Ass."

In the winter and spring of 1786, Jefferson shepherded the Ass through the thickets of international diplomacy. The main concern was obtaining permission from Empress Catherine II of Russia to travel through her lands. At the time only Russia and the Ottoman Empire required passports for visitors. Ledyard wanted to go without a passport, but Jefferson and the Marquis de Lafayette counseled him to wait for permission. "You see," Ledyard told his cousin Isaac, "I have so many friends that I cannot do just as I please." Jefferson spoke with Count Ivan Simolin, the Russian minister to France, while Lafayette contacted Count de Vergennes, France's foreign minister; Marquis de Castries, the French minister of the navy; Louis Philippe, Count de Segur, the French ambassador to Russia; and Baron Frederich Melchior von Grimm.

Grimm was the key contact. The longtime minister at Versailles for the Duchy of Saxe-Gotha, Grimm was a special confident of Empress Catherine II of Russia. She subscribed to *Correspondence Litteraire*, his periodical publication of his letters and literary criticism, and considered him an unofficial Russian representative in France. In a letter to Grimm, Lafayette enclosed a note from Jefferson and a plan of travel from Ledyard. Confidently if not naively proposing that the journey "will take no more than two years," Ledyard said he would lead a small party of a scientist and "two strong and robust domestics" and that the total cost would not exceed five hundred louis d'or ($60,000 in 2005). Jefferson's letter, dated 9 February 1786, spoke of Ledyard's "spirit of enterprize which has distinguished his whole life. He has genius, an education better than common, and a talent for useful & interesting observation. I believe him to be an honest man, and a man of truth. To all this he adds just as much singularity of character." Lafayette translated Jefferson and Ledyard's contributions into French and then added his analysis of the scheme: "All that I have been inclined to recognize in the ardent traveler makes me believe that Her Imperial Majesty will be satisfied with him. It has not been a year since I saw him for the first time, but the inquiries that I have made about him have all been favorable. This officer is completely preoccupied by his dominant passion, that of remarkable voyages, and with his personality I would believe him to be made expressly for that which he proposes."

Grimm passed along the packet to St. Petersburg, and hopes were high that permission and financial and logistical support would come from Catherine II. Lafayette, acting as a middleman, obtained almost 600f from Baron von Grimm as an advance from the empress to support the project. The marquis quietly covered the rest to make it a full 600f (or $3,500 in 2005) and passed the money to Jefferson, who handed it to Ledyard. In addition, over the course of the year, Jefferson gave Ledyard a total of 476f for living expenses.

Beyond money, Jefferson offered two outlandish ideas, taken from Ledyard's Tahitian tattoos, on how to make scientific observations. Worried that natives might rob or even murder Ledyard if he carried exotic tools like pen, ink and paper, Jefferson suggested as a "method of recording certain important observations" that Ledyard should "prick certain Characters into his own skin." These shorthand reminders would then be indelibly etched upon his body and prevent him from having "to carry implements of any kind" besides, of course, tattooing tools. The other notion was to decipher latitude without carrying the necessary astronomical equipment. Ledyard was to have the English foot tattooed on his arm and use it to make the required calculations. Since Ledyard kept a detailed journal on his trip around the world and never seemed to take a longitude measurement himself, it appeared that he ignored Jefferson's bizarre body art schemes.

Bursting with excitement about his plan, Ledyard wrote his cousin Isaac for the first time in five months: "My last Letters by the Fitzhughes of Virginia left me in the Metropilis of France, the verry football of chance and I have continued so untill within a verry few days of the date of this Letter. All the distresses that you can imagine incident to such a situation, have most faithfully attached themselves to me: they are now gone, and once more I greet you with a chearful heart. . . . In about fourteen days I leave Paris for Brussells, Cologne, Vienne, Dresdon, Berlin, Varsovie, Petersburg, Moscow, Kamchatka Sea of Anadivy, Coast of America." For Ledyard, there was a patriotic element to his itinerary. Although he had spent just two of the past twelve years in America, Ledyard felt a citizen of his native country:

> I die with anxiety to be on the back of the American States, after having either come from or penetrated to the Pacific Ocean. There is an extensive field for the acquirement of honest fame. A blush of generous regret sits on my Cheek to hear of any Discovery there that I have not part in, & particularly at this auspicious period: The American Revolution invites to a thourough Discovery of the Continent and the honor of doing it would become a foreigner. But a Native only could feel the pleasure of the Atchievement. It was necessary that an European should discover the Existance of that Continent,

but in the name of Amor Patria. Let a Native of it Explore its Boundary. It is my wish to be the Man I will not yet resign that wish nor my pretension to that distinction.

Waiting was Ledyard's most common occupation since leaving the Cook expedition, and he knew how to get comfortable. Flush with cash, he moved out of Paris to Saint-Germain-en-Laye, a rural retreat a dozen miles from Paris that boasted a number of foreign residents, including Thomas and Mary Barclay, the U.S. consul to France and his wife, and William Short, Jefferson's private secretary. He went for a four-mile run every day in the Saint-Germain forest, getting so fit he joked that he was a Houyhnhnm, one of the clever horses in *Gulliver's Travels*. One spring day he walked twelve miles into Paris in the morning and returned in time to have midday dinner at the Barclays'. Another time, he told Jefferson about a frightening experience walking home from Paris in the evening. "I heard a horse stumble and fall and a person give one groan. I sprang into the wood to see what was the matter and found a man down under his horse and both so entangled together that neither could rise. In making a sudden strong effort to disengage the man I so strained my loins that I have ever since been confined to my room, but am better. The man was much hurt."

In April 1786 Ledyard predicted he would receive word from Catherine II, but it was not until midsummer that matters came to a head. In July Jefferson learned that Lafayette was about to leave Paris for two months and quickly wrote to the marquis, asking him to go to Grimm and get more money for Ledyard. Lafayette did his bidding and a few days later reported that Grimm did not want to advance any more money and had advised Ledyard "not to Throw a way Any other opportunity."

Grimm's premonitions soon proved correct. The empress denied their request. Her reasons stemmed from another of the enormously coincidental facts that fate threw across Ledyard's path. Catherine had just sent out the Billings expedition. Commanded by Joseph Billings, a sailor from the *Discovery*, the expedition was the Russian response to the Cook and La Perouse voyages. In August 1785 the empress ordered "A Secret Astronomical and Geographical Expedition" aimed at exploring the northeast edge of Siberia and the Aleutians. Officially it was a state secret, but with the supervision of the St. Petersburg scientific community and the departure that autumn of dozens of the expedition's officers—including three English-men—word soon leaked out. For Catherine II, Ledyard simply was some-one tardily trying to join her not-so-secret-anymore expedition: "Mr. Ledyard would do well to take another route than that of Kamchatka, be-cause, as far as this [Billings] expedition is concerned, there is no longer a way to reach it. Besides, everything that has been written about this [Billings] expedition is completely false and a chimerical dream: there never has been a party on foot, and it all comes to the expedition of Captain Billings and of the personnel selected by him and Pallas. Let the American have the money you have given or promised him; but don't throw my money out the window in the future: I do not know those people at all and have had nothing to do with them up to now." Grimm, perhaps embold-ened by the powerful names behind the Ledyard plan, asked her to recon-sider, but she wrote back: "Je vous ai dit tout ce que j'avais a dire sur le Sr Ledyar" ("I have told you all I had to say about Mr. Ledyard.")

On 15 August 1786, Jefferson went to the usual Tuesday gathering of foreign ministers at Versailles. Grimm told him about Catherine II's rejec-tion. The next day Jefferson wrote to Ledyard, giving him the news and adding that he hoped Ledyard could switch itineraries and explore the American continent from the east coast instead. The same day Ledyard wrote to Jefferson, but not from his bucolic home in Saint-Germain. He was in London.

His exit from Paris, after fifteen months, was as hasty as his entrance. At six in the morning one day in July, a visitor named Sir James Hall came to Ledyard's boardinghouse. Hall was a young Scottish baron and geologist on his way home after a three-year European tour. Ledyard had met him three or four times in Paris that summer. At one dinner Hall had, Ledyard wrote, "expressed the highest Opinion of the Tour I had determined to make and said he would as a Citizen of the world, do any thing in his power to pro-mote it." Now at dawn Hall was there to help. Hall saw some coins on Led-yard's bureau and asked how he was doing financially: "If fifteen Guineas, interrupting the answer he had demanded, will be of any service to you, there they are and put them on the Table—. I am a traveller myself and tho' I have some fortune myself to support my travels, yet I have been so

situated as to want money which you ought not to do." Hall not only supplied money, he sent a letter to Ledyard in early August about a ship leaving from London for Nootka Sound. With no news yet from Catherine II
and the urge to travel overwhelming, Ledyard dashed to London.

John Ledyard arrived in London in time to witness a short-lived but
intense British passion for the Northwest fur trade. Six ships had gone out
in 1785 for Nootka Sound: four had fitted out in India and two, the *King
George* and *Queen Charlotte*, in London. The first four went illegally, without the sanction of the East India Company, the ancient and all-powerful
business conglomerate that had a monopoly on British trading rights east
of Cape Town. (The four from India sailed under Portuguese colors.) The
King George and *Queen Charlotte*, on the other hand, carried royal names
and Union Jacks. Unlike in the United States, where the only governmen-
tal support for the fur trade came in the form of a letter of recommendation given to the *Empress of China*, British officialdom actively encouraged
the fur trade. Richard Etches, a seasoned London tea and wine merchant,
asked the EIC for a charter of exclusive trade on the American coast. In
August 1785, after complex negotiations involving the admiralty, Etches received a five-year, non-exclusive license. He immediately sent out the *King
George* and *Queen Charlotte*, christened by Sir Joseph Banks in honor of the
present heads of state and under the command of two Cook officers,
George Dixon and Nathaniel Portlock, with a son of John Gore's on board.

A year later, when Ledyard arrived in London, Etches was preparing another state-sanctioned royal couple, the *Prince of Wales* and *Princess Royal*,
for Nootka. The ships, commanded by James Colnett, a veteran of Cook's
second voyage, sailed from London on 23 September 1786. Sadly, Ledyard
was somehow unable to secure passage to Nootka aboard Etches's ships.

Instead, Ledyard tried to sail on an illicit expedition that did not have
the approval of the East India Company. The ship, called the *Harriot* and
captained by J. Bruce, was due to leave London in mid-August. Sir James
Hall introduced Ledyard to the ship's owners, who warmly welcomed the
Cook veteran. One of the officers in charge was another Cook man, and he
too was pleased to have Ledyard's company. The *Harriot* was scheduled to
sail around Cape Horn and land at Nootka, "from thence I mean to make
an attempt to cross the continent to Virginia." Ledyard told his cousin.

Hall also gave Ledyard twenty guineas to outfit himself. "I bought two great Dogs, an Indian pipe and a hatchet," he told Thomas Jefferson. Ledyard knew this was a strange and meager set of belongings. "My want of time as well as more money, will prevent my going otherwise than indifferently equipped for such an Enterprise," he wrote. "It is certain I shall be more in want before I see Virginia." But he asked, "why should I repine?" The dogs were for company, protection and hunting. There would have been many lonely interludes, and the faithful love of a canine companion would mean a great deal. Seaman, a black, one-hundred-and-fifty-pound Newfoundland dog, traveled with Meriwether Lewis to the Pacific and back; he caught squirrels, mountain goats and antelope and barked when bears prowled near their campsites. The hatchet could be used to cut firewood and help fashion a temporary shelter. The peace pipe was the piece de résistance. Even with unlimited time and money, Ledyard would have rejected the idea of a massive expedition, with porters snaking in a long line behind him. Ledyard wanted to move fast and light. During the four years with Cook, he saw the inherent dangers of traveling in groups. A ship like the *Resolution* or a large expedition gave the illusion of security. Expensive equipment attracted thieves and large numbers of people aroused suspicions. Traveling in a small group meant being nimble and flexible and, most of all, dependent on locals for support. The best way to introduce oneself was using the old tradition of the peace pipe, which although it was not common west of the Rockies, was a staple of conversation across the Great Plains. When he listed his ports of call in North America, Ledyard gave the Sioux and Chippewa. The native people of North America would be his way stations.

Ledyard's departure date with the *Harriot* was postponed until September. In the meantime, he took in the sights of London. The great city, teeming with nearly a million residents, was the capital of the world. The Thames handled more traffic than any other river in Europe. The famously convoluted streets were dark and dirty, loud with the clang of iron wheels on cobblestones and pierced by the call of hawkers. London was more expensive than Paris and had greater extremes of rich and poor, mansions in Belgravia and scores of abandoned children sleeping in Hyde Park. For Ledyard, though, Paris was a home and London was merely a base camp from which to launch expeditions. After delighting in the Palais-Royal, he was less enchanted by the mobs in Covent Garden, the pleasures of Vauxhall and Ranelagh Gardens or the extensive library of books and newspapers at the Chapter Coffee House in Paternoster Row. "I cannot submit to a haughty eccentricity of manners so prevalent among the English," he wrote. "They have millions of Virtues but damn their vices, they are enormous." He complained of the "proud insolent stiff English Tavern" and found himself reacting violently to some Englishmen. He told Jefferson, a fellow Anglophobe: "Everything is a cabal, even on the streets. Fortunately for me I understand well to give some punches and have literaly been obliged to thrash 5 or 6 of those haughty turbulent & very insolent people: one of them at the theatre where I assure you one is still more liable to insult than in the streets even." It sounded less fractious in a letter to his cousin Isaac, where he mentioned "Boxing some Puppy at the Theatre a la mode d'anglais," but nonetheless the scrapping indicated that his nerves were short.

Thrashing and punching were not his only reactions to Londoners, and Ledyard did make a couple of friends. "I am received with the greatest politeness in London," he told his cousin, adding in reference to his unauthorized exit from the British navy in 1782, "yet I am a deserter in London. What a world this is." London defined him not as a marine gone missing but as a man who had been with Captain James Cook. It was an elite, close-knit fraternity. "We find no small Satisfaction in talking over the eventful History of our Voyage and are happy beyond Measure when any of our old Companions come to see us from other Ships which they do as often as they can," wrote David Samwell, the *Resolution*'s surgeon, in 1781. "We are perhaps somewhat partial to one another, for it is an article of Faith with every one of us that there never was such a Collection of fine Lads take us for all in all, got together as there was in the *Resolution* & *Discovery*."

Sir Joseph Banks was a Cook man nonpareil. Banks was a baron, president of the Royal Society and one of the most powerful figures in Britain. The great panjandrum of Western science, he had funded and sailed on Cook's first voyage and thereafter, with a tutelary, renaissance spirit, had instigated dozens of expeditions and projects. He lived in a sixteen-thousand-square-foot pile at 32 Soho Square, with marbled chimneys, lantern skylights, twenty servants and an original portrait of Cook in the front parlor. Banks and Ledyard, both having reveled in the pleasures of Polynesia, no doubt traded stories and compared tattoos. Ledyard, like many other explorers, spent many afternoons in Banks' giant second-floor library, poring through volumes of history and science and pondering other worlds while listening to the rustling of the carriage horses stabled below.

Colonel William Smith, the secretary to the American legation in London, became another important contact. Smith had first run into Ledyard at Jefferson's in Paris. In June 1786 Smith married his boss's daughter, Nabby Adams, the daughter of John and Abigail. Ledyard visited the Smiths several times at their house on Wimpole Street near Regent's Park. In September the colonel, acting as minister plenipotentiary in John Adams's absence, detailed Ledyard's proposed route around the world in a letter to John Jay, the secretary for foreign affairs for the Continental Congress:

> It is a daring, wild attempt—and I have my doubts of his success—but finding him determined to pursue the subject, I thought he had better do it in the way he now is, than bind himself in any manner to his people—he embarked the last week free and independent of the World, pursuing his plan unimbarassed by Contract of obligation—if he succeeds, and in the Course of 2 or 3 years, should visit our Country by this amazing Circuit, he may bring with him some interesting information,—if he fails, and is never heard of—which I think most probable, there is no harm done—he dies in an unknown Country, and if he composes himself in his last moments with this reflection, that his project was great, and the undertaking, what few men are capable of—it will, to his mind, smooth the passage—he is perfectly calculated for the attempt—he is robust and healthy—& has an immense passion to make some discoveries which will benefit society and insure him, agreable to his own expression, 'a small degree of honest fame.'

Doubting that the *Harriot* would ever leave the Thames, Ledyard asked Smith for a letter of introduction in case he decided to travel overland to Nootka. With Catherine II's rejection, Ledyard and Smith thought that an eighteenth-century version of an American passport might suffice in Russia. "Mr Ledyard's object is to enquire into the natural History of the Countrys through which he may pass for the Extension of Science and the Benefit of Mankind," wrote Smith in the letter.

All Persons whom it may concern are requested to give him every necessary passport and Protection to enable him to compleat his Tour with despatch, and that he may be protected from every delay or detention, not Justified by the Laws of the place where he may be. M. Ledyard's good character & Conduct, it is expected will ensure him civility & respect and the great Object he has in view be a particular reason why the friends of Merit and of Science should aid him with their countenance and protection: he having also spent several years past in pursuit of objects which contribute largely to render him fit, for this Enterprize and particularly having accompanied the late celebrated Capt Jas. Cook on his last voyage are points, which exclusively of Mr Ledyard's personal merit it is hoped will ensure him the passports & protection requested.

The U.S. passport came into use, for the *Harriot* proved to be a red herring. In late September, at the same time that the *Prince of Wales* and *Princess Royal* were leaving port, customs officials seized the *Harriot* and everything aboard, including Ledyard's belongings, was impounded. "I am obliged in consequence to alter my route," Ledyard sputtered to Isaac, "& in short, every thing—all my little Baggage shield Buckler lance Dogs— Squire & all gone—. I only left—left to what—to some damned riddle I'll warrant you."

Immensely frustrated at yet another setback, Ledyard swung into action. In November 1786, reverting to his original plan, he announced that he would travel overland from Europe through Russia to Kamchatka and across the Aleutians to Alaska and Nootka. If exploration of North America were his goal, it would have been much easier for Ledyard to sail back to the United States and travel overland from the east coast. Jefferson clung to the option of starting in Kentucky, as seen in a 1 September 1786, letter to Ezra Stiles, the president of Yale: "A countryman of yours, a Mr. Lediard who was with Capt. Cook on his last voiage, proposes either to go to Kamschatka, cross from thence to the Western side of America, and penetrate through the Continent to our side of it, or to go to Ketucke, and thence penetrate Westwardly to the South sea. He went from hence lately to London, where if he found a passage to Kamschatka or the Western coast of America he would avail himself of it; otherwise he proposed to return to our side of America to attempt that route. I think him well calculated for such an enterprise and wish he may undertake it." Ledyard insisted on going east rather than west. His pride was wounded after Catherine II's rejection and he wished to learn more about Siberian natives, but the main reason was he wanted that "small degree of honest fame." He wanted to walk around the world.

Like generations of explorers after him, Ledyard focused on courting supporters. He had cultivated a powerful set of backers in Paris, giants like Lafayette and Jefferson, and in London he did the same. Chaperoned by Joseph Banks and William Smith, Ledyard met with various aristocrats in an effort to drum up funds. By the end of November, Banks and Smith raised a formal subscription for Ledyard's expedition. Three other men signed the subscription, including John Walsh, a longtime member of the Royal Society and veteran of the Indian colonial service, and Dr. John Hunter, the Scottish dentist who coined the words *molars* and *incisors*. Smith, worried that requirements of the London subscription might disrupt Ledyard's itinerary, added an addendum, "that he should not be under the necessity of reporting to them the discoveries he may make in America, will make such advances of Cash as will enable him to move upon principles of economy free from those shackles which they appear disposed to confine him with." Other gentlemen not on the subscription list contributed as well, and by the end of the month, Ledyard had charmed London to a tune of £50 ($7,000 in 2005).

"I am indeed a very plain Man, but do not think that mountains or oceans shall oppose my passage to glory while I have such friends in remembrance," Ledyard told Jefferson. "My heart is on fire—ye stimulate, & I shall gain the victory." At the end of November 1786, six years since he sailed up the Thames at the end of the Cook voyage, John Ledyard sailed down the Thames on his next passage to glory.

The United States was founded upon the notion of doing the undoable and dreaming the magnificent. Ledyard's idea to circumambulate around the globe was pure American. He had sailed around the world, something very few had accomplished. Now he would walk around the world, which no one had done. Bernard DeVoto, the twentieth-century American historian, wrote in a letter to Catherine Drinker Bowen: "If the mad, impossible voyage of

Columbus or Cartier or La Salle or Coronado or John Ledyard is not romantic, if the stars did not dance in the sky when the Constitutional Conven-
tion met, if Atlantis has any landscape stranger the other side of the moon
any lights or colors or shapes more unearthly than the customary homespun
of Lincoln or the morning coat of Jackson, well, I don't know what romance
is. Ours is a story mad with the impossible, it is chaos out of dream, it began
as dream and it has continued as dream down to the last headlines you read
in a newspaper. And of our dreams there are two things above all others to
be said, that only madmen could have dreamed them or would have dared
to—and that we have shown a considerable faculty for making them come
true. The simplest truth you can ever write about our history will be charged
and surcharged with romanticism, and if you are afraid of the word you better start practising seriously on your fiddle."

Walking the world was a ludicrous dream. It meant crossing unmapped
lands, through kingdoms, nations and lawless lands, across dozens of rivers,
over snow-capped mountain passes, alone except for two dogs. It was, in
the eighteenth century, nearly impossible. He knew nothing about the geography of the American west and was not nearly as experienced in wilderness travel as he would need to be. Traveling alone, he would necessarily be
unable to carry sufficient presents to make friends and pay Indians to guide
him. He had read books on biology, history, geology, geography and soci-
ology but would mostly rely on his ingenuity, hardiness and charm. It was
crazy. Ledyard knew it. "If you cannot call me mad," he told his cousin
Isaac on the eve of his departure, "say I am thus." He had fifty pounds, a
wool cloak, two dogs, a hatchet and a pipe. He had, as his subscription said,
"public & private Letters as Vouchers for his character." He had little else.

Ledyard was always ambivalent about his chosen career as a traveler. He
complained of missing his friends and wrote hundreds of letters from
abroad, each filled with professions of friendship and love. In Paris, knowing that his "seven year's ramble" from 1773 had expired, he told Isaac "I shall
be absent from my friends for 4 or 5 years, perhaps 6 or 7: this is not an exhilarating reflection applied to the circumstances of any man not condemned to the gallows: applied to myself it is as bad as the gallows. I have
been cheated of life, & hereafter shall be only to live for my friends." He
prayed in his letters for his family, blamed himself for their disappointments

and setbacks and spoke of his guilt in not providing for them. In a letter to Isaac, he quoted Virgil, saying there was nowhere in the world he would rather be than "stretching out at your ease under the shade of a beech tree." He thought that he had been "formed by nature and education to move in the small circle of domestic life," and amidst the continual dislocation of the traveling life, he latched onto any tangible memento of home. "How very valuable the least trifle becomes in certain situations," he told his cousin, pointing to two buttons Ben Ledyard's wife had given him in Middletown. He had lost one, but the other had been on his sleeve ever since.

Fate so often conspired to thwart Ledyard that he frequently felt he should give up his dreams and return to Groton or Southold. There were tantalizing "if onlys" that cobwebbed his past paths: if only he had received his rightful inheritance, if only Parker had not stolen money, if only La Perouse had not been sailing in 1785, if only the *Harriot* had cleared customs. Ledyard often bemoaned his bad luck and spoke of the "malice of fortune" and "the maloccurences of Fate." but he knew it went both ways. "The Strumpet has kissed me as often as she has kick'd me." He knew the theory that what did not kill you made you stronger. Columbus had waited years before receiving permission to sail. Cook had carried coal in Whitby cats before sailing to the South Seas. Speaking of good and bad luck, Ledyard experienced so much of both that they "eventually rendered me so hardy as to meet either without an extra palpitation."

Thus, with a hopeful heart, Ledyard took passage to the continent. He wandered across the Low Countries and into the German principalities. He caught an open-air ferryboat down the Elbe River, which turned out to be a miserable trip. After all the troubles with timing in the past and the phrase "too late in the season" repeatedly ringing in his ears, it was ironic that on his first major adventure since leaving Cook he chose the worst time to depart. An early winter blizzard slammed into the ferry and for forty hours Ledyard, bundled in his new wool cloak bought in London, endured the shawling snow. One of his dogs died in the storm.

In Hamburg, Ledyard and his one remaining canine companion stayed at a tavern run by a Scottish couple named Parrish. Ledyard told them of his plans to go to St. Petersburg. They said that another American traveler named Colonel William Langborn had passed through their tavern with the same destination. They described him, according to Ledyard, as "a Gentleman—a very good kind of man and an odd kind of man who had travelled much, had lately left him for that Place, took only a Shirt in his Pocket and always went on foot." A letter arrived at the tavern from Langborn. When he had left Hamburg, Langborn had asked the Parishes to send his luggage to Copenhagen, but after two months it had not arrived. Ledyard decided to go rescue Langborn. In his letter to the Parishes, Langborn "complains exceedingly of the awkwardness of the situation," wrote Ledyard to William Smith on 20 December 1786. "He says it makes People suspicious of him. Whether he left money in his trunk or Papers necessary to negociate Bills I cannot say, but he intimates a want of money from the want of his Trunk. I will fly to him with my little all and some clothes and lay them at his feet. At the moment I may be useful to him: he is my Countryman, a Gentleman, a Traveller. He may go with me on my voyage. If he does I am blessed; if not I merit his attention and am not much out of my way to Petersburg."

No one had a monopoly on being a lone, eccentric pedestrian. A traveler named John Stewart, known as Walking Stewart, was a British man who walked over vast stretches of Asia in the 1780s. Stewart had befriended Wordsworth in Paris and De Quincey in Bath and, according to the *Encyclopaedia Britannica*, "cut a curious figure by wearing Armenian dress." Walking Stewart, it turned out, nearly met Ledyard, as he was wandering through Scandanavia a few months after Ledyard. Langborn was an even closer doppelganger. A wealthy Virginian and Martha Washington's cousin, Langborn had been Lafayette's aide-de-camp during the war. In 1783 he sailed to Europe and spent his days walking forty or fifty miles from place to place, rambling across much of Great Britain and continental Europe. Bumping into the same people Ledyard knew, Langborn saw his old friend Lafayette in Paris, got Jefferson to give him a letter of recommendation and dined with William Smith and John Adams in London. (Lafayette, writing to George Washington, said that Langborn was "the same queer fellow you know him to be.") Ledyard had planned to travel in a small group—in his February 1786 passport proposal, he stated he would take a scientist, "as well as two strong and robust domestics"—and having nearly crossed paths with Langborn in Paris and London, Ledyard thought this fellow pedestrian would be a boon companion.

Arriving at Copenhagen at Christmastime, Ledyard found the colonel in destitute circumstances, without money, clothes or friends. Ledyard had ten guineas and spent most of it on resuscitating the colonel. Despite his providential arrival, Ledyard could not persuade Langborn to join him. "He will write to you when it suits his humor," Ledyard told Smith, "which tho good and like other peoples when applied to others yet left to himself is very Singular. I see in him the Soldier (which predominates), the Countryman and the generous friend... I asked to attend him through his Route to Petersburgh—no—I esteem you but I can travel in the manner I do with no man on Earth." Ledyard and Langborn went their separate ways. For the next ten years Langborn walked around Europe in a manner very similar to Ledyard's. Besides a favorite dog, as the *London Chronicle* reported in 1789, "this gentleman's equipage consists of a pocket compass, a hatchet, a pair of pistols, a sword and a shirt in his pocket to change the one on his back." In both Austria and Spain, Langborn was thrown in jail on suspicion of being a spy. In late 1796 he returned to Virginia, married a seventeen-year-old girl, and ten years later bailed Aaron Burr out of jail during his treason trial in Richmond.

Ledyard, meanwhile, leapt into the wintry chasm of Lapland. He looked at a map and figured the quickest way to St. Petersburg was through Sweden and Finland. He jumped the narrow Oresund to Sweden. North of Stockholm he tried to cross the Gulf of Bothnia to Finland. Sadly he found that the ice had not frozen solid, and his fifty-mile shortcut across the Gulf turned into a twelve-hundred-mile trek around it. He walked through Lapland, the vast region of northern Sweden and Finland. He had just his English cloak for protection against the snow and cold. "I traveled on foot with it in Danemarc, Sweeden, Lapland, Finland & the Lord knows where," wrote Ledyard when he sent the cloak to Isaac in 1788. "In opulence & in poverty I have kept it, slept in it, eat in it, drank in it, fought in it, negociated in it: it has been thro every scene my constant & faithfull servant." Ledyard traveled initially on a new road along the Gulf and then on the Norrstigen, the old king's highway complete with guesthouses and horses for rent. He reached Tornio near the Arctic Circle and then came down the Finnish side of the Gulf.

Ironically, it was to be the only major segment of his journey on foot, and it was easily the most difficult. Nothing he had done or would do matched the undiluted horror of his solo march through Lapland. The two months spent trudging through the bitter cold was a singular ordeal. "Never did I adopt an Idea so fatal to my happiness," he wrote a few months later. He had little money, no common language and no map. He ate reindeer, drank vodka and boarded with the Lapps, Western Europe's last nomadic people. The sun barely crested the horizon for much of the first weeks of his trek. The drifting snow covered all traces of road. The temperature dove below zero degrees. To travel, he probably used Lapp wooden skis and grass-stuffed boots, with their up-curving toe, to slide along the snow. He found Swedes in particular very hospitable: "If the inhabitants [of the rest of the world] were all Sweeds (for instance) I could eat, drink, sleep & travel at my ease." Ledyard looked by with fondness at the people he met along the trip and with anger at their governments. "Upon the whole, mankind have used me well, & tho I have as yet reached only the first stage of my journey I feel myself much indebted to that urbanity which I always thought more general than many think it to be," Ledyard wrote in March 1787, "& was it not for the villianous laws & bad examples of some Governments I have passed thro I am persuaded that I should have been able to have given yo still better accounts of our fellow creatures." A year later Ledyard's former colleague, John Paul Jones, also attempted to cross the Gulf of Bothnia in winter. Jones, saying that Ledyard's route was impossible as "by the far north, the roads were impracticable," chartered a thirty-foot open boat and Swedish boatmen and sailed for four stormy days before landing in present-day Estonia. Traveling alone, Ledyard had no Swedish sailors to talk to, and at some point in his midwinter trek he began to talk out loud. While a struggling divinity student in Connecticut and Long Island, Ledyard had sometimes rehearsed his sermons while walking in the woods. Now in Lapland, he kept his spirits up by practicing his French. On the long walks between villages, he lectured the snow-plastered tree limbs and any animals within earshot, as he told Thomas Jefferson: "It is a most extraordinary language: I believe that wolves, rocks, woods & snow understand it, for I have addressed them in it & they have all been very complaisant to me."

In mid-March 1787 Ledyard arrived in St. Petersburg. He was half-frostbitten, bruised and battered, his shoes ripped, his luggage consisting of just one extra shirt and his dog dead.

Taking a boat up the Neva River, Ledyard came upon a mirage. Eighty-four years earlier, the place had been a marshy delta of the Neva dribbling into the Baltic Sea. In 1703 the Tsar Peter started his "Window to the West," naming it Sankt Pieter Burkt, and by the time Ledyard arrived St. Petersburg was as cosmopolitan a city as any in the world. Since 1714 building with stone outside St. Petersburg was forbidden, so the contrast between the forlorn wooden huts of villagers outside town and the cold permanence of the city was dramatic. Peter and subsequent Tsars channeled the meandering Neva into canals, with cut embankments of red Finnish granite. Ledyard gazed at the Winter Palace, the grand, quarter-million-square-foot, one-thousand-roomed mansion that stretched five hundred feet along the southern bank of the Neva. Across the river were the gray granite walls of the Peter and Paul Fortress, where the Tsar's prisoners were held. Ledyard strolled up and down the fashionable, three-mile long, fully paved Nevsky Prospect. He took a cup of tea from a street vendor's steaming samovar. Then he moved into the *Angliiskaia naberezhnaia*, the English embankment.

Along the southern bank of the Neva, opposite the forbidding fortress, stood a line of three-story brick warehouses owned by English merchants. Behind the warehouses was Old Isaac Street, the heart of the thriving expatriate community. In a city of two hundred thousand people, thirty-two thousand foreigners lived in distinct districts, and although the British numbered less than fifteen hundred, they exerted a centrifugal force upon the city. British products were the rage, and many stores, including four of them named "English Shop," sold English coal, linens, buttons, guns and cognac. In the English embankment was the English Inn (run by a Scot), where Ledyard probably stayed. There were coffee houses, subscription libraries, the English Club (founded in 1770 and now with three hundred members) and an Anglican church.

Although brutalized by his Lapland journey, Ledyard quickly revived with the help of Sir Joseph Banks' letters of introduction. He drew twenty guineas on the account of Banks through Brown & Porter, an English merchant firm in town. Ledyard was such a unique figure, the firm wrote to Banks to ask "whether & how far Mr. Ledyard's expectations of pecuniary assistance will be fulfilled," adding that "it would be a pity to stop the man in his progress after having advanced so far." He also used Banks as a means to immediately introduce himself to Peter Simon Pallas. Ten years older than Ledyard, Pallas was the Joseph Banks of Russia. He was from Berlin, but after finishing his medical studies in Leyden he had moved to London and written so learnedly about zoology that at age twenty-three he had become a fellow in the Royal Society. From 1767 to 1774 he had led a scientific expedition to Siberia commissioned by Catherine II. Afterwards he was a professor of natural history at the imperial St. Petersburg Academy of Sciences, the author of numerous books and the director of the Billings expedition. Ledyard called Pallas "an homme de Bois," or a man of the woods, suggesting that for all his city polish Pallas was also a traveler at heart.

Pallas was equally impressed with Ledyard. He wrote that summer that Ledyard had a "restless and nearly savage character," adding "he was used to living on little and enduring all kinds of hardships, almost like the savages of his fatherland. He always travelled dressed after the manner of American hunters, in a simple jacket, with a headgear of polished leather. He did not burden himself with baggage, and he never thought about the future. No man was less anxious about his life and his fate." They regularly dined together at Pallas's apartment, joined by fellow members of the Academy and Pallas's greyhound, Albertini.

On 19 March 1787, Ledyard wrote Jefferson from St. Petersburg in an optimistic tone. "I cannot tell you by what means I came to Petersbourg, & hardly know by what means I shall quit it in the further prossecution of my tour round the world by Land: if I have any merit in the affair it is perseverence, for most severely have I been buffeted—&yet still am I even more obstinate than before—& fate as obstinate continues her assaults. How the matter will terminate I know not: the most probable Conjecture is that I shall succeed, & be kicked round the world." He dined that day with Pallas in typical Ledyard style: "I dined in a shirt that I had worn four days—I have but two: & I suppose when I write you next I shall have none." Jefferson received the letter in June and soon wrote to a mutual American friend in Paris, John Banister. In a paragraph that summed up Ledyard the American Traveler, Jefferson said: "I had a letter from Lediard lately dated at St. Petersburg. He had but two shirts, and yet more shirts than shillings. Still, he was determined to obtain the palm of being the first circumambulator of the earth. He sais that having no money they kick him from place to place and thus he expects to be kicked round the world."

"This Auro[r]a Borealis of a City," Ledyard called St. Petersburg, grew brighter as spring approached. The sledding hills built on the Neva melted. The giant bonfires on the shores burned away. At Easter the city exploded into a ferris-wheeled, carouseled carnival. Ledyard wandered the docks and talked with the captains of the four U.S. ships that lay in the harbor that spring.

He also fell in love with a German woman. The German community was one of the largest in St. Petersburg—the English Club's minutes were taken in German—and through Pallas, Ledyard met many attractive love interests. "You may think if you please that the passion I had for my charming little blue-eyed german lass is no more," Ledyard wrote to Pallas in October 1787, "but you will be deceived—it keeps pace with my other passions: kiss her for me, you or doctor Reiniggs. I wish I could die to night at her feet, or higher up—kiss her for me & assure her of my esteem." Ledyard was completely smitten with her. Two months later, while wintering out in eastern Siberia, Ledyard was even more effusive in another letter to Pallas, speaking of "a kind of soft sentimental pain that I am sure has originated from a pair of blue eyes I saw at your house: indeed why should I hesitate to say I love her. I have so often mentioned in my letters to you: I am not content to be always King: if she was here I would resign my scepter to her. Speak kindly of Anthony yet who have not seen a Cleopatra. It is not a modern observation that there is in madness itself a pleasure that none but madmen can conceive of. Who can despise the chains of love but an Anchorite. I feel inclinced to be a slave to my German lass." As with Rebecca Eells of Stonington, Ledyard turned his back on love in St. Petersburg. He tantalizingly never mentioned even the name of this German woman, how he met her, what she was like, what places they visited or how wrenching their goodbye was. If he was tempted to stop his journey and settle down in St. Petersburg, he never suggested such a scenario. Despite his avowals of love, he did not mention her after leaving Russia. The fact that Ledyard could stop his ceaseless movement for a moment and fall in love reveals another side of his personality, yet when he moved on, he showed the strength of his desire to travel. His love of women was no match for his wanderlust.

As spring arrived, Ledyard struggled to leave. In an attempt to get the passport Catherine II had denied a year earlier—"without which I cannot stir," Ledyard said—he applied to the English and French embassies (there was no official American diplomatic representative in Russia until 1804) and dined with the Portuguese ambassador. The Comte de Segur, the French ambassador, refused to issue a passport. He could not appeal to Catherine II. She had been gone since the first of the year on her Potemkin village tour of the Crimea and would not return until mid-July. "My spirits are bad," he told William Smith on 15 May 1787. "My heart is ill:—it is oppressed: I think too severely: my designs are generous—why is my fate otherwise." Suddenly, Ledyard's fate changed. By chance he met a Russian officer who was on the staff the grand duke Nikolai Pavlovich's two-thousand-soldier-strong private army. The grand duke, Catherine's son, actively opposed his mother's rule because she had not, as tradition demanded, allowed him to become Tsar when his father had died. Granting permission to someone his mother had denied was an easy decision. On 20 May the St. Petersburg gubernatorial administration issued a passport to John Ledyard, Esquire, for passage through Ekaterinburg, Korkino, Kolyvan, Irkutsk and Okhotsk to America. His purpose, as stated in the passport, was to obtain information relating to natural history while traveling through Siberia on his way to America. Once he had the passport, Ledyard went with Pallas to the post office to obtain a travel order for free passage from St. Petersburg to Irkutsk. Pallas had hired William Brown, a Scottish physician returning to Siberia along the post office route, to carry supplies for the Billings expedition and arranged for Ledyard to accompany Brown as a "Messenger."

On the first of June, Ledyard and Brown left St. Petersburg and, riding post, reached Moscow on the sixth. On the way they overtook the grand duke and his entourage, heading to Moscow to meet the empress when she arrived from the Crimea at the end of June. Perhaps Ledyard politely waved to the future Tsar and thanked him for the passport. After less than two days in Moscow, enough time for Ledyard to be robbed of fifty rubles, they left for Siberia.

12

Double Relish—Siberia

SIBERIA, IN ITS SHEER SIZE, is the Pacific Ocean of the globe's landmass. Alone, it boasts one-twelfth of the world's land, and the entire United States could comfortably fit into its boundaries. Stretching from Central Asia to the Arctic and from the Urals to the Pacific, it contains desert, mountains, steppe, taiga, tundra, dozens of major rivers and mountains and the world's largest body of freshwater, Lake Baikal.

Like European settlers on the east coast of America heading west, Russians inexorably migrated east across their continent from Moscow, settling new towns, battling natives, cutting roads and eventually reaching the Pacific in 1648. The watershed moment was in October 1581 when Cossacks conquered Sibir, the capital of a major Mongol principality. For Russians, Sibir (meaning "sleeping land" in the Tatar language) became the etomological source for *Sibirskaia zemlia*, the land of Siberia.

Siberia also suggested a dark, forbidden place. In Moscow and St. Petersburg, native Siberians—a Mongol-Turkic mix—were called Tartars, the extra *r* making it close to the Greek *tartarus*, meaning "hell." In the seventeeth and eighteenth century, Russia gobbled up Siberia, expanding the empire at a rate of sixty thousand square miles a year, led by the promyshlenniki chasing the black fur of the sable. The only product imported into Siberia was exiles banished by the Tsar; their numbers increased tremendously after the death sentence was abolished in 1753.

In the eighteenth century an extensive Siberian infrastructure evolved, especially in the wake of the Bering, Pallas and Billings expeditions. Peasants, miners, nomads, Cossack frontiersmen, Russian merchants, refugees and military officials mixed with a myriad of native Siberians including Buryats near Lake Baikal and Sakha in the Lena River valley.

Information about Siberia was still scarce. While browsing Sir Joseph Banks's library in London and that of Pallas in St. Petersburg, Ledyard read a number of relevant books. Banks owned a copy of Chappe d'Auteroche's *Voyage en Siberie*, translated into English in 1774. D'Auteroche, a French astronomer, traveled to Tobolsk in 1761 and wrote a book so famously critical of Russian governance in Siberia that Catherine II had a rebuttal published. Ledyard also saw John Bell's *A Journey from St Petersburg to Pekin: 1719–22*, an account written by a Scottish doctor and published in 1763. More reliable was Pallas's own three-volume account of his seven-year sojourn in Siberia, the standard reference book for Siberian natural history, but it was not that useful for Ledyard since it was written in German. Ledyard waded through the nine-volume *History of the Turks* by Abulgazi-Bagadur, but it was more than a century old, barely covered the native Siberians and, as Ledyard said, "I do not remember any thing like Philosophic Research or Information in his History." Thomas Pennant, a regular correspondent of Banks and Pallas, wrote three books on zoology that referenced Russia. Two long-out-of-date descriptions of Siberia came from Cornelius de Bruyn, who traveled through much of Russia from 1701 through 1703, and Georg Wilhelm Steller, who was on Bering's second expedition in the early 1740s. Ledyard was not impressed. "Steller ought to have been hung and Le Bruyn burned," he wrote in his diary. "Such Travellers in Countries of such immense extent and replete with those circumstances that lead boldly into the most remote History of Man & of Nature have only furnished matter to feed the pampered Vanity of Buffon & of airy Hypothesis." William Coxe, an Englishman who advised Pallas on the Billings expedition, issued the seminal 1780 *Account of Russian Discoveries between Asia and America* and in 1784 a best-selling two-volume *Travels*, but both did not have much to say about Siberia. Ledyard, as the first American to travel across Siberia, was traveling relatively blind.

The dream was to walk the world, but it was clear that it would be impossible to walk Siberia. The distances were too vast: four thousand miles from St. Petersburg to Irkutsk, the capital city of eastern Siberia, two thousand more to the Pacific. Going on foot would take years, especially considering the intensely cold and snowy Siberian winters and the equally dangerous springtime, when swollen rivers swamped lowlands. Ledyard did not have the money to exist for six or seven years in Russia.

Instead he had, via Pallas's intervention, a free lift all the way to the Pacific. Ledyard rode in a kibitka, a leather-hooded three-horse-drawn coach shaped like a large cradle. Russian distances were calculated in versts, about two-thirds of a mile, and along the trakt, as the 1760s-built Moscow-Irkutsk highway was known, every thirty versts or so was a small village and a post station where kibitka drivers switched horses and where travelers could eat and spend the night. The kibitka system, though rudimentary, was effective, and over a hundred thousand people worked along the trakt, maintaining the road, caring for the horses and carriages, handling the mail and serving as *iamshchiki,* or coachmen. Despite the steady succession of post stations, the kibitka reminded Ledyard of the Cook voyage: the tedium of waiting, the monotonous, barely changing view and the isolation of a self-enclosed vehicle. "Kabikta travelling is the remains of Caravan travelling," he wrote. "It is your only home—it is like a Ship at Sea."

Ledyard and Brown passed Nizhni Novgorod, Russia's third-largest city, followed the Volga River and after four hundred miles reached Kazan. They stayed a week in Kazan, an old Russian town with mosques, a university and a row of shops on what was called Sunday Street. Leaving Kazan, Ledyard and Brown rode past deeply forested hills of the Ural Mountains to Ekaterinburg, where the Romanov family was killed during the Russian Revolution. A busy industrial city, with gun, anchor and iron foundries and paper mills, Ekaterinburg was the first stop after crossing the Urals and the last town before Siberia proper. They pressed on to Tobolsk, across the Tobol River from ancient Sibir. Tobolsk boasted the first fort east of the Urals and the first monastery in Siberia, but by the time Ledyard arrived it had lost some of its frontier charm. Crude fisherman's shacks mingled with brick houses for the town's officials, and spring floods had created malarial swamps at the edges of the town.

After three days in Tobolsk, Ledyard and Brown spent nine hard days crossing the desolate Baraba steppe. A wooded land dotted with hundreds of lakes and marshes, the Baraba was filled with nomadic Tatars. On 23 July they reached Barnaul on the Ob River where Brown lived. Ledyard billeted at the house of the city's treasurer. "Treated with great Hospitality," wrote Ledyard "but obliged to sleep in my Cloak on the Floor, as I have done ever since I left Petersburgh." After four nights, he took rooms at another house. The night after he switched, the treasurer's house burned to the ground, along with twenty-four other houses.

Brown took Ledyard to dinners with the governor of the city, judges and retired army officers, all of whom were quite interested in meeting the American traveler: "I am a curiosity myself in this country: those who have heard of America flock round me to see me: unfortunately the marks on my hands procures me & my Countrymen the appelation of wild men. . . . We have however two Stars that shine even in the Galaxy of Barnowl, & the healths of Dr Frankling & Gen'l Washington have been drank in compliment to me at the Governors table: I am treated with great hospitality here—hitherto I have fared comfortably when I could make a port any where—but when totally in the Country I have been a little incommoded: hospitality however I have found as universal as the face of Man."

Being midsummer, the weather was very warm. The Ob, a three-thousand-mile-long river, meandered past in a slow, brown ooze. "The mornings here are exceedingly hot: a serene cloudless sky—and a dead Calm." Only in the evenings was there much of a breeze. Ledyard wrote Jefferson and Lafayette from Barnaul, sent care of Pallas (he also enclosed for Pallas a rhinoceros leg bone found on the banks of the Ob). Ledyard also told Jefferson that the Tatars and Native Americans were the same people. The theory was first mooted in the sixteenth century, and in 1645 a Jesuit missionary in Mexico guessed that Native Americans had "crossed some narrow stretch of sea." Very few people had spent substantial time with both Native Americans and Siberians, so Ledyard spoke from experience, not conjecture. Furthermore, since Ledyard knew the geography of the North Pacific, especially the fact that Bering Strait was a mere fifty miles in width, he was one of the first to hint at the idea, later accepted as fact, that Native Americans had immigrated across the Bering Strait.

After a week, Ledyard left Barnaul: "At nine Oclock waited on the Goernor with my passport—He was well pleased with it, gave me a Corporal to conduct the affairs of the Mail; told me I had nothing to do but sit in my Kabitka; and mustered up French enough to say, 'Monsieur, Je vous souhaite un bon voyage.'" Ledyard said a warm farewell to Brown, and for the first time since March he was alone.

Three days later, having traveled nearly three hundred miles, Ledyard arrived in Tomsk. He found the local peasants very hospitable, and after giving him barley soup, milk, onions, bread and kvass, a Russian rye and malt drink, they would accept no payment. He had dinner with the governor, a Frenchman named Tomas Villeneuve, who claimed to be the son of the duc d'Orleans. He "kept me drinking strong Liquors until 1. Oclock and departed quite fuddled: but did not think myself so much so as I really was. I never was so ill after a debauch as I have been to-day. . . . Took a walk towards evening and bathed in the fine river Tomsk,—felt better after it." Villeneuve had been in Siberia for a quarter century and had forgotten much of his French. "I asked him if the town or its environs afforded any thing curious in natural History: his answer was that there were in it,—thieves, liars, rascals, whores, rogues, and villains of every description. . . . I was convinced that he was one himself."

Shambling out of Tomsk, Ledyard crossed the Yenisei River at Krasnoyarsk and again got drunk with a local commander. The weather soured. "Driving with wild tartar horses at a most rapid rate over a wild and ragged Country," Ledyard wrote in his diary. "Breaking and upsetting Kabitkas—beswarmed by Musquetoes—all the way hard rains and when I arrived at Irkutsk I was and had been the last 48 hours wet thro' and thro'—and one complete mass of mud."

On 15 August 1787, exactly two and a half months after leaving St. Petersburg, a mud-splattered Ledyard arrived at the Siberian capital city of Irkutsk. (He had made excellent progress. Martin Sauer, an Englishman on the Billings expedition, had taken a month longer when he made the same trip the year before.) Irkutsk, on the banks of the Angara River forty miles from Lake Baikal, was a substantial town. A meticulous counter, Martin Sauer estimated there were twenty thousand citizens living in twenty-five hundred houses there, twelve stone churches, one cathedral, two monasteries, a hospital, a divinity school, a library and a theatre. In the center of town stood a square of brick buildings that was the Irkutsk market, and outside town was a massive brandy distillery, three salt works, a glassblowing factory and an eleven-loom textile mill.

Exhausted by his trip, Ledyard postponed seeing the sights. He spent a day resting in his rooms. "I shrewdly suspect by what I see from my poor little talc window," he wrote in his diary, "that I shall even here find all the fashionable follies—the cruel ridiculous extravagance, and ruinous éclat of Petersburg." Ledyard then got a shave for ten kopecks and, using letters of reference from Peter Simon Pallas and a Dr. Reiniggs of St. Peterburg, gained immediate entrée to Irkutsk's small but furiously competitive upper classes. He had dinner the second day with three Germans and a Frenchman who had once lived in Quebec. All were exiles, a part of what Ledyard estimated to be a throng of one hundred and fifty deportees in Irkutsk represented the whole range of exiles: religious dissenters, Polish and Swedish rebels, serfs, vagrants, bandits and revolutionaries. "Not a day passes scarcely," wrote Ledyard, "but an exile of some sort arrives here."

Ledyard met with Ivan Iakobi, the governor-general for all of eastern Siberia, and the bishop of Irkutsk, Mikhail Mitkevich, but his closest companion was an old friend of Pallas, Aleksandr Karamyshev. A student of Carl Linnaeus in Sweden, Karamyshev was a chemistry professor and colleague of Pallas at the St. Petersburg Academy of Sciences until 1779, when he moved to Irkutsk to run the local bank. Karamyshev had Ledyard to dinner almost every day at his house and allowed him free run of his extensive library. He took him to a small museum that housed a few curiosities. Most were marvels like the skin of a Chinese goat, but one in particular brought back memories: a piece of Hawaiian bark cloth that the *Resolution* had left in Kamchatka in 1779. Karamyshev gave Ledyard some Siberian apples and appleseeds, which he in turn posted to Pallas and Lafayette. He taught him about Siberian culture and introduced him to local Buryats. Related to Genghis Khan's Golden Horde that had swept through Asia, the Buryats were a formidable nomadic Mongol race. Ledyard learned that the Buryat had only recently abandoned their traditional shamanism for Tibetan Buddhism after missionaries from Lhasa came to the Lake Baikal region. They wrote in vertical columns, lived in felt-covered gers (yurts) and burned dried camel dung for fuel. Ledyard, an early adherent to phrenology, measured their heads.

A good host, Karamyshev guided Ledyard on a two-day sightseeing trip to Lake Baikal. They dined there with Erik Laxmann, a Finnish naturalist, chemistry professor and glass-factory owner. After meeting with Laxmann and touring his glass factory, Ledyard took a cruise on the lake in the rain. The lake is a mind-boggling four hundred miles in length and so deep it contains a fifth of the world's fresh water. Ledyard may have seen Baikal's freshwater seals, but focused on the depth of the lake; he fruitlessly tried to sound the bottom with a fifty-fathom line.

In Irkutsk, as in Barnaul, Ledyard felt like a celebrity. Officers saluted him in the streets. Leading citizens invited him to dinner. Although his clothes were ragged, they must have had some value, for the woman doing Ledyard's laundry filched some of his shirts. "At this place I am in a circle as gay, rich, polite and scientific, as if at Petersburg," he wrote to William Smith. "I drink my French and Spanish wines: and have Majors, Colonels, and Brigadiers, by Brigades, to wait on me in the town, and disciples of Linnaeus to accompany me in my philosophic walks. In Russia I am treated as an American with politeness & respect and on my account the healths of Dr. Franklin and General Washington have been drunk at the tables of two Governors; and at Irkutsk the name of Adams has found its Way. Among the middling Class of People, I am a kind of Phenomenon, among the peasants a right down wizard."

After ten days, Ledyard left for Yakutsk, the last major town before the coastal mountains. Governor Iakobi had shown him charts of the province and, although Ledyard's travel order terminated in Irkutsk, arranged for him to continue to go east by the postal system. Iakobi, Ledyard wrote, "told me I should [be] particularly well accomodated—wished me a good and successful voyage,—and that my travels might be productive of information to mankind." Iakobi handed Ledyard a letter of introduction to Grigorii Marklovskii, the commander of Yakutsk: "With this letter the American 'gentleman' John Ledyard comes to you traveling from St. Petersburg through this country to America for the acquisition of knowledge and information about natural history in all its departments. He is a pretty good man." Iakobi also gave Ledyard a genial travel companion, Erik Laxmann's son Adam, who was a district police officer and fluent in Russian.

The restorative sojourn in Irkutsk finished, Ledyard was again in great haste. "I am on the wings," he told Smith, adding that he wanted to reach Yakutsk and cross the mountains to the coast before winter descended; otherwise he would have to go on a sledge drawn by dogs or reindeer, he supposed. The weather did not bode well. Some nights in Irkutsk the temperature dropped below freezing, and on the second night out of Irkutsk he suffered a severe frost that numbed his feet. Leaves were falling off trees. Kibitka travel had lost none of its charm during Ledyard's break in Irkutsk, and he found his carriage was "run away with by these cursed unbroke tartar horses." More than once Ledyard and Laxmann had to jump out of the kibitka as it hurtled off the road.

After three months and four thousand miles, Ledyard reached the end of the kibitka line at Kachuga. He and Laxmann boarded a boat for the next leg down the Lena River. The Lena, one of Russia's great waterways, snakes its way more than twenty-seven hundred miles from near Lake Baikal to the Arctic Ocean. They hired a *dosihennik*, a flat-bottomed, one-masted, forty-foot boat, and headed northeast into the least known region of Russia. (It remains so today, as the Trans-Siberian Railway, built in the 1890s, goes southeast from Irkutsk and avoids the Lena River valley completely.) They passed through forests of birch, pine, poplar, fir and larch, rarely seeing signs of humans. Ledyard sent Karamyshev fossils, one containing what he thought was the leg of an elephant. They occasionally bought food from peasants along the shore. One of the crew stole their brandy and "got drunk and impertinent," wrote Ledyard. "I was obliged to handle him roughly to preserve order." Another crewman deserted. Autumnal chills swept the boat. One night Ledyard manned the helm of the batteau during a snow squall and came down with the worst cold he had ever suffered. Another night, in an occurrence replete with symbolism, Ledyard's ink froze.

On 18 September 1787, just as delegates in Philadelphia signed the U.S. Constitution, John Ledyard reached the frontier village of Yakutsk. Just three hundred miles below the Arctic Circle, Yakutsk was as far north as Ledyard had been since he slogged through Lapland at the beginning of the year. Ledyard could be proud. In less than ten months, without using a ship, he had covered one hundred and thirty degrees of longitude or 40 percent of the world. He had gone across Europe and Asia at its widest point and was just five hundred miles from the Pacific.

He stopped. The damning phrase again rang in his ears: too late in the season.

Winter had come. Ice choked the Lena. Six inches of snow lay on the ground. Ledyard and Laxmann disembarked from the *dosihennik* two miles above the town on the left bank of the Lena and took a sledge into town. Ledyard immediately delivered his letters of recommendation to Marklovskii, the Yakutsk commander. Marklovskii escorted Ledyard to a guesthouse, where they discussed in French Ledyard's plans to cross the mountains to Okhotsk. Marklovskii listened to the weather-beaten traveler and then said, as Ledyard recorded, "the first service I am bound to render you is to beseech you not to attempt to reach Okhotsk this winter." He declared it was impossible, that winter had already closed the trail to Okhotsk. This was not exactly true. Billings and two of his officers in his expedition left Okhotsk on 12 September, just six days earlier, to travel back to Yakutsk, arriving on 13 November. But they were fully versed in Siberian climate and culture and had unlimited funds to pay for food and assistance. For the lone, impoverished traveler who had only been in Siberia since the summer, it would have been as foolish as his Lapland fandango. Ledyard had less than two pounds sterling and hardly any winter clothing. The route through the Stanovoy Mountains was notoriously brutal. Ledyard, in his own inimitable style, told Marklovskii he was going anyway. "I almost rudely insisted on being permitted to depart immediately & was surprized that a Yakutee Indian & a tartar horse should be thot incapable to follow a Man educated in the Lat'd of 40."

Forty degrees latitude in Connecticut was quite different from sixty degrees in Siberia. For three days the two men argued. To seal his testimony, Marklovskii brought in as a supporting witness an old trader who regularly traveled to Okhotsk. The trader told Ledyard of the hardships he would face. "I was obliged however severely I lamented the misfortune to surrender to two such advocates for my happiness," Ledyard wrote to William Smith in October 1787. "The Trader held out to me all the horrors of the winter here & of the severity of ye journey in the best season, & ye Command't the goodness of his house & the society here all of which would be at my service." Marklovskii offered another reason besides the weather for halting Ledyard. In his letter of recommendation, Iakobi had said that Ledyard intended to join the Billings expedition. "For this reason I request you humbly to receive Mr. Ledyard with as much favor as possible, and in all his desires uniformly to render him assistance in every possible way and to deliver him to the above-mentioned Expedition without the slightest delay." Billings had passed through Yakutsk in August and was planning to return in the autumn, so Marklovskii told Ledyard he was not only preventing the American from certain death but also allowing him to meet Billings in the quickest manner.

"I will declare that I never was so totally at loss how to accommodate myself to my situation," Ledyard told Smith. With no money, no clothes, no connections and no permission, he had no choice in the end but to submit. Financially, it was dicey. He had already borrowed money from his friends' creditors across Europe, and now there was the question of how to pay for eight months of expenses without an inch of territory gained. To Smith he spoke optimistically about his enforced layover in eastern Siberia: "It is certainly bad in theory to suppose that the seasons can triumph over the efforts of an honest man. . . . The only consolation I have of the argumentative kind is to reflect that him who travels for information must be supposed to want it, & tho a little enigmantical it is I think equaly true that to be traveling is to be in error." It was a satisfaction, he said, that he could soak up the culture of a hitherto mostly unknown region. Privately in his journal, though, Ledyard sounded a more desperate note. After his first meeting with Marklovskii on 18 September, he wrote:

> What alas! shall I do for I am miserably provided for this unlooked for delay. By tarrying the winter I cannot expect to resume my march until May, which is 8 months. My funds! I have but two long frozen Stages more and I shall be beyond the want or aid of money, until emerging from her deep deserts I gain the American Atlantic States and then thy glow'ng Climates. Africa explored, I lay me down and claim a little portion of the Globe I've viewed—may it not be before. How many of the noble-minded have been subsidiary to me or to my enterprizes: and yet that meagre devil POVERTY who hand in hand has travelled with me o'r half the globe—and witnessed what Oh ye feeling Souls!—the tale I'll not unfold—'twould break the fibrils of your gen-

tle hearts. . . . This is the third time I have been overtaken and arrested by winter and in both the others by giving time for my evil genius to rally her hosts about me have defeated the Enterprize. Fortune thou has humbled me at length, for I am this moment the slave of cowardly solicitude, least in the womb of this dread winter, there lurks the seeds of disappointment to my ardent desire of gaining the opposite Continent. I submit.

Resigned to his enforced hibernation, Ledyard settled in for a long winter's nap. Borrowing money from Marklovskii on Pallas's credit, Ledyard outfitted himself with winter clothes. As only a dandy like Ledyard would, he later sent some of the clothes to his cousin Isaac accompanied by detailed praise. He bought a Sakha coat "made of the Rein deer skin & edged with the dewlap of the moose; perhaps you will wear this yourself in winter: it is made for a riding coat & I have rode both horses & deer with it." He purchased two hats, a Siberian red fox cap for six rubles and a Russian white ermine and blue fox hat for twenty-five rubles; an eight ruble pair of reindeer skin boots; and gloves made from the feet of foxes and lined with rabbit for five rubles. A Yakutsk friend gave him a second Sakha coat and reindeer socks. The coat was "made of a spotted Rein deer calf," Ledyard wrote. "The dark boarder is a dark skin & as they are rare among the Rein deer so it is there put for ornament. The edging is the same as the surtout: you will observe on the inside of the skin a number of spots: these were occasioned by a small insect bred there from the eggs of a species of fly & which together with the vast numbers of musquestoes obliges this charming animal to migrate annualy N & S as the seasons require."

"These cloaths were not all that I wore last winter in Siberia," Ledyard wrote Isaac. "I wore many more & froze my nose & ears after all. You have no Idea of the excessive cold in those regions." Yakutsk was in the middle of a region that outside of the Antarctic was the coldest on earth. He had a mercury thermometer that froze solid on 19 November (mercury freezes at minus 40 degrees Fahrenheit). It snowed regularly, though rarely at night. The stars came out at half past two in the afternoon. The sky was a dismal gray during the few hours of sunlight and reminded Ledyard of sailing with Cook in northern Alaska. "The upper region is a dark still expanded vapour with few openings in it," he wrote in his diary. "In the lower Atmosphere there is a constant succession of snow-blown Clouds floating over head resembling Fogg-Banks." Due to the cold, there were no wells in Yakutsk. Locals stacked cakes of ice in their yards like cords of wood, bringing them inside one by one to melt. Sakha herders brought their milk to market in frozen chunks. Locals used glass or cow skins as windows, but a two-inch film of ice soon covered either. The most common sound was the melting and freezing of ice: "The Houses & Rivers keep a continual Cracking & all Nature groans beneath its Rigour."

Yakutsk, "town of the horse people," was officially a hundred and fifty years old. According to Martin Sauer, it had three hundred and sixty-two buildings, five churches, a cathedral and a monastery. The streets were irregular and unpaved. The winter pace was languid. Most people stayed indoors huddled by a peat-burning stove. The only spurt of heart-pounding effort was when people rushed out of their weekly hot baths; completely naked, they plunged themselves into the Lena or wallowed in the snow. "Their Dance is accompanied or rather performed by the same odd twisting and wreathing of the hips as at Otaheite." The excitement of the season came in November when a church caught fire and burned.

While waiting for spring in Yakutsk, Ledyard assimilated what he had seen throughout his trip and wrote in his journal. Apparently he had the intention of publishing a book on his travels that verged on becoming a guide book: at one point he wrote that Yakutsk "is the last place where you will be able to make any enquiries, therefore let them be extensive." Laxmann and Ledyard wrote up a Lena River itinerary of towns and distances, noting the places where they procured supplies. Ledyard tossed off tidbits of information on dozens of topics in his journal. Sometimes he wrote so briefly that it seemed he was either disinterested in the subject but felt obligated to include it, or that these were rough notes that later would be amplified. He skipped from topic to topic; deliberately left pages blank for future additions; threw out fragmented thoughts, questions, a smattering of facts and figures, and digressions of all sorts; and eventually admitted that he was not "certain whether I ever wrote a Line regularly."

The majority of his notes concerned the people of Siberia. He wrote about geology, archeology and politics, but he was innately drawn to "my Brethern & my Sisters in this world." He spent many afternoons visiting the homes of local people. He examined the journal of a Russian officer who had lived with the Sakha for two years. The Sakha, a race also descended from the Mongols, had stubbornly resisted Russian rule and were able to practice a good deal of local autonomy. They maintained a shamanistic religion (the word shaman was from the Tungus, native Siberians who lived north of the Sakha) and had highly developed oral epics. In the winter they lived in log cabins, with windows made of mica and doors of leather. Ledyard investigated their wedding ceremonies and hunting techniques. He saw the Sakha, and thought they resembled the Cherokees, fished on the Lena at night with torches, much like the Tahitians did in the Pacific. He found that the Sakha took their children to study the night sky in order to learn navigation and weather prediction. In researching native Siberian languages, he learned that his earlier effort to learn native Alaskan languages at Unalaska in 1778 had been a farce. He remembered that he had been "walking one day on Shore with a Native who spoke the Russ language. I did not know it. I was writing the names of several things. I pointed to the Ship supposing he would understand that I wanted the name of it; he answered me with the Words Ya Snaiu, which in Russ is I know. I wrote a Ship. I gave him some snuff, which he took & held out his hands to me for more, making use of the Word Malinko, which signifies in Russ little. I wrote more." Now, a decade later, he understood that one of the pitfalls of anthropology was misinterpretation.

During his stay in Yakutsk, Ledyard developed quite unusual views about the human race. He argued that the nations that "commix and intermarry most with other nations are the handsomest." After discussing the different skin colors in Siberia, he quietly predicted Darwin and the theory of evolution: "The difference of Colour in Man is not the effect of any design in the Creator; but of causes simple in themselves, and will perhaps soon be well ascertained—It is an extraordinary circumstance but I think I ought not on that account to conclude that it is not a Work of Nature. . . . The Result is that I think this difference is the mere effect of natural Causes, & of the most [powerful] of these, that of Generation."

Ledyard found himself favoring the Tatars over the Russians. The Russians in Siberia were extremely jealous, lacking in virtue, messy and "the most consummate Scoundrels in the Universe," he wrote, echoing Chappe d'Auteroche's comments from a quarter century before. Siberia was "a

Nursery of the most infamous Characters in her Dominions," and he found "the rankest vices to abound [here] as much as in their Capital." Russian officers were "worse than the vilest miscreants in the armies of Cortez or Pizaro." The native Siberians, on the other hand, pleased him. They kept their houses neat and had a pleasant disposition. "I observe that there is one continued flow of Good nature & Chearfulness among the Tartars—They never call names & abuse each other by words." They were "a people whose wants and occupations are but few, whose minds necessity has not tortured almost to disstraction for the means of preservation on account of difficulties which the Luxury of Civilization hath created even for its ordinary members, he who with a happy indifference can endure a State of privation, whose apprehensionss are not racked with the Legends of future purgations, and whose heaven is peace and leisure." He went on:

> The Tartar however situated is a voluptuary: and it is an Original and striking trait in their Character from the Grand Signor to him who pitches his tent on the wild frontiers of Russia & China, that they deviate less from the pursuit & enjoyment of real sensual pleasure, than any other people. . . . Would a Tartar live in Vive le Roi? Would he spend ten years in constructing a Watch? Or twenty in forming a Telescope? . . . [The Tatar] is a lover of Peace—no Helen, & no System of Religion has ever yet disturbed it. He is contented to be what he is. Never did a Tartar I believe speak ill of the Deity, or even his Fellow Creatures. He is hospitable & human—He is constantly tranquil & cheeful— He is Laconic in Thoughts, Word & action—They do not prostitute even a Smile or a Frown any more than a European Monarch. This is one reason (& I think the greatest) why they have been constantly persecuted by nations of another Disposition & why they have always fled from before them & been content to live any where if they could only live in Peace.

In only one way were the Siberian and the Russian on the same plateau as everyone else in the world. In Yakutsk Ledyard penned his famous paean to women, words that would later appear in articles, books, broadsides and almanacs and put into poetry:

> I observe too that the Woman wherever found is the same kind, civil, obliging, humane, tender being; that she is ever inclined to be gay & cheerful;

timorous & modest; that she does not hesitate like Man to do a generous action of any kind. . . . The Woman is never haughty, arrogant or supercilious; full of courtesy & fond of Society; ecconomical, ingenious; more liable, in general, to err than man, & in general have more virtue & perform more good actions than him. . . . That I never addressed myself in the Language of Decency & Friendship to a Woman whether civilized or savage without receiving a decent & friendly answer—even in english Billingsgate. With Man it has often been otherwise. In wandering over the barren plains of inhospitable Denmark; thro' honest Sweden & frozen Lapland; rude & churlish Finland, unprincipled Russia & with the Wandering Tartar, If hungry, dry, cold, wet or sick, Woman has ever been so friendly to me and uniformly so. And to add to this Virtue so worthy the appellation of Benevolence; those actions have been performed with so free & kind a manner, that if I was dry I drank the sweetest draught & if hungry eate the coarse Morsel with double relish.

Spending eight months in a tiny frontier town was not easy for the free-spirited Ledyard. "Without any violence to the metaphor, or pedantic affection," he wrote to William Smith in October 1787, "I declare to you that to leave Yakutsk with respectability & to reach Okhotsk alive will be to pass a Scilly & Charibdis that I have never yet encountered." In November, with the sun barely rising over the horizon, he slipped into hibernation. He stopped writing in his journal, except for a daily temperature entry. He grew bored with the citizenry of Yakutsk. "My mind is equally an epicure," he told Professor Pallas, "& when I am among those who ought to be good, nothing will satisfy it but the feast of reason & the flow of soul, but it has still more reason to complain than my heart. . . . I might as well look for figgs & grapes here as information." Occasionally, he lashed out at those around him. Martin Sauer, who lived with Ledyard for three months and liked him, admitted that "Ledyard's behavior, however, had been haughty. . . which certainly made him enemies." Ledyard scrapped with his housemate Laxmann, twice feeding bread to Laxmann's dogs, which annoyed the Finn. "The Lesson I gave him on the occasion has almost cured him," Ledyard wrote arrogantly in his diary. "but I have told him to beware how he disturbs my peace a third time by his rascally passion & he has done it. I remarked that this observation may appear trivial to an European. I observe also that I am not fond of trivial Observations." His relationship with Marklovskii never recovered from their initial battle of wills over going to Okhotsk. One afternoon Ledyard took Marklovskii's dog for a walk. "He expostulated with me so seriously about it that I could not believe him in earnest," Ledyard recorded in his diary. "I told him so & I told him that whatever declaration he might make to the contrary I woud not believe it." Gavriil Sarychev, a naval officer in the Billings expedition, found Ledyard eccentric and his plan of walking around the world without money, maps and winter clothes quite absurd, but reserved his harshest words for Ledyard's attitude toward Marklovskii. The commandant had fed and clothed Ledyard. "The only return which Mr. Ledyard made for this extraordinary hospitality, was to calumniate and abuse every one; and finally challenge his benefactor for remonstrating with him on the impropriety of his behavior. Finally, after a reminder of decency to him, he dared to challenge the commandant to a duel." The prospect of bloodshed enabled both parties to reach a settlement, but Ledyard's use of the old feudal system of defending one's honor by dueling revealed a stunning pugnacity.

As the darkness of the season descended, the tension eased. First Christian Bering, the nephew of Vitus and a lieutenant in the Billings expedition, arrived in town. Then in mid-November Captain Joseph Billings himself appeared. Even though Ledyard and Billings each had heard of the other's presence in Siberia, it was still an extra-special moment. Here in an ice-clad village in deepest Siberia, two men who had sailed around the world together grasped hands. They had not seen each other in more than seven years. Billings kindly allowed Ledyard to board with him and his pregnant mistress. In a twelve-page letter to Pallas in December, Ledyard called it "peculiarly satisfactory. . . . I think myself the happiest of the two: tho I dare say Cap' Billings thinks himself so. We absolutely contend about it, being perpetually engaged in a reciprocity of services from morning to night."

Billings, a Londoner, had sailed as an able seaman on the *Discovery*. He switched over to the *Resolution* in September 1779, so it was likely that he and Ledyard were well acquainted. A bit of a scurrilous character, Billings had spent time in 1783 in the King's Bench debtor's prison before Sir Joseph Banks bailed him out. His expedition, personally chartered by Catherine II to explore the Pacific coast of Russia, had yet to accomplish much. There were delays in transporting supplies and building ships, and he had lost several hundred horses while moving stores. His French naturalist, Patrin, had taken ill and returned home. In his one stab at discovery, Billings had inconclusively explored the East Siberian Sea, running into ice not far from their launch at the mouth of the Kolyma River. Some of his staff wanted to travel onward, and Billings, unsure of his command, forced his officers to sign a written statement declaring it was more prudent to turn back. Many of his men had scurvy. The surgeon, Michael Robek, suffered severe frostbite in his hands and feet. Ledyard, in his letter to Pallas, reiterated his doubts about Billings that he had voiced in St. Petersburg. "He is as rough in his address as a Russian bear. . . [and does] not know the theory of good breeding tolerably well. He tells me that he is determined not to go to Heaven in such an awkward plight." But, overall, Ledyard thought Billings was judiciously running the expedition and, most importantly, was treating the native Siberians humanely.

Ledyard threw his lot with Billings. After Christmas, Billings returned to Irkutsk to examine a deposit of guns, clothing and medicine waiting for the expedition. Ledyard decided to join him, which meant heading fifteen hundred miles in the wrong direction in midwinter. He despaired of reaching North America otherwise. There appeared to be very little movement from Siberia directly to Nootka Sound. It might take him years to hopscotch across the fifteen-hundred-mile-long Aleutians via the promyshlenniki just to reach the inhospitable Alaskan coast. Billings, on the other hand, agreed to carry Ledyard directly to Nootka. The only catch was a further delay. Billings planned to spend 1788 getting his supplies to the Asian coast and building his expedition's ships, and 1789 exploring the Korean peninsula. He would not be going to Nootka until 1790.

With two years to kill, Ledyard offered Billings his services in exploring the Kolyma River valley. "We have talked about it, but nothing is decided," Ledyard told Pallas. The security offered by associating with a well-funded expedition pleased Ledyard, but the delay of another two years upset him, as he told Pallas: "The Idea [of waiting] does not fully satisfy me: if one could live a hundred years in the full possession of all the powers—a le bonheure—5 or 6 years spent in traveling on this [continent of

Asia] previous to my visiting the other Continent would not be so much thought of—but the melancholy reverse of 60 or 70, with 36 substracted from! And then besides there is another Continent still less known than America that demands a visit from me—the Gods have a right, for ought I know, to shorten my life: but not to curtail my fame." It was a curious decision for an explorer bent on crossing America, but in Yakutsk in the bleak midwinter, the assurance of support and an eventual lift to Nootka was a more rational option for a weary lone traveler than hopscotching across the Aleutians.

On 29 December 1787, Billings, Martin Sauer, Ledyard, Robeck and two other officers boarded dog-pulled sledges and raced up the frozen Lena in the dark. In three weeks they were back in Irkutsk. Ledyard and Billings boarded together. Billings still kept quiet about the expedition, adhering to Catherine II's wish for secrecy, as Ledyard told Pallas: "A sense of delicacy on my part & a tenacious adherance on his part to what I suppose to be his duty to the expedition forbids me the freedom to ask any particular question & him to speak of it in any other Manner than as he pleases voluntarily to do." Loneliness struck Ledyard hard in Irkutsk and he sought comfort. To give examples of the Sakha language, he wrote down a couple of sentences in his diary: "To a girl to go with me—will you go and live with me at Kamschatka. I want a woman to go and live with me at Kamschatka." As he planned to spend the following winter in Petropavlovsk, it was not surprising that he was practicing his lines to secure a female companion. "The genius of my enterprize sleeps for the moment," he wrote Pallas in January 1788. "Peace be unto it sleeping or waking: it is an innocent spirit. It is also an amorous one when at ease, & during this recess from the hot pursuits of fame do not be surprised if among other of its lububrations you find it sporting in the world of love—not algebraically, mathematicaly, nor altogether seriously, but some how platonicaly, by accident, from necessity." He had, apparently, already let go of the memory of his St. Petersburg blue-eyed love.

With three months to go before returning to Yakutsk, Billings and Ledyard planned to tour Lake Baikal. In the meantime, Ledyard felt uncomfortable. Six months later he looked back fondly on his midwinter sojourn in Irkutsk. "I was happy," he told a Scottish friend. "Every difficulty was done away: in the language of my dear Sauvages I had a cleary sky & smooth waters." But at the time he was less confident. On 25 January 1788, he wrote to Sir Joseph Banks: "I am among a bad People: I cannot tell you how bad they are. . . . I can form no connections: except the Society of my old Shipmate Capt. Billings, who is very friendly to me. I am as much alone as I should be on one of the Andes."

13

Common Flag of Humanity— Banished

ON 18 DECEMBER 1787, the personal secretary for Empress Catherine II, A. V. Khrapovitskii, sat at his desk in St. Petersburg and wrote of the day's events. In one sentence Khrapovitskii revealed that the machinery to change John Ledyard's life had been irrevocably set into motion: "It is ordered to send back the American John Ledyard, making his way from Ohotsk to America, from that place; he was a naval cadet with the famous Cook." Three days later Catherine II formally issued the order for Ledyard's arrest and banishment from the Russian Empire. She directed Ivan Iakobi, the Russian governor in Irkutsk, "to send him off under proper supervision, without causing him trouble," to Moscow, then Smolensk, Polotsk and the border with Poland, where he was to be left "with the warning that he not dare henceforth to appear anywhere within our Empire."

In July 1787 when the empress got back to St. Petersburg after her tour of the Crimea, she probably heard about Ledyard from a number of people, including her friend Pallas. Knowing that Ledyard had disobeyed her express orders must have upset her. Not only was Ledyard, to whom she had denied a passport, in her country, but he was traveling with a bona fide passport issued by her recalcitrant son. Ledyard told his cousin Isaac he was arrested because of "a mixture of jealously, envy & malice" and safely back in London he told a friend that "the great Catherine is but a little queen. She banished me from private pique: personal malice." No doubt Catherine II must have been annoyed with the American traveler.

But it was more than just a personal feud. Catherine II feared Ledyard might meddle in the Russian fur trade. His stated goal was to explore North America, the western littoral of which was producing tens of thousands of rubles a year in income for her treasury. Furthermore, for years Ledyard had publicly sought to set up a fur-trade factory in the Pacific Northwest, which would be in direct competition with the Russian promyshlenniki and their fur stations in Alaska. "You were wrong, if you don't mind, to strike off my accounts the very small expenditure for the American, Ledyard," the empress wrote on 26 November 1787, to her correspondent in Paris, Baron Grimm. "Regarding Ledyard, Discovery for others is not always Discovery for us." International interference in the North Pacific was a very real fear. Cook's voyage had disturbed the empress—hence Khrapovitskii's mention that Ledyard had sailed with Cook—as had the news of a French version of Cook, the La Perouse expedition. Besides sending the Billings expedition to chart the North Pacific, Catherine II also planned to dispatch four ships from the Baltic to protect her new Alaskan colonies; only war with Sweden prevented those ships from sailing. One eyewitness, Martin Sauer, wrote that the imperial guards had accused Ledyard of being a French spy. Perhaps Catherine II believed he was on the way to a rendezvous with the French at Kamchatka, where La Perouse landed in September 1787.

Catherine II's gravamen was Ledyard's actions in Irkutsk during ten fateful days in August 1787. On 18 August Ledyard had innocently written in his diary: "Went this morning to see a Merchant owner of a Vessel that had passed from Kamschatka to different parts of the Coast of America." On Unalaska in 1778 Ledyard became the first American to meet the Russian promyshlenniki, and now, nine years later, he was the first to know the greatest of them, Grigorii Shelikhov. In 1784 Shelikhov, a Ukrainian-born trader, had set up the first permanent Russian colony in Alaska on Kodiak Island, and was the motivating force behind the Rossisko-Amerikanskaia Kompaniia, the imperial behemoth founded in 1799 and modeled on the East India Company. The RAK maintained fur-trading bases across Alaska, as far south as eighty miles above San Francisco and even on Kauai in Hawaii. In 1787 Shelikhov was temporarily living in Irkutsk after a four-year tenure in Alaska and had just presented Governor Iakobi a detailed business plan for the RAK. According to Ledyard, their meeting went well. They compared charts of the North Pacific. Shelikhov told him some facts about the Russian fur trade, and Ledyard concluded by writing that Shelikhov "offers me a passage" in a ship leaving Okhotsk for the Aleutians the following summer.

Shelikhov, however, saw the meeting in an entirely different light. Afterwards he gave Iakobi a long memorandum entitled "Notes on Conversations with John Ledyard" that acidly condemned the American traveler. He said Ledyard pestered him "with ardent curiosity" about the Russian fur trade's history and present status. He said Ledyard had told him that ten thousand Europeans had been living north of California for many years. "He uttered these words as a threat," wrote Shelikhov. Ledyard also had apparently claimed that on the Cook voyage they had traded for sea-otter pelts with native Alaskans living at 73 degrees latitude and had made them subjects of King George III. "This is where he revealed himself as incorrect," Shelikhov wrote, saying that those people never hunted sea otters and had for a long time been "subjects of the Russian Scepter." Shelikhov believed that Ledyard probably had not been on Cook's voyage, for his descriptions of Kamchatka and the Aleutians seemed second-hand. "And he evaded many such questions of mine by similar obscure and confusing replies." When they talked about Ledyard's plans of walking across America from Nootka Sound, Shelikhov told him that the natives there "were bellicose and always engaged in merciless warfare with one another." Ledyard instantly changed his itinerary and told Shelikhov he intended then to travel from California.

As with Shelikhov, Ledyard naively believed that his interactions with the governor of eastern Siberia, Ivan Iakobi, had gone swimmingly. "Our conversation was merely respecting my going with the Post," Ledyard wrote. Iakobi "wished me a good and successful voyage, and that my travels might be productive of information to mankind." Actually Ledyard had sunk himself. On 7 November 1787, Iakobi sent a substantial letter to Aleksandr Bezborodko, the acting foreign minister in St. Petersburg. Mirroring Shelikhov's notes, Iakobi's report harshly condemned Ledyard: Iakobi had told Ledyard that the Pacific Northwest Indians "could by reason of their savage nature make difficulties for him" and that Ledyard had quickly said he would then proceed from California; that Ledyard had "expressed avid curiosity" and asked "ingenious questions" about the Russian fur trade; that Ledyard claimed ten thousand Europeans lived in Alaska; and that they had argued about under whose flag the natives of northern Alaska owed allegiance. Iakobi even doubted whether Ledyard was an American and felt that he had clear proof that he was an Englishman because of Ledyard's "inconsistent behavior and statements." Perhaps, Iakobi hypothesized, "he was sent here to reconnoiter this area for the English."

Not waiting for advice from St. Petersburg, Iakobi had decided to keep his eye on Ledyard. "So as not to betray my suspicion of him by an untimely refusal," Iakobi let Ledyard continue on to Yakutsk. But to stall him, Iakobi sent a secret order to Marklovskii, the commander of Yakutsk, to convince Ledyard to spend the winter there and "while giving him a friendly welcome, not let the least of his shifty undertakings escape his observation." The only hint of this second, secret letter—a hint which Ledyard blithely ignored—was a kibitka delay. Ledyard expected to leave Irkutsk on a Monday but Iakobi told him the post would not be ready to leave until Wednesday. In the intervening forty-eight hours, Iakobi sent his secret orders to Marklovskii. With his report, Iakobi enclosed letters of Ledyard's addressed to Peter Simon Pallas and to England, as well as "a secret and special letter" from Karamyshev, the Irkutsk banker. In conclusion, Iakobi said that "sending him back to St. Petersburg will pose no difficulty" and recommended that Her Imperial Majesty be informed about this matter.

Whatever the misapprehensions arising from a sputtering mix of languages and translators, Shelikhov and Iakobi clearly came away from their conversations with Ledyard thinking he was a loose cannon apt to blow up their fur-trading system. The fact that Ledyard had discussed the fur trade in such a relentlessly candid and combative style with men who clearly had a stake in it suggested that he did not have tact. Fur had been the idée fixe of his post-Cook life. He had spent years singing about pelts, cargo, ships and profits, so it was natural to join in concert with men who were experts. He should have known better, however, since they could not have possibly thought Ledyard as innocent as he really was. It was one thing to be pumped full of grand visions, but it was quite another thing to never relinquish them.

Moreover, he did not just talk but he argued. "Singular," the term his friends repeatedly used for Ledyard, might have been a polite codeword for what today we would diagnose as bi-polar disorder or manic-depression. Ledyard exhibited classic symptoms of the mental illness: his days spent in bed, his mood swings, his shopping sprees, his rash exits, wildly bizarre entrances, his intense garrulousness and his physical feats. As if he knew he was not well, he kept walking away from his family, friends and women he loved before he blew up at them and ruined it all. In a way, Ledyard's restlessness can be seen not as something innate in his personality, but as a reaction to his roller-coaster emotional make-up.

When he did not or could not run away, he revealed a volcanic temper. By his own admission, he burst into rage at a startlingly large number of people. He argued with his grandfather, his Ledyard cousins in Bristol, Mai in Tonga and Laxmann in Yakutsk. He thrashed theatre-goers in London and his boatman on the Lena. He challenged Marklovskii to a duel. Some of this anger was innate, but some of it was learned watching Captain Cook. For nearly three years he saw close at hand how a leader dealt with tension, or a blocked path, by bursting into a deck-clearing fury. Cook's rages led to acute measures—cutting off ears, flogging backs, kidnapping, clamping into irons, burning down villages—and Ledyard had those extremes as a model for handling obstacles. His intemperate self-destructive personality now crushed his greatest dream.

They came, as they always do, in the night. On 31 January 1788, Ivan Iakobi received the arrest order from Catherine II. The following evening Russian policemen led by the commander of the Irkutsk police burst into Ledyard's rooms and arrested him.

News of the arrest quickly spread through town. A legal secretary came to the home of a military officer, where Martin Sauer was playing cards, and said there was rumor of an order had to arrest an Englishman in the Billings expedition. Sauer laughed, as he was the only Englishman in Irkutsk besides Billings himself. Then two guards came and asked Sauer to come to the police station. "Here I found Mr. Ledyard under arrest," wrote

Sauer. Ledyard told Sauer he had sent for Billings, but Billings would not come. Sauer left the station and went to Billings's house. He returned a short while later with the deadly reply: Billings would do nothing. He lived in fear of Catherine II—hence the signed statement he had forced his officers to sign the previous summer—and told Sauer, as he later recalled, "that it was an absolute order from the Empress and he could not help him." As a token of his friendship, Billings gave Sauer a few rubles and a fur-lined pelisse to take to Ledyard. Sauer brought these to Ledyard and then fetched the prisoner's clothing, most of which was newly washed and still dripping wet. "Ledyard took a friendly leave of me," wrote Sauer, "desired his remembrance to his friends, and with astonishing compsure leaped into the kibitka and drove off with two guards, one on each side." In thirty minutes, Ledyard later told Sir Joseph Banks, he had gone from a traveler occupied in the common mundane task of washing one's clothes in a tub to a prisoner of the empress of Russia sitting in a kibitka rumbling west. He managed to gather some of his possessions, but had to abandon many of his personal papers.

After fourteen months of grinding exertion heading east, Ledyard now involuntarily sped west. Two guards and a commanding officer sat in the half-open kibitka with him, talking in Russian. They traveled almost nonstop, halting only to change horses and have an occasional meal. During the day the swirling wind and deep chill hounded him. At night he slept in the kibitka or, if he was lucky, on the floor of the rest houses. Only twice from 13 February until 19 March did he manage to take off his clothes and sleep in a bed. In Nizhni Novgorod just east of Moscow, Ledyard wrote of staying "in a vile, dark, dirty, gloomy, damp Room; it is called quarters: but is a miserable Prison. The Soldiers who guard me are doubly watchful over me when in a Town, tho' at no time properly. So thro' their consummate Indolence & Ignorance, for every day I have it in my power to escape them, but tho' treated like a felon, I will not appear one by flight."

Ledyard had to pay for his own food, though he barely ate in the twenty days from Irkutsk to Nizhni Novgorod and called himself "emaciated." He had no idea where he was going or why he was imprisoned. The lack of habeas corpus frustrated Ledyard. "Was I guilty of any the least thing against the Country or any thing in it, or was there even a Crime alledged against me, I could suffer with some patience or at least resignation." Instead, he was faced with being "seized, imprisoned and transported in this dark and silent manner with no cause or accusation but what appears in the mysterious wisdom which is pictured in the face of my Serjeant." In the summer it had taken Ledyard ten weeks to travel from Moscow to Irkutsk; now in winter, with the power of the empress behind them, the guards spirited Ledyard that distance in thirty-three days.

Half benumbed by the horror of his situation, Ledyard managed to scribble a few notes on Siberian culture, but he mostly bemoaned his fate. "Take Physic pomp," he wrote, recalling King Lear's advice. "Cure yourselves, you great men." Ledyard's free spirit chafed in detention. "Loose your Liberty but once for one hour, ye who never lost it, that ye may feel what I feel," he wrote. "Altho' born in the freest Country of the World, Ideas of its exquisite Beauties & of its immortal Nature that I had never before. Methinks every Man who is called to preside officially over the Liberty of a free People should once—it will be enough—actually be deprived unjustly of his Liberty that he might be avaricious of it more than of any earthly possessions."

While in Yakutsk, Ledyard had praised Catherine II's rule in Siberia, speaking of her humanity and generosity. Now he slammed her: "My anxious hopes are once more blasted, the almost half accomplished wish! What secret machinations have there been? What motive could direct this? But so it suits her royal Majesty of all the Russians and she has nothing but her pleasures to consult. She has no nation's Resentment to apprehend, for no State's, no Monarch's Minister am I, but travel under the common flag of humanity. Commissioned by myself to serve the World at large, and so the poor, the unprotected wanderer must go where sovereign will ordains." He never recorded any thoughts of betrayal by Iakobi and Shelikhov and just once referred to Karamyshev after the arrest as "The Scoundrel." Ledyard's focus on the empress was so great that he felt Catherine II was attacking the United States in arresting one of its citizens. "I consider Resignation as Cowardice," he wrote. "Nor will I set the base Example, debase my honour, or sin against the Genius of my noble Country. They may do wrong & treat me like a Subject of this Country, but by the Spirits of my great Ancestors, & the ignoble Insult I have already felt, they shall not make me one in Reality." Despite his professions of love for the United States, Ledyard had been born a British subject and had enjoyed just eighteen months in America as a U.S. citizen. Ledyard might have an American accent, but he was the prototype for a new breed of explorer, someone who wanted to discover new lands not for the greedy hands of a particular country's merchants but for the sake of discovery. The world was his tribe and he sailed under humanity's ensign.

In Moscow the guards brought Ledyard before a general named Eropkin for a brief interrogation. Eropkin never told Ledyard the crime for which he had been arrested, and within hours he was leaving Moscow, with a driving snowstorm blowing his kibitka like a kite. Catherine II had ordered the guards to escort Ledyard to Petr Passek, the governor-general of the Russian border region, in what is today Belarus. When they reached Polosk one windy night, they learned Passek was nearly two hundred miles south in Moghilev. Ledyard, "weak & ill with fatigue," was asleep in the kibitka when they came to Polosk and only woke up when they stopped at the first post station on the road to Moghilev. Ledyard panicked, as he recalled: "I was frantic. My want of Information left me ignorant of any other Subject to vent my rage against except the one called Fate, which I could never comprehend & could therefore never gain any kind of satisfaction of. But from habit & the custom of Europe I cursed it wherever it was. I was never before sensible of a weakness of body. I fell down in my rage on the floor & slept until daylight."

Two days later, Ledyard pulled up at Passek's residence. He was told to wait in the kibitka. After a half hour he was taken into the house and, after cooling his heels another half hour in an anteroom, was led into Passek's bedroom. Passek, in the guise of a monarch, was lounging in bed, chatting with a Catholic priest sitting on a sofa. He was in his sixties and wore a curled wig. Speaking French, he offered Ledyard tea and told him that his orders were to escort Ledyard out of the empire, and that Ledyard was forbidden to enter it again. He added that it had been impudent of Ledyard to try to pass through Russia without permission. With indignation, Ledyard demanded that Passek inform him of his crime. Passek ignored Ledyard's request and proceeded to wax eloquently about Catherine II's good works, adding, according to Ledyard, "that whatever Reasons her Majesty had for her proceedings, she had only politely told me that my

Visit to her Dominions was disagreable & desired me to discontinue it." Passek added that he had never been a prisoner and began to say that that Catherine II had long arms. "Yes by God General yours are very long Eastward," Ledyard replied. "If your Sovereign should stretch the other Westward she would never bring it back again entire, & I myself would contend to lop it off." With that, he stormed out of the house.

"O Liberty! O Liberty! How sweet are thy embrace," Ledyard wrote in his diary on the evening of 18 March 1788, when he reached the border with Poland. He was taken across a river and deposited at the house of a Jewish family. When his portmanteau was brought into the house, he discovered a final insult: his coachman had snatched five rubles from his baggage. Ledyard spent four nights in the border town. The Russian officers at the border post gave him wine, lemons and bread and invited him to smoke a pipe. The commandant "choaked me with congratulations on my Deliberation from Confinement; bowed, smiles, complimented. Lyed, swore & protested with all the ease & grace of his Predecessor Sinon." The most delicious moment was when Ledyard took off his lice-ridden clothing and stepped into his first bath in five weeks. A steam bath in Unalaska had been one of Ledyard's first interactions with Russians ten years earlier, and now it was one of his last. "Very dirty, & fond of the Russian hot Bath," he wrote in his diary that day. "It was a great Luxury to me. I was reanimated after half an hour spent in it."

For forty rubles Ledyard hired a Russian trader to carry him to Konigsburg (Kaliningrad) on the Baltic Sea; not trusting him, Ledyard made him sign a contract and took his passport. A young man whom Passek had sent to act as an interpreter also arrived. Traveling through Poland, despite the accoutrement of a paid driver and interpreter, was not easy. Some nights Ledyard slept in the kibitka because the stage houses were so badly appointed or filled with people suffering from smallpox. Rain had washed away some of the roads and at times he gained just a mile each hour.

On 28 March 1788, Ledyard came to Vilna, the capital of Lithuania. "The first Salutation was by two dirty, wretched-looking Soldiers from a decayed, smoaky log-buit Guard house, who wanted to know if I had any Merchandize in my Kabitka. Being answered not, they then wanted to know if I had any money to spare." After shedding the roadblock guards, Ledyard went into Vilna and stayed a few days. He walked around the hills on its outskirts and was very pleased to find a town inspector out examining the public works.

Freedom, springtime and hot baths invigorated Ledyard and his libido returned. He complained that Polish women's figures were undetectable under their thick dresses and that he was unable to view "a Work of Nature as expressly formed to attract Attention, Admiration, Esteem & Love." In Vilna he met a Jewish woman from Danzig, one of "the beautiful daughters of Israel," and decided to travel with her into Prussia. He dismissed his driver and translator, the former of whom predicted that the kibitka horses would fall ill from coming into contact with his Jewish girlfriend. "One of the many Instances of Russian Superstition," noted Ledyard, adding that the driver also pinched two rubles from Ledyard's luggage. "The last View I had or ever wish to have of a Russian was of a Thief."

Upon crossing into western Europe, Ledyard wrote that he felt the same rapture he did when seeing his mother in Southold in 1782 after their eight-year separation. In late April he and his Danzig girlfriend arrived in the coastal town of Konigsburg. He found a merchant who would take the good name of Sir Joseph Banks credit and obtained five guineas. He wrote a letter to Banks, telling him of the loan and of his "miserable journey, in a miserable country, in a miserable season, in miserable health, and a miserable purse." In a few weeks he arranged passage to England and, leaving his girlfriend, departed for England. By the end of May he was back in London where, eighteen months and fifteen thousand miles earlier, he had started.

On Monday, 9 June 1788, nine men gathered at St. Alban's Tavern off Pall Mall. They were members of the Saturday's Club, a London dining society that met intermittently, often, as was the case this afternoon, on a Monday. During the meal the conversation turned to Africa. Someone said that with the completion of the Cook voyages nothing worthy of research—the poles excepted—needed to be accomplished by sea. By land, it was another story. Men were exploring west of Canada, and Asia had seen its share of wanderers, but the map of African interior was still largely blank. Henry Beaufoy, one of the men present, wrote a few months later, that "ignorance must be considered as a degree of reproach upon the present age. Sensible of this stigma and desirous of rescuing the Age from a charge of ignorance, which, in other respects, belongs so little to its character," the men decided to take action. In the clatter of dishes and calls for more claret, they formed the Association for Promoting the Discovery of the Interior Parts of Africa.

The men of the society, known more concisely as the African Association, were culled from the thin tip of London's intellectual pack. Seven of the twelve members of the Saturday's Club were fellows of the Royal Society and had written essays variously on rhubarb, fisheries and brewing furnaces. All but two of the twelve were politically active as members of parliament. Six were Scots, two were Irish, all were prosperous and prominent. Besides Sir Joseph Banks, the other animating force in the association was Henry Beaufoy. He was the son of a London wine merchant, a Quaker, a committed abolitionist and a Whig in the House of Commons.

On the following Friday four of the men—Banks, Beaufoy, Lord Rawdon, a young army officer destined to become governor-general of India, and Andrew Stuart, a lawyer who served on the Board of Trade—met at Banks's home in Soho Square as an executive committee to run the African Association. They set annual dues at five guineas. Banks became the first treasurer and Beaufoy the secretary. They passed a motion authorizing Banks to approach the Home Office to solicit the services of Simon Lucas, then an interpreter for Asian languages at the Court of St. James, in exploring North Africa.

More explorers were needed to make the Association viable. With unusual good timing, John Ledyard appeared. As soon as he reached London, he headed to Soho Square to consult with Banks. The discussion between the vagabond traveler and the knighted naturalist must have been topsy-turvy: the harsh disappointment and wasted money of the Siberian venture supplanted by the startling possibilities of the African Association. Ledyard had always thought of exploring Africa, and, after all the bad luck trying to reach Nootka Sound, a change of focus seemed appropriate. The real determinant for Ledyard was money. Here was a ready and robust supply of cash for Africa, whereas he probably felt unable to ask Banks—or anyone else—for more support to continue his around-the-world scheme.

Carrying a letter from Banks, Ledyard went to Beaufoy's home. "Before I learnt from the note the name and business of my Visitor," wrote Beaufoy in 1790, "I was struck with the manliness of his person, the breadth of his chest, the openness of his countenance, and the inquietude of his eye." After introductions they went into Beaufoy's parlor to look at maps of Africa. Ledyard told him of his plan to traverse the continent. Showing him the route he thought best, Beaufoy traced a line from Cairo south and west to the supposed course of the Niger River. Ledyard thought he was singularly suited for the adventure. Beaufoy asked when he could leave and Ledyard famously replied, "Tomorrow morning."

Beaufoy calmly said that it would take a few weeks to prepare for the expedition and lent him thirty guineas. On Tuesday the seventeenth, the committee for the African Association met again at Banks's house. Ledyard's proposal, with his voyage with Cook and his Siberian journey taken as "unquestionable proofs, in the opinion of the Committee, of his ardour in the pursuit of Geographical knowledge," was accepted by the committee.

The next fortnight was a blur of activity. "I have not time to do any thing," Ledyard wrote in a letter to his cousin Isaac. "I want to talk a month with you without interruption," he wrote to a Scottish friend, but said he could only speak for a minute. Visitors streamed to his lodgings at the Green Man & Still, a busy inn on Oxford Street. He rushed from dinner to dinner as honored guest, especially at a grand meal with the entire African Association membership. Ledyard had striven for years to become famous and now his Siberian adventure and pending African trip had made his name. Despite the failure of his grand plan to walk around the world, Ledyard had cemented his career as an adventurer and he proudly told his cousin that in London he was "somewhat known to fame & by accident to money." To his cousin he claimed that "no other Man has seen as much of Asia & America" as he had. "Behold me the greatest traveler in history," he told his mother. "An eccentric, irregular, unafraid, unaccountable, curious & without vanity, majestic as a comet."

Many newspapers reported on his upcoming adventure, with the *Times of London* calling him "an enterprising character." The crowning act was when the association hired Carl Fredrik von Breda, a young Swedish pupil of Sir Joshua Reynolds, to paint Ledyard's portrait. Breda painted Ledyard standing next to a map of Africa. Ledyard's Connecticut friend, the painter John Trumbull, declared the painting to be "not only a perfect likeness but good painting." When Ledyard had copies made for his family in America and for a wealthy landowner who also lodged at the Green Man & Still, though, they did not turn out well. He told Isaac "It is an old stupid devil of a thing (and looks exactly like Avery the taylor on Groton bank). It was taken by a boy, who is as dumb & deaf as the portrait. . . . they are done in water & are mere daubings." In a poignant move, Banks hung the Breda portrait in Somerset House, the new headquarters for the Royal Society in London and the same building where eight years earlier Ledyard had collected his pay after the Cook voyage. The portrait eventually returned with Breda to Sweden and later was lost, but in 1788 it proved to be one prominent manifestation of Ledyard's renown.

Ledyard did not wholly lose his senses. He tried to copy a transcript of his Siberian journal—"the few rude remarks I have made in my last tour"— but ran out of time. He studied medicine with a fellow of the Royal Society and good friend of Banks, Dr. John Hunter. A surgeon and anatomy instructor who had sponsored Ledyard's Russian adventure, Hunter maintained at his Leicester Square residence a comprehensive museum of animal and human specimens, including a kangaroo from Cook's first voyage. Hunter's tutelage, Beaufoy wrote, allowed Ledyard to "accomplish himself in Physic as far as the shortage of the Education would allow."

Money, for the first time in his adult life, was no longer a problem. Ledyard bumped into James Jarvis, an American coin minter and old friend who had lent him 100 livres in Paris. Now uncharacteristically holding a full wallet, Ledyard tried to repay him but Jarvis declined. On 26 June Beaufoy and Banks met as the committee with Ledyard and approved a further payment of seventy guineas, making a total of one hundred guineas. Banks also reimbursed Ledyard for all of his outfitting and living expenses, including £8 pounds 8 shillings for "6 fine shirts," £5 pounds 15 shillings for a suit, £4 pounds 12 shillings sixpence for his lodgings at the Green Man & Still. Ledyard, unable to resist, went around London doing more than simply collecting necessities for a trip through Africa. While buying hatchets, boots, a hat and pistols, he also acquired a half dozen pairs of silk stockings, white cravats, silk handkerchiefs, a watch and a waistcoat. The grand total for the London leg of his African Association adventure was £158. In four weeks Ledyard had managed to spend the 2005 equivalent of $21,000.

Ledyard's profligacy stemmed in part from his financial models. He had the unerring ability to become business partners and close friends with men who were reckless with money. Robert Morris and William Duer went to debtor's prison. Daniel Parker embezzled hundreds of thousands of dollars and fled to Europe. William Smith, John Adams's son-in-law, abandoned his wife and twice went to jail—once for debt and once for trying to liberate Venezuela. Jarvis failed to produce a single copper coin despite a lucrative contract with the U.S. government, fled his creditors and suffered through years of suits. Even Thomas Jefferson, despite his genius, was perpetually short of money, and when he died in 1826, one hundred and sixty slaves had to be sold to cover his debts.

Despite his fancy outfits and full wallet, Ledyard was not well. Fifteen years earlier he had written, "my Body becomes a substitute for cash, and pays my travelling charges." He tried to deny that his body's account now was empty. Knowing that Jarvis, on his way to New York, might comment on his ragged state to the Ledyard cousins, he told Isaac that "I am now in as full bloom & vigour as 37 years will afford any Man—Jarvis says I look much older than when he saw me at Paris 3 summers ago which I readily believe. An American face does not wear well like an American heart." At the border to Poland, he admitted, he might have been "dissappointed, ragged, penniless: and yet so accustomed am I to such things I declare my heart was whole." In his letters home, Ledyard was doggedly optimistic as usual. He spun through stories from Siberia, deliberately leaving out the worst of the Lapland adventure or his Russian banishment.

To those who knew him now, however, the African adventure looked something like a death wish. He was drained and exhausted. On the morning of 30 June 1788, Ledyard went to Henry Beaufoy's house to say farewell to him and Banks. He evidently realized, as Beaufoy remembered him saying, that he would probably not make it out of Africa alive:

> I am accustomed to hardships. I have known both hunger and nakedness to the utmost extremity of human suffering. I have known what it is to have food given me as charity to a madman; and I have at times been obliged to shelter myself under the miseries of that character to avoid a heavier calamity. My distresses have been greater than I have ever owned, or ever will own to any man. Such evils are terrible to bear; but they never yet had power to turn me from my purpose. If I live, I will faithfully perform, in its utmost extent, my engagement to the Society; and if I perish in the attempt, my honour will still be safe, for death cancels all bonds.

Over the course of the last five months John Ledyard had gone from far eastern Asia, where he was contemplating his summer on the Pacific Coast, to western Europe where he was leaving for Africa. It was a stunning volte-face, and somehow, beneath the bravado of the majestic comet and the heart that was whole, he must have known it was too much for any man to bear.

14

I Go Alone—Grand Cairo

ON THE FOURTH OF JULY 1788, the author of the Declaration of Independence celebrated the twelve-year anniversary of its official signing with his usual dinner for the Americans in Paris. That day Thomas Jefferson received a regret to his party from a man he thought at that moment was striding across the hills of California. John Ledyard was in Paris.

Jefferson had last heard from Ledyard the previous June, when he got a Ledyard letter posted in St. Petersburg. Evidently he had not received the letters Ledyard wrote to him from Barnaul and Irkutsk, possibly because of Iakobi's censoring. Since returning from Russia, Ledyard, perhaps embarrassed at his failure, had not written to Jefferson.

Now, on the Fourth, Ledyard was bedridden with a cold and a fever in his rooms at the Hotel d'Aligre, a fashionable inn on rue d'Orleans near the Palais-Royal. (Stendhal mentioned it in *The Red and the Black*.) Jefferson replied to his note, and Ledyard managed to rouse himself out of bed and struggle over to Hotel Langeac to dine with Jefferson. That night Ledyard told him the whole story and outlined his plans for Africa. Jefferson was upset that Ledyard had contracted to explore for a British organization and for a while their conversation was strained. As a way to save face,

Ledyard made a promise: even with the probability that Africa would kill him or permanently end his traveling itch, he pledged, as Jefferson told James Madison two weeks later, that "if he escapes through this journey, he will go to Kentuckey and endeavour to penetrate Westwardly from thence to the South sea."

The next day, almost as if it were an assignment, he wrote Jefferson a memorandum on what he learned in Russia. For Ledyard, such a note was typical of Enlightenment thinking: "We now a days seek truth not only for its own enchanting beauty, but from a principle tho not more valuable yet more generous, viz the pleasure of communicating it to one another. The soothsayers, magicians, phrophets & priests of old would think us as errant fools, as we think them knaves." Then he laid down his theories: that the difference in skin color was because of nature, not God; that the native Siberians and Americans were one people, the Americans having come over from Asia; and that all of mankind descended from one common ancestor. These ideas later became accepted, but at the time they were considered odd, if not wrong-headed. The only time Ledyard might have erred was when he said that the mechanism for spreading all the races around the globe was "a general deluge," as related in the Bible.

Ledyard spent ten days in Paris, visiting other friends and old haunts. Then he took a coach down to Marseilles, the old Mediterranean entrepôt. Jefferson had recommended that Ledyard contact Stephen Cathalan, Jr., a Marseilles merchant and friend who later became a U.S. vice-consul. Ledyard went to him upon arrival and asked for an introduction to a captain of a ship bound for Alexandria. Cathalan was "exteriorly polite," Ledyard later told Jefferson, but at the same time mysteriously "strove to prevent my embarking." Cathalan took Ledyard to the local chamber of commerce, and Ledyard spent a frustrating day meeting with officials who gave him no assistance. The last ship of the season was about to depart and Ledyard, after just two days in Marseilles, managed to hitch a lift on it without any help from Cathalan or the city officials. For once his luck held and he was, by mere hours, not too late for the season.

On Tuesday, 5 August, just thirty-four days after leaving London, John Ledyard arrived at Alexandria. It was an astonishingly quick transit and that day he dashed off a self-congratulatory note, datelined Alexandria, to Henry Beaufoy. The letter reached Beaufoy in October and he relayed the surprising news to Banks, adding that "the ardour with which he proceeds in his Mission, & the kindness which he bears the Society, are favourable to our hopes & prove in the strongest manner the propriety of the choice we have made."

After the fortnight crossing the summery Mediterranean, the view of Alexandria from the sea was spectacular, with the fabled town rising above fine beaches. But as the ship pulled into the small harbor reserved for Christian ships, it was less impressive. Named after its founder, Alexander the Great, Alexandria had been at one point the largest city in the Western world, the center of Greek and Jewish culture, home to Euclid the mathematician and the famous two libraries that contained close to a million books. Julius Caesar had occupied the city, as did Augustus after the suicide of Antony and Cleopatra. But by the time Ledyard arrived, its Roman-era population of three hundred thousand had shrunk to twelve thousand. Almost all the remnants of its glory days, like the celebrated lighthouse on Pharos, one of the seven wonders of the ancient world, had either disappeared or were underwater. A granite shaft, called Pompey's Pillar, and the twin red granite obelisks, named Cleopatra's Needles, were the only extant proofs of Alexandria's epic history. "They are both & particularly the former [Pompey's Pillar] noble subjects to see & contemplate & are certainly more captivating from the contrasting deserts & forlorn prospects around them," Ledyard told Jefferson. "No man of whatever turn of mind can see the whole with't retiring from the scene with a 'sic transit gloria Mundi.'"

Thus passes the glory of the world, and in 1788 Alexandria was a backwater transit station. Ledyard spent two weeks there and summarized what he saw in a series of splenetic nouns: "Alexandria at large forms a scene wretched & interesting beyond any other that I have seen: poverty, rapine, murder, tumult, blind bigotry, cruel persecution, pestilence." He did however dash off another letter to Beaufoy, dated 9 August, with the news that he was "in good spirits" and that he might accompany a caravan of Nubians who annually traded with "a nation called Yalott who are said to live near the shores of the atlantic." Ledyard told Beaufoy he was confident about this information, since in 1785 he had taken some vocabulary words from an Englishman who had lived in West Africa with a tribe called Joloft.

With these good prospects, Ledyard headed towards Cairo. On 19 August under a bright full moon, he took passage north along the coast accompanied by an English merchant named Hunter. At sunrise he was at Rosetta, where he spent a dozen days before sailing with Hunter up the Nile.

An aficionado of rivers ever since his paddle down the Connecticut, Ledyard had cruised down the Elbe in a snowstorm and the Lena when it was crackling with ice. He knew two Thames Rivers, the Avon, the Volga, the Ob, the Seine, the Ompompanoosuc, the Yenisei, the Rhone, the Hudson and the Delaware. When confronted with the world's greatest river, he could not hide his disappointment. He enjoyed looking at the multitudes of boats, with their cargos of onions, watermelons, dates, livestock, dogs and camels (who lay down on the deck) and listening to the sailors' music in the evenings, but the Nile did not impress him. "You have heard & read much of this River—& so had I," Ledyard wrote Jefferson. "But when I saw it I could not concieve it to be the same. It is a mere mud puddle compared with the accounts we have of it: What eyes do travellers see with— are they fools or rogues? For heavens sake hear the plain truth about it." He told Jefferson that the Nile looked similar to the Connecticut and that the accounts of its annual flooding were hyperbole.

Curious about Egyptian people, Ledyard disembarked with the captain of his felucca whenever they stopped at a village. He was stunned by the poverty. "The villages are most miserable assemblages of poor little mud huts, flung close together without any kind of order, full of dust, lice, fleas, bed-bugs, flies, and all the curses of Moses: people poorly clad, the youths naked; in such respects they rank infinitely below any Savages I ever saw."

On 6 September 1788, Ledyard landed outside of Cairo and rode into the city on the back of a donkey. He went first to the home of the Venetian consul, Carlo Rosetti. A longtime advisor to the ruling Beys of Egypt, Rosetti was also the chargé d'affaires for the British consul, George Baldwin. Rosetti served him dinner and then sent him out to look for lodging. Unable to find anything suitable, Ledyard went to a monastery run by Spanish brothers of the Order of Recollects of St. Augustine. The convent was a popular hostel for the few European travelers and Catholics from Damascus who came to Cairo.

Continuously occupied for two hundred generations, Grand Cairo, as it was then known, was the oldest city Ledyard had visited. Many millennia had made Cairo the most layered civilization on earth, with decayed remnants of earlier eras peeking out from contemporary stones like half-peeled slivers of an onion. Crumbling detritus built up so quickly that street levels rose at the rate of two feet every hundred years. Beginning in AD 640, Islam subsumed the city's earlier reincarnations as Memphis and Heliopolis. An Islamic royal precinct at the northern end of the city, called al-Qahira, after the planet Mars, was too hard for European traders to pronounce, so they began calling the city Cairo.

Like Alexandria, Cairo was in moldering decline when Ledyard arrived in 1788. It had been ruled since 1517 by the Ottoman Turks. Despite the fiery independence of the Mamelukes, the mercenary cavalry corps who governed Egypt, Cairo was a provincial garrison town. With a population of a quarter million, there were scarcely any wheeled vehicles. Minarets competed in Cairo's skyline with the city's hundred-foot-high dumps. There were three hundred organized guilds in Cairo, including one for thieves. The plague visited on average once every three years, and the city's most prosperous citizens were often connected to the incessant waves of death: mystics, astrologers, undertakers and used-clothes merchants. Wealthy Cairenes lounged in caiques and smoked hashish and opium, and the poor lived in the narrow, winding cul-de-sacs that allowed neighbors to talk from their windows but forced them to walk miles if they wanted to meet.

Centuries of myth—especially *Tales of a Thousand and One Nights*, first translated into English at the beginning of the eighteenth century—gave Westerners the impression that Cairo was an exotic tumble of sights and sounds. Nothing could be further from the truth, according to Ledyard. People in London wanted black magic and mystery, but what he saw was mundane. An Englishman, Ledyard wrote in his diary, might ask him what an Egyptian woman looked like and he could make up some bewitching description or tell him "to take notice of the first company of Gypsies he saw behind a hedge in Essex." He saw mummies. He met Coptic Christians. He heard women ululating, which reminded him of frogs. He was in no mood to confabulate. "Cairo is a wretched hole & a nest of vagabonds. Nothing merits more the whole force of Burlesque than both the poetic &

prosaic legends of this country. Sweet are the songs of Egyptian paper. Who is not ravished with gums, balms, dates, figgs, pomegrannates with the circassia & sycamorrs with't knowing that amidst these one's eyes, ears, mouth, nose is filled with dust eternal, hot fainting winds, lice, bugs, musquetoes, spiders, flies, pox, itch, leprosy, fevers, & almost universal blindness." Ledyard bitterly lashed out against the ancient glorifiers of Egypt—Thucydides, Homer, Herodotus. He told Jefferson to burn their books and laugh at their stories, for everything was false, exaggerated and a stranger to historical fact. Even with "your curiosity & love of Antiquity," Ledyard told Jefferson, he would never spend three months in Egypt.

Three months was half of Ledyard's sentence, though. The autumn was stifling hot and reminded him of Philadelphia in summer. The few Europeans, mostly French and Italians, wore turbans, caftans and slippers to blend in, and although Ledyard followed suit, he still found the atmosphere poisoned by bigotry and fear. Being a Christian, Ledyard wrote, was "very, very humiliating, ignominioius, and distressing." The Nubian caravan fell through and Ledyard hunted around for another means into the interior. He still had cash. The African Association had directed George Baldwin, the British consul in Cairo, to give Ledyard up to £80. That was the limit, not only because the association was a brand-new organization, but because Ledyard had argued against a large, well-financed operation, as Beaufoy wrote: "The Committee are persauded, that in such an Undertaking Poverty is a better protection than Wealth, and that Mr. Ledyard's address will be much more effectual than money, to open to him a passage to the Interior of Africa."

Baldwin proved to be a colorful person with whom to pass the time. A former East India Company representative, Baldwin had first come to Egypt in 1773. Seeing a possibility of cutting shipping time from India to England, he attempted to bring goods from India across the sands of Suez to the Mediterranean, in violation of the Ottoman ban on Christian ships sailing up the Red Sea. He was imprisoned, escaped, and in 1786 returned to Cairo as British consul. He liked to say that he composed a glass of water from the Ganges, the Thames and the Nile and drank it on the top of the pyramids.

Despite such global elixirs, one of Ledyard's stumbling blocks was geography. His first route, as he told his cousin in early June, was to go from

Cairo to "Mecca on the Red sea: beyond is unknown & my discoveries begin." To his mother he added Jerusalem to the itinerary. Beaufoy then sketched for him a line on a map, running from Sennar, the Moslem kingdom in present-day eastern Sudan, across to the Niger. At the end of June 1788, the African Association published the official plan: From Mecca, "he shall cross the Red Sea, and taking the rout of Nubia, shall traverse the Continent of Africa, as nearly as possible in the direction of the Niger, with which River, and with the Towns and Countries on its border, he shall endeavour to make himself acquainted—and that he shall return to Britain by the way of any of the European Settlements on the Western Coast." The reason for placing Mecca on the itinerary was partly grounded in ignorance about where it was in relation to Africa, but was also to take advantage of the annual caravans that carried pilgrims on the Haj. James Bruce, the Scot who had spent three years in Ethiopia and claimed to have found the source of the Nile, told Sir Joseph Banks in 1789 that he was afraid that Ledyard's path across Africa was too high or too low. "Very lucky he will be if he ever comes back; but I confidently say he shall not, nor do anything worthy of repeating, even tho' he had language," Bruce added negatively.

Once on the ground in Africa, Ledyard tried to fill in his itinerary's gaps. For weeks he made inquiries about the regions to the south and the caravans that crossed them, but it was hard to learn more than bits of hearsay. "It will appear very singular to you in England, that we in Egypt are so ignorant of countries which we annually visit," Ledyard told the African Association, saying that the Egyptians can "sing, dance and traffic" without needing a map. Early in his stay, Ledyard became acquainted, via the good graces of Rosetti, with a minister to one of the most powerful Mameluke beys in the city. The bey promised letters, support and protection through Nubia to Sennar, whose capital lay on the Blue Nile. The best way to learn about African geography, Ledyard discovered, was to go to the slave market where the merchants and caravan leaders congregated. In the beginning he was treated badly, for Christians were not allowed to buy slaves, but after taking with him one of Rosetti's Egyptian underlings, the merchants were less rude. The slave market became a useful source of information, and without spending a pound he learned a lot about the interior of Africa. One day he counted two hundred slaves, mostly women, for sale, a part of the estimated twenty thousand slaves annually brought to Cairo. He was told they came from a place fifty-five days' journey west of Sennar, in present-day Chad. He asked some of the female slaves if he would be treated well in their country. They told him yes, "that they should make a King of me, and treat me with all the declicacies of their country."

King for a day sounded fine, but political upheaval prevented Ledyard from assuming his throne. Almost as regular as the flooding of the Nile were coup d'états. Mameluke upstarts constantly revolted against their Mameluke governors. One insurrection occurred when Ledyard was in Cairo. A bey named Amurat rebelled against Ishmael Bey, the current leader. Amurat and his cohorts took over Upper Egypt and massed seven thousand troops just three miles south of Cairo. The city was in uproar, according to a *Times* of London correspondent writing in October: "These disputes render the roads impassable and the caravans cannot proceed, being exposed to the fury of the Arabs, whose depredations and cruelties Amurat encourages and protects." In November the situation worsened. Famine threatened as farmers fled their fields. Mutton prices soared to fifteen French sols per pound. Christian merchants in Cairo and Alexandria, the *Times* reported, "were in a very oppressed and critical situation."

In the middle of the turmoil, Ledyard made final preparations to leave. In November he contracted with a merchant to accompany a caravan to the Blue Nile at Sennar, a journey he reckoned was six hundred miles and would take a month. From there he aimed to join a caravan west to the mythical kingdom of Wangara in western Sudan, the Niger, Timbuktu and on to the Atlantic coast.

On 15 November 1788, Ledyard wrote his final letter. It was addressed to Thomas Jefferson. He said he was leaving in a few days: "I travel from here SW about 300 leagues to a Black King: there my present conductors leave me to my fate—beyond (I suppose) I go alone. I expect to cut the Continent across between the parralels of 12 & 20 N Lat." He told Jefferson that if he survived he would probably return to France. "I shall not forget you," he ended his letter. "Indeed it would be a consolation to think of you in my last moments. Be happy. I have the honor to be with esteem & friendship y'r Excellency's most obed't & most humble Servant, J. Ledyard."

The spring of 1789 was one of the most thrilling in European history. William Blake wrote the *Songs of Innocence,* and in the first week of May, Louis XVI opened the Estates General, the first step towards the French Revolution.

Among the friends of John Ledyard, the news raced around that he was dead. Rumors emerged out of Egypt and in early May London newspapers, including the *European Magazine & London Review,* reported on the death of Ledyard in Cairo. In Paris Thomas Jefferson saw the obituaries and wrote anxious letters to friends in London asking for more information. In one letter to Thomas Paine, Jefferson said he had just received Ledyard's poignant letter dated 15 November 1788. This contradicted the rumor of his death there in January, Jefferson told Paine, as Ledyard must have been far in the interior of the continent by January. If Sir Joseph Banks had no solid news after September, then Jefferson's letter of 15 November would seem to gainsay any death.

On 17 June Thomas Paine wrote to Jefferson, telling him what Banks had said: "We have lost poor Ledyard—he had agreed with certain Moors to Conduct him to Sennar. The time of their departure was arrived when he found himself Ill and took a large dose of Emetic Tartar, burst a blood vessel on the operation which carried him off in three days. We sincerely lament his loss." The same day Paine wrote to Banks to ask for more information, telling Banks that Jefferson believed Ledyard was still alive.

The next day Paine followed up with a second letter to Jefferson. That morning Paine had received a reply from Banks. Inside Banks's letter was a copy of a letter Henry Beaufoy had written to Banks that morning. Reports from Egypt were buried in this letter inside a letter inside a letter. The first report was written by Rosetti, the Venice resident, to Hunter, the British merchant, dated 27 January in Cairo, and the second was from George Baldwin, the British consul, to Beaufoy, dated 4 March 1789, at Alexandria. Both letters evidently reached London in mid-June and "from the general correspondence of those two Accounts," Banks concluded, "Mr. Beaufoy apprehends that no doubt can be entertained of the Melancholly fact which they announce." The rumors were true. Ledyard was dead.

On the day of the caravan's departure, Baldwin wrote, "bad weather or other causes occasioned delay as happens to most caravans. Mr Ledyard took offence at the delay and threw himself into a violent rage with his conductors which deranged something in his system." Rosetti said the caravan leaders felt the wind was not right. The political instability, with rebel Mamelukes attacking caravans, probably also played a role in the delay. Since time immemorial, travelers have suffered departure delays. Ledyard had traveled around the world by a stunning variety of means—from Russian postal carriage to sledge to Hartford sulky to dugout canoe to a four-hundred-ton blue-water ship—and should have been inured to waiting by now. Instead, his temper boiled over. In Belarus Ledyard's rage at logistical snafus had been so strong he had passed out; in Cairo, probably suffering from dysentery, he felt sick to his stomach. "He was seized with a pain in his stomach occasioned by Bile," wrote Rosetti. Distressed at the sudden pain, he took an emetic to induce vomiting. "But he took a dose so strong," wrote Baldwin, "that as at the first or second effort of its operations to break a blood vessel." Normally, his robust constitution could withstand the dosage, but in his weakened state, he succumbed.

He died in three days, according to Baldwin; Rosetti said six. He probably was at the monastery, in his stone-walled room. The squalor of the scene—the all-too-familiar threadbare sheets, the gray light filtered through a dirty window, his straw-colored hair plastered against his pale, damp face—was a bleak, anonymous ending. The date Rosetti gave was 10 January 1789. John Ledyard was only thirty-seven years old.

Epilogue

During his lifetime John Ledyard was a slippery, elusive person. In the last seventeen years of his life, only twice did he stay in a single place for more than six months. He had a dozen personas, each one of which summed him up for a certain segment of society: he was the renegade Dartmouth dropout, the Connecticut sailor, the marine from the Cook voyage, the circumnavigator, the writer, the would-be fur trader, the wanderer of Siberia, the solo adventurer for the African Association. When he died, these various guises coalesced into the romantic, doomed explorer.

News of Ledyard's death filtered to America in the autumn of 1789, but it was not confirmed until the summer of 1790. A flurry of newsprint ensued. *The Essex Journal & New-Hampshire Packet* published a lengthy obituary which other newspapers reprinted. The *Quarterly Review* and the *Universal Asylum and Columbia Magazine* ran articles on Ledyard. Journals like the *American Museum* and the *Columbian Gazetteer* published elegies written for Ledyard; the latter, written by "Anna," was entitled "A Wreath offered to the neglected Sod of Ledyard—the Celebrated Pedestrian Traveller." John Foster, an American critic, wrote about Ledyard in a popular essay "On Decision of Character." At the same time the African Association, under the editorship of Henry Beaufoy, published a book on the society's first years. Beaufoy devoted two chapters on Ledyard that served as a substantial source of biographical information for other writers. (Beaufoy gave equal weight to Simon Lucas, Ledyard's twin explorer, for his explorations were mildly more successful than Ledyard's—he spent five days traveling outside Tripoli before retreating because of rumors of marauding Arabs.)

Beaufoy cobbled together Ledyard's comments on native women into an encomium that circulated widely, often in the form of a poem after an 1802 Rhode Island almanac put it in verse. *The Edinburgh Encyclopedia* included an entry on Ledyard in its Africa section, as did both of the standard contemporary American biographical dictionaries. Everyone effusively praised Ledyard. "He was as bold as a lion, and gentle as he was bold," said the unnamed *Essex Journal* writer, who apparently knew Ledyard.

His cousin Isaac Ledyard was the first keeper of the Ledyard flame. Even before he died, Ledyard's prose began to appear in American magazines. Isaac contributed an excerpt from his June 1788 letter from London to the *American Magazine* in October 1788, and submitted the rest of the letter in August 1790. Mourning the passing of his beloved cousin and seeing the public interest in his life, Isaac decided to publish a *Life & Letters* of Ledyard. He began to compile Ledyard's papers, and in 1790 he wrote to Henry Beaufoy in order to obtain Ledyard's journals from Russia and "the papers that were with him at the time of his death." Beaufoy declined to send them, saying he had not yet finished perusing them. Ledyard wrote again, and this time Richard Price, a Unitarian minister and leading political theorist, replied in Beaufoy's stead. Throwing up more obstacles, Price said that Beaufoy did not want to give up the papers without assurances he would no longer be obligated to Ledyard's heirs. Since the papers were the property of the African Association, Isaac would also have to get permission from the other officers and a letter of reference. Isaac wrote to Sir Joseph Banks, giving John Jay and John Adams as references, asking for Banks's intercession with Beaufoy and inquiring about any property that might have been in Ledyard's possession in Cairo—"tho ever so inconsiderable in itself, it would be highly valued for his sake by his mother & a sister." Banks replied that he could not help, that Ledyard had left his Russian papers with Beaufoy to be returned if he survived and to be retained "as testimony of gratitude for favors received" if he died. The African papers, Banks said, were the property of the African Association. No property of Ledyard's ever made it back from Cairo to London, Banks added, saying that he died only with "Medicines & trinkets" as "he originaly determin'd to travel without money or other valuables which he justly thought would serve no purpose but to render him the object of plunder & ill usage."

Eventually, Banks and Beaufoy, through the intercession of William Smith, did send Isaac transcripts of his cousin's papers. Isaac had the copy of his Breda portrait engraved for mass production, and in the autumn of 1792 told friends that he was on the verge of turning the manuscript into proof sheets. Isaac struggled, however, with the question of using Ledyard's 1783 memoir of the Cook voyage, as he told a Hartford friend: "I do not mean to dishonor the Traveler's history with a penurious & inelegant Edition." He was a perfectionist and struggled to discern the necessary from the irrelevant.

After a few years of dithering, Isaac turned to his brother-in-law, Philip Freneau, for help. Freneau, who had married Eleanor Forman, the sister of Ben Ledyard's wife, was now a major poet and pro-Republican newspaper editor. A Princeton man, he wrote acclaimed verse on the Revolution and on such events as the *Empress of China* leaving New York Harbor. In the summer of 1797 Freneau ran advertisements for subscribers for his Ledyard book in his newspaper, the *Time Piece and Literary Companion*. The book was to be "handsomely bound and lettered," about two hundred and fifty pages long, and priced at twelve shillings. The *Pennsylvania Gazette* reported that the book would be interesting since "Ledyard was a man of a strong original cast of mind, and an accurate intelligent observer of human nature."

Subscribers evidently flocked to the edition, and Freneau composed a manuscript that contained many of Ledyard's letters and lengthy commentary. Isaac worked closely with Freneau and obtained some of Ledyard's letters from Thomas Jefferson. In March 1798 Isaac, who had earlier promised to "have subscriptions on foot in each State," sent Jefferson some subscription forms for him to forward onto "proper persons in the Southern States." He said the book was now prepared for the press and eagerly awaited as it "has been loudly called for from almost every part of the Union." At the same time Freneau ran a detailed announcement about the book in the *Time Piece*. The book, titled, *The Interesting Travels of John Ledyard: With a Summary of His Life*, was now almost five hundred pages long and the price had risen to two dollars. It was to "be printed on fine paper, with a new type, ornamented with a full length portrait of the Author, in the attitude of taking leave, on his departure for Africa," referring to an engraving of Ledyard taken from the copy of the Breda painting. Freneau was confident about the book: "The solicitude expressed by the public for this long expected Work; the character of the Author, and the celebrity of the travels, render unnecessary, to most Americans, encomiums which are ordinarily used in recommending books to public patronage." There were delays in printing. In August 1798 Freneau again ran announcements about the book, but it never appeared. In 1821 Isaac's youngest son Daniel Ledyard explained that his father "concluded, with the advice of his friends, to abandon this intention, the account of his travels being to[o] incomplete to answer the public expectation."

Thomas Jefferson remained one of Ledyard's leading champions. With the expansion of the fur trade on the Pacific Coast, Jefferson's interest in the west increased. In 1792 the *Columbia*, the first American ship to sail around the world, found (and gave its name to) the Columbia River. Jefferson naively hoped that with the discovery of a second major river of the West, there might be an easy portage between the Missouri and the Columbia for an all-water route across the continent. In 1793 he again lent his name to an effort to explore the American west. Andre Michaux, a French botanist, announced he was going to walk overland to the Pacific. When he approached the American Philosophical Society in Philadelphia, Jefferson, the APS's president, avidly took up the effort. He helped raise a subscription for Michaux and sent him a long memorandum on possible research interests along the way. Michaux had reached Kentucky when it was revealed that he was a secret agent for the French government. Jefferson had him recalled. Believing that a solo explorer would not be successful, Jefferson as U.S. president decided to launch a larger expedition called the Corps of Discovery, captained by Meriwether Lewis and William Clark. Even at the turn of the nineteenth century, Jefferson knew little about the American west. He still thought the Blue Ridge Mountains were the tallest on the continent and that mammoths, giant sloths and even volcanoes might be found out west. In the 1814 history of the Lewis & Clark Expedition, Jefferson wrote that Ledyard and his failed journey in Russia had been an original catalyst for the expedition.

Ledyard's reputation might have eased into a comfortable obscurity if not for the obsessive passion of his first published biographer, Jared Sparks. Born in Connecticut three months after Ledyard died, Sparks apprenticed to a carpenter until at age twenty he managed to get a scholarship to Exeter. To earn money he tutored boys in Havre de Grace, Maryland, and was there when the British sacked the town during the War of 1812. His report on that incident appeared in the *North American Review* and helped launch his literary career. At age twenty-six he graduated from Harvard, and after a period as a Unitarian minister in Baltimore and chaplain for the House of Representatives, he became the editor of the *NAR*. Like many American boys of the time, he grew up idolizing Ledyard. In 1815, in fact, he wrote in vain to the African Association to see if he could complete Ledyard's itinerary. Beginning in 1820 with a visit to Thomas Jefferson at Monticello, Sparks began collecting materials for a biography of his hero. After a few visits to the Ledyard family in New York, he was able to obtain the papers of John Ledyard in their possession. He ran newspaper advertisements requesting help, corresponded with Ledyard's friends in America and Europe and visited Groton, where he met Ledyard's half-sister and saw a lock of Ledyard's hair.

In 1828 Hilliard & Brown in Boston published *Memoirs of the Life and Travels of John Ledyard from his Journals and Correspondence*, by Jared Sparks. The book created a tremendous sensation. A London edition was soon released; a year later Hilliard & Brown printed a second edition and a Leipzig publisher released a German translation. As editor of the *North American Review*, Sparks held a lofty position within the U.S. literary scene, and many people paid attention to his first biography. Booksellers regularly advertised *Memoirs of the Life and Travels* in local newspapers. Dozens of magazines reviewed his book or quoted excerpts, sometimes tens of thousands of words long. One journal, the *Southern Review* in Charleston, even reviewed one of the reviews.

The reviews were not uniformly positive. A number of critics chastised Sparks for writing, in reference to Mai, that "there has never been a more idle scheme of philanthrophy, than that of converting a savage into a civilized man. No one attempt, it is believed, has ever been successful." Others quibbled about the lack of footnotes. One reviewer in the *Christian Monthly Spectator* chastised Sparks for not quoting Ledyard more liberally, arguing that the three-hundred-and-twenty-five-page book was too short and that Sparks was flogging it "for a price that ought to procure five hundred pages."

After Sparks's biography appeared, Ledyard stayed in the public consciousness. In part this was because of the fame of his Boswell. Sparks wrote life & letter biographies of Gouverneur Morris (three volumes, 1832), George Washington (twelve volumes, 1837) and Ben Franklin (ten volumes, 1840), and collected two series of correspondence of the Revolution (twelve volumes, 1830, and four volumes, 1853). His biggest sellers were eight biographies he wrote for the twenty-five volume *Library of American Biography*. First published in 1834–1838, this series sold more than a hundred thousand copies in its first fifteen years. To cap his career, Sparks was president of Harvard from 1849 to 1853. With such a notable figure as his chief publicist, Ledyard stayed a household name throughout the nineteenth century, and Little, Brown published new editions of the Sparks biography in 1847 (as a part of the *Library of American Biography* series) and 1864.

For all his tangible accomplishments, Ledyard's most profound legacy was that he forged a new, American archetype: the heroic explorer. Before him, Americans did not by and large travel for the sake of discovery. Exploration was either piecemeal, hesitant and mostly a matter of getting just to the next mountain range, or it was focused on specific scientific tasks, financial gains or geopolitical advantages. The most active explorers in North America were officers in the Hudson Bay Company and French *voyageurs*, or mountain men and fur traders who explored the Great Lakes region. Ledyard, on the other hand, had a global outlook. He was not content with going beyond the bend; he wanted to go around the world. Furthermore, those Americans who did wander—like Daniel Boone, the frontiersman; Conrad Weiser, the Indian go-between; and John Bartram, the botanist—went on piecemeal, halting journeys that did not capture the public's imagination. Ledyard talked of walking the world. Explorers who covered great distances usually were not adept at writing up or publicizing their exploits. John Carver, for instance, explored the upper reaches of the Mississippi in 1766 and 1767, but took eleven years to write his memoirs and died a pauper. William Bartram, John Bartram's son, undertook a four-year excursion in the mid–1770s to the American south and west. But his book was not published until 1791, and, though popular, it did not spur him on to further travel. It took a unique person, who combined tremendous endurance, brilliant vision and public relations expertise, to alter the American perception of exploration.

Ledyard became the patron saint of visionary explorers. In 1820 a sea captain, John Cochrane, attempted to follow Ledyard's path on foot around the world; Cochrane reached Kamchatka, but was unable to proceed on to North America. Herman Melville mentioned Ledyard in *Moby-Dick*, imagining that "the mere crossing of Siberia in a sledge drawn by dogs" had ensured that Ledyard had no way "of attaining a high social polish." In the 1850s Bayard Taylor, America's first travel writer, retraced much of Ledyard's steps; while cruising the White Nile in the Sudan, Taylor christened his boat the *John Ledyard*. In 1866 Mark Twain used Ledyard's 1783 *Journal* as a sounding board when he wrote travel essays from Hawaii. Periodically, a collection of profiles on *The Most Celebrated Voyages* (1803), *Lives of Celebrated Travelers* (1844), *Distinguished American Explorers* (1859), *Gallant Vagabonds* (1926), *Famous Pioneers* (1963) and *Fifty Intrepid Americans* (2003) would appear, offering Ledyard as a prime example. In 1939 and 1946 two more biographies appeared on Ledyard, both of which were redolent with romantic mythmaking.

Henry David Thoreau perhaps more than anyone else understood the lure of Ledyard's story. He often referred to him in his diaries and, most hauntingly, summed up Ledyard's persona in his 1849 *A Week on the Concord and Merrimack Rivers*: "There stands a gig in the gray morning, in the mist, the impatient traveler pacing the wet shore with whip in hand, and shouting through the fog after the regardless Charon and his retreating ark, as if he might throw that passenger overboard and return forthwith for himself; he will compensate him. He is to break his fast at some unseen place on the opposite side. It may be Ledyard or the Wandering Jew. Whence, pray, did he come out of the foggy night? And wither through the sunny day will he go? We observe only his transit; important to us, forgotten by him, transiting all day." Ledyard's ingrained restlessness, his unknown itinerary and his drive to keep moving at all costs became his signature legacy. For many generations, he was a thrilling but slightly forlorn figure.

Today, more than two hundred and fifty years since his birth, there are a number of ways to touch the spirit of John Ledyard. In his hometowns of Groton, Hartford and Southold, there are the well-tended graves of his grandparents, parents, siblings and other kinsmen. In Hanover there is a constellation of Ledyardiana: his plaque on the banks of the Connecticut next to the clubhouse of the Ledyard Canoe Club, near Ledyard Free Bridge, down the hill from Ledyard National Bank and Ledyard Lane. Fittingly, the one place in America named after him is in Alaska. In 1975 the federal Board on Geographic Names gave the name Ledyard Bay to a one-hundred-and-twenty-mile bight between Point Lay and Cape Lisburne at 69 north latitude—not far from the farthest point north that Ledyard ever reached.

There is no grave for John Ledyard. In 1789 in Cairo, he was, according to Henry Beaufoy, "decently interred in the neighborhood of such of the English as had ended their days in the capital of Egypt." No tombstone survived into the nineteenth century, despite the ardent searches of a number of Ledyard enthusiasts. In the 1840s Jared Sparks tried in vain to erect an obelisk to Ledyard in Cairo. Not having a monument at his final resting place, though, somehow suits Ledyard. He was too volatile to have his image be flattened, chiseled and sunk into one patch of soil.

His feats were astounding. He sailed on the greatest circumnavigation in the age of sail. He took an epic land journey across a third of the world. He covered more territory than any native-born American before him. His failures were inspiring. He never established a fur-trading company, but his work led to the China trade and the opening of the Pacific for the United States. He never crossed the continent, but Thomas Jefferson, encouraged by his attempt, launched the Lewis & Clark expedition. Ledyard was the first American to see the west coast of the continent, Alaska and Hawaii. He had famous friends like Jefferson, Cook, Lafayette and Banks.

In the fullness of time we see Ledyard not merely for his feats and his failures, his firsts and his friendships, but for his incandescent dreams. Jefferson said he was a man of genius but he had too much imagination. It is that overflowing, unmanageable, penetrating, elastic imagination which places him at the core of a nation's psyche. Too much imagination is the American ethos. Ledyard wanted to go to unmapped places and discover new lands. He wanted the thrill of first contact. He wanted to plumb the mysteries of history and geography in the field, not in the armchair in a library. He wanted to do something no one else had ever done and walk around the world. Today, his seven-year ramble still continues. John Ledyard is in the wilderness of every American explorer's mind, full of passion and hope, burning to see the next horizon.

Acknowledgments

I have been blessed with the best possible advocate in Joseph Regal, my literary agent. During the entire adventure, he unwaveringly believed in John Ledyard and in me.

Basic Books was fantastic. Chip Rossetti was a steady and sure-footed editor who saw to the heart of the story. I also warmly thank Joe Bonyata, David Shoemaker, Holly Bemiss, John Sherer, and Beth Parker.

In tracking down traces of Ledyard, a marvelous murmuration of librarians guided me: at Dartmouth's Rauner Special Collections Library in old Webster Hall, Joshua Shaw, Barbara Krieger and, above all, Sarah Hartwell; Loraine Baratti and Joseph Ditta at the New-York Historical Society; Hali Keeler and Lois Geary at the Bill Memorial Library in Groton; Judy Kelmelis at the Groton Public Library; Mary Beth Baker at the Avery Copp House in Groton; Milly Perry at the First Church of Christ, Congregational, in Groton; Vanessa Hansen at the Whitaker Historical Collection in the Southold Free Library; Clara Bjerknes at the Southold Historical Society; the librarians at the G. W. Blunt White Library in Mystic Seaport; William Stingone and John D. Stinson in Manuscripts and Archives at the New York Public Library; Barbara Austen and Sharon Yusba Steinberg at the Connecticut Historical Society; Megan Davis and Pat Schaefer at the New London County Historical Society; Valerie-Anne Lutz, Roy Goodman and Robert S. Cox at the American Philosophical Society; Rachel Onuf at the Historical Society of Pennsylvania; Sharon Cooney at the Lorenzo State Historic Site; Joe Maldonado at the British Library; Paul Cooper and the indefatigable Neil Chambers at the Natural History Museum in London; Godfrey Waller and Peter Meadows at the Cambridge University Library;

Annie Ridgeon at the James Caird Library at the National Maritime Museum in Greenwich; Kimberly Nusco at the Massachusetts Historical Society; and Martha Whittaker at Sutro Library.

Throughout the past five years, my friends and family were tremendously supportive. Debbie and Jim Zug went beyond the role of parents to read the manuscript, help with translations, dispense encouragement and always lend a discerning, interested ear. At the National Geographic Society, Lisa Thomas coordinated and Carl Mehler produced the two fabulous maps. I thank all those who paddled with me down the Connecticut in Ledyard's wake, especially Edward J. Gilmartin and Taylor H. Ricketts. Leslie Hulse, Peter H. Quimby, Adrianne Pierce and Tara Bray Smith donated their linguistic skills for translations. Jay Heinrichs, Robert McCracken Peck and Jim Collins read early drafts of the manuscript and offered perceptive suggestions and comments; Jim in particular championed the book since we first discussed it one fine summer afternoon in New Hampshire long ago. I benefitted from conversations with Ledyard historians Jere R. Daniell, Sinclair H. Hitchings, Alan Thomas Ledyard, Theckla Ledyard, William Spengemann and Jerold Wikoff. For following up false leads: Irene Axelrod at the Peabody Essex Museum; Dorrie Hanna at the Mystic River Historical Society; Ian Graham at Bowdoin College; Joanna Bowring at the British Museum; Margaret Sherry Rich at Princeton University; David Kuzma at Rutgers University; Hannah Cunliffe, who did research for me in England; and, most of all, Mikael Ahlund, Clara Anderson, Joanna Corden, Michelle Facos, and James G. Harper, who searched for the missing Carl Fredrich von Breda portrait of Ledyard. Many thanks also to Joseph C. Baillargeon, Rose Marie Belforti, Ian Boreham, Brigitte M. Botnick, Vanni Cappelli, Colin Colloway, Robert Demaria, Barbara E. Dunn, Bill Goring, Colby Loud, James H. Merrell, Kate Seibold, Peter Lane Taylor, Evan Thomas and Eric Tulman. Alexis B. Miron, Wendy and Jeff Brown, Gwyneth and Robert Loud, Judith and Abram T. Collier, Megan and David B. Zug, Jr., Laura Z. and Peter H. Quimby, Robby Legg, Grace Cutler and Douglas Rogers and Leslie Hulse and Mark Stafford benevolently billeted me during my research peregrinations.

Whether walking around the world or around the eighteenth century, I have had the greatest traveling companions. Livingston lit the trail with his curiosity and joy. This book is lovingly dedicated to Rebecca, his mother and my wife. At every step of the way, she helped make this a Sustaining Book.

A Note on Sources

In order to be as faithful as possible to the sense and meaning of the prose quoted in this book, as well as to emphasize the distinctive styles and raw immediacy of the writers, I have retained the original spelling and punctuation in almost every instance.

Primary sources on John Ledyard are remarkably rich and varied for an untitled eighteenth-century figure. The home for Ledyard studies is at Rauner Special Collections Library at Dartmouth College. For over a century Dartmouth has assiduously gathered Ledyardiana: a three-volume copy of the *Life & Letters* manuscript composed by Philip Freneau and Isaac Ledyard, which includes one version of his Russia journal and as copies of forty-odd letters of Ledyard's; a dozen original letters, as well as a number of original letters relating to Ledyard; the Beaufoy transcript, another version of his Russia journal; numerous books, articles and correspondence about Ledyard; and the extensive papers of Sinclair H. Hitchings, a mid-twentieth-century Ledyard researcher.

There are two other essential repositories. One is the New-York Historical Society, which preserves two dozen original letters of Ledyard's; other original letters; Ledyard's original itinerary in eastern Siberia; a fragment of his Russia journal; the original 1786 subscription for Ledyard's walk around the world; Ledyard's original comparative chart about Native American languages, given to Thomas Jefferson; Ledyard family papers; general correspondence; and a bound volume of genealogical notes made by descendent Ledyard Lincklaen. The other is Houghton Library at Harvard University. The Jared Sparks collection contains Sparks' commonplace books; diaries; research notes and correspondence; an early draft of his biography; and most importantly, Ms. 112, which is a bound volume of Sparks' research and interview notes, musings, correspondence, copies of Ledyard's letters and newspaper clippings.

Other original letters are held at the Boston Public Library, the Whitaker Collection at Southold Free Library, the Historical Society of Pennsylvania, the American Philosophical Society and the Library of Congress. The Connecticut Historical Society keeps a copy of the *Life & Letters* manuscript, as well as original Ledyard family correspondence. The New York Public Library has the papers of Samuel Forman and the Ledyard family. The G.W. Blunt White Library at Mystic Seaport has a 1785 invoice of Ledyard's brothers Thomas and George. The First Church of Christ in Groton has the original baptismal and membership records for the Ledyard family. The New London County Historical Society has original legal papers and the Nathaniel Shaw papers. The Southold Historical Society hold Ledyard family papers.

In England, the Cambridge University Library holds original material on the African Association. The Natural History Museum has copies of four Ledyard letters, as well as the Dawson Turner copies of correspondence of Sir Joseph Banks. The National Archives (the old Public Records Office) has log books, muster books and journals from the Cook voyage; Guy Carleton's 1783 correspondence; and custom and intelligence records. The British Library has letters to Sir Joseph Banks.

The original 1783 book was reprinted, with editing, extensive annotation, and insightful essays, by James Kenneth Munford and Sinclair H. Hitchings (Corvallis: Oregon State University Press, 1963). That same year, Quadrangle Books in Chicago also produced a facsimile edition of the 1783 *Journal*. Extracts from Ledyard's African journal can be found in [Henry Beaufoy] *Proceedings of the Association for Promoting the Discovery of the Interior Parts of Africa* (London: C. Macrae, 1790). Another essential book by and on Ledyard is Stephen D. Watrous, editor, *John Ledyard's Journey through Russia and Siberia: The Journal and Selected Letters* (Madison: University of Wisconsin Press, 1966).

There are a number of biographies of Ledyard: Jared Sparks, *Memoirs of the Life and Travels of John Ledyard from his Journals and Correspondence* (Boston: Hilliard & Brown, 1828; London: Henry Colburn, 1828; Boston: Hilliard & Brown, 1829); *Life of John Ledyard, the American Traveler* (Boston: Charles C. Little and James Brown, 1847; Boston, Little, Brown, 1864); Kenneth Munford, *John Ledyard: An American Marco Polo* (Portland, OR: Binsford & Mort, 1939); and Helen Augur, *Passage to Glory: John Ledyard's America—The Life and Travels of the First Man to Envision America's Destiny in the Pacific* (Garden City, NY: Doubleday, 1946). None of these biographies are trustworthy, with imagined scenes, gaps in research and florid language. Sparks was notorious for revising original letters, a practice that Augur replicated. Munford later repudiated his own biography. See also Zakhar Dicharov, *Neobychainye pokhozhdeniia v Rossii Dzhona Lediarda-amerikantsa* (St. Petersburg: Nauka, 1996).

Hundreds of books include essays on Ledyard. The most insightful is Larzer Ziff, *Return Passages: Great American Travel Writing 1780–1910* (New Haven: Yale University Press, 2000). See also A[ndrew]. Kippis, *Captain Cook's Voyages, with an account of his life during the previous and intervening periods* (1788; New York: Alfred A. Knopf, 1924); William Mavor, *An Historical Account of the Most Celebrated Voyages, Travels, and Discoveries from the Time of Columbus to the Present Period* (Philadelphia: Samuel F. Bradford, 1803)—"When we contemplate the vast extent of his former travels, the hardships which he endured with such amazing fortitude, and his unshaken resolution to devote the remainder of his days to the public benefit, fearless of sickness, dangers, or death itself, we sincerely hope, that our generous readers will honor his arduous attempts with the smile of approbation, while the warm tear of regret bedews his Egyptian grave"; George L. Craik, *The Pursuit of Knowledge under Difficulties* (1830; London: George Bell & Sons, 1876); Thomas Bingley, *Tales about Travellers: Their Perils, Adventures, and Discoveries* (New York: Wiley & Putnam, 1844); James Augustus St. John, *The Lives of Celebrated Travellers, vol. 2* (New York: Harper & Brothers, 1844)—"To the young mind which makes companions of its own dream, solitude is sweet, as it favours their growth, and throws a gorgeous mantle over their deformities"; Samuel M. Smucker, *The Life of Elisha Kent Kane and of Other Distinguished American Explorers* (Philadelphia: G.G. Evans, 1859); Charles C. B. Seymour, *Self-Made Men* (New York: Harper & Brothers, 1877); W. C. Prime, *Among the Northern Hills* (New York: Harper & Brothers, 1895); Henry Beston, *The Book of Gallant Vagabonds* (New York: George H. Doran, 1925)—"The gallant vagabond is not the man with the sun helmet and the file of native bearers; nor is he the wastrel who drifts down-stream and sees the world as he goes; the real prince of vagabonds is the wayfarer with scarce a penny in his pocket who fights his way upstream to see where the river rises, and crosses the dark mountains to find the fabled town. His curiosity is never purely geographical. . . . The vast loneliness of the sea which comes when twilight fades and night begins, blue, cloudy islands seen at dawn, the sounds of rushing brooks in the quiet of green valleys, strange folk making strange music under the moon,—all this he had hungered to see, all this he had seen. He had achieved his ambition in spite of every barrier, he had girdled the earth on a sixpence and a ha'penny"; Don C. Seitz, *Uncommon Americans: Pencil Portraits of Men and Women Who Have Broken the Rules* (Indianapolis: Bobbs-Merrill, 1925); Fred Lockley, *Oregon Trail Blazers* (New York: Knickerbocker Press, 1929); Eleanor Early, *Behold the White Mountains* (Boston: Little, Brown, 1935); Jeannette Mirsky, *The Westward Crossings* (New York: Alfred A. Knopf, 1946); Ernest S. Dodge, *New England and the South Seas* (Cambridge: Harvard University Press, 1965); Ian Frazier, *Great Plains* (New York: Farrar, Straus & Giroux, 1989); and Tony Horwitz, *The Devil May Care: Fifty Intrepid Americans and Their Quest for the Unknown* (Oxford University Press, 2003).

At least two poets have written on Ledyard: Benjamin W. Ball, "Ledyard's Soliloquy" in *The Merrimack River, Hellenics and Other Poems*, edited by Frederick F. Ayer (New York: G.P. Putnam's Sons, 1892)—"The earth's vast surface is/The Page my restless eyes would fain peruse/By light of sun and star in every clime"; Richard Eberhart, "John Ledyard," *Collected Poems 1930–1986* (New York: Oxford University Press, 1988)—"Only death remains/To tell us/How great we were/Speaks the voice of the voyager/From fading bronze letters,/Great with desire."

There are three notable juvenile books on Ledyard: ["*A Yankee*"], *The Adventures of a Yankee: or the Singular Life of John Ledyard; with an Account of his Voyage Round the World with the Celebrated Captain Cook* (Boston: Carter, Hender and Babcock, 1831); Best line from the children's book: "He was unusually fond of adventure; and although I know not that he was vicious or ugly, he was wild and frolicksome." S. G. Mantel, *Explorer with a Dream: John Ledyard* (New York: Julian Messner, 1969); and Laurie Lawlor, *Magnificent Voyage: An American Adventurer on Captain Cook's Final Expedition* (New York: Holiday House, 2002). See also Agnes Danforth Hewes, *The Codfish Musket* (Garden City, NY: Doubleday, Doran, 1937) and Franklin Folsom, *Famous Pioneers* (Irvington, NY: Harvey House, 1963)—"Exciting thoughts raced through John's very handsome, very blond head. Indians might inhabit all of America! This meant he might have friends anywhere in America. These friends could help him if he wanted to cross the continent."

For academic journal articles on Ledyard, see Henry A. Tirrell, "Ledyard the Traveller" in *The Records and Papers of the New London County Historical Society,* vol. 3, no. 2 (1912); Eufrosina Dvoichenko-Markov, "John Ledyard and the Russians," in *The Russian Review*, vol. 11, no. 4 (October 1952); Sanford H. Bederman, "John Ledyard: Early American Traveler" *Bulletin of the Georgia Academy of Science*, vol. 29 (June 1961) and "The Ethnological Contributions of John Ledyard," *Georgia State College School of Arts & Sciences Research Papers*, no. 4 (July 1964); and Donald Jackson, "Ledyard and Lapérouse: A Contrast in Northwestern Exploration," *Western Historical Quarterly*, vol. 9, no. 4 (October 1978).

For magazine articles on Ledyard, see *The Western Journal of Agriculture, Manufactures*, vol. 3, no. 1 (October 1849); T. M. Eddy, "John Ledyard," in *Ladies Repository*, 1854; James Parton, "The Yankee Traveller, Ledyard," in *Wood's Household Magazine*, vol. 11, no. 2 (August 1872); E. M. Halliday, "Captain Cook's American," in *American Heritage*, December 1961; Bertha S. Dodge, "John Ledyard, Controversial Corporal, 1751–88" *History Today*, September 1973; John Brinton, *Aramco World Magazine*, November/December 1980; and Richard Sassaman, "The Slave of Accident," *American History*, April 1999.

Dartmouth has been an avid interpreter of Ledyard's life. *The Dartmouth Alumni Magazine* has often published articles on Ledyard: James D. McCallum, "John Ledyard and His Russian Journal," March 1927; Edward Connery Lathem, "A Wayward Freshman: Some Recollections of John Ledyard, 'that wondrous Adventurer' as an undergraduate," February 1963; and Jerold Wikoff, "The Man Who Could Not Arrive," Summer 1993, as well as June 1906, March 1921, August 1926, November 1927, March 1928, January 1931, and April 1940. *The Dartmouth*, the daily undergraduate newspaper, also has regularly reported on Ledyard, including: H. E. P[arker], "John Ledyard," in February 1874; 22 October 1886; 8 January 1906; 14 June 1907; 19 May 1926; 11 September 1939; 1 and 15 October 1943; 22 January 1962; and 16 and 17 May 1977. See also, Charles Manley Smith, "John Ledyard" in the *Dartmouth Literary Monthly*, vol. 5, no. 3 (November 1890). Two undergraduates wrote theses on Ledyard: Leland J. Stacy, "John Ledyard 1751–1788: Traveler, Explorer, Chronicler or Geographer?" 1953; and Marsha Rich, Williams-Mystic Program, 1977.

For newspaper articles on Ledyard, see *North American Review*, April and July 1824; *Biography*, 4 March 1826; *New-York Mirror*, 1 October 1836; *The New-Yorker*, 2 May 1840; *Every Youth's Gazette*, 26 March 1842; *Dwights American Magazine*, 18 April 1846; *Scientific American*, 7 July 1849; *Yale Literary Magazine*, June 1851; *Putnam's Magazine*, June 1855; *Saturday Evening Post*, 28 October 1871; *Brooklyn Eagle,* 30 December 1881, 18 November 1883, 8 May 1890, and September, 1927; *Boston Herald,* 4 July 1919; *New Haven Register*, 1 October 1939; *Hartford Times*, 10 May 1943; *New York Times Book Review*, 31 August 1952; *Hartford Courant*, 7 July 1957; and *Valley News*, 19 April 1983.

Notes

Prologue

xiv **fur-clad bodies:** "They all sung in concert in a wild Manner," wrote David Samwell in his diary on 29 March 1778, "which some of our sailors compared to that of a Brother Tar on board who it seems in his time had cryed Potatoes about London."

Chapter 1—Ocean's Briny Waves

1 **roots were in Long Island:** For more on the history of Southold and Long Island, see Benjamin F. Thompson, *History of Long Island: From Its Discovery and Settlement to the Present Time* (two volumes, 1843; repr., Port Washington, NY: Ira J. Friedman, 1962); Epher Whitaker, *History of Southold, Long Island: Its First Century* (1890); August Griffin, *Journal* (1857; repr., Orient, NY: Oysterponds Historical Society, 1983); Frederic Gregory Mather, *The Refugees of 1776 from Long Island to Connecticut* (Albany: L. B. Lyon, 1913); Harvey M. Lawson, *History and Genealogy of the Descendants of John Lawson* (Southbridge, MA: Central Massachusetts Printing, 1931); and Clarence Ashton Wood's three articles on Ledyard in *Long Island Forum*, September and November 1953 and March 1954.

2 **reverend's grandson:** Reverend John Youngs's son Thomas Youngs moved to Oyster Bay, Long Island, and nine generations of Youngs lived in his home there. Today Youngs Memorial Cemetary has been subsumed by the Theodore Roosevelt Sanctuary, the oldest National Audubon songbird sanctuary in the country, founded in 1923, and the place where Roosevelt was buried in January 1919.

2 **village of Groton:** For more on Groton and New London, see Frances Manwaring Caulkins, *History of New London, Connecticut, From the First Survey of the Coast in 1612 to 1852* (New London, 1860); Emily S. Gilman, ed., *The Stone Records of Groton*

(Norwich, CT: Free Academy Press, 1903); Joshua Hempstead, *The Diary of Joshua Hempstead: A Daily Record of Life in Colonial New London, Connecticut: 1711–1758* (1901; repr., New London: New London County Historical Society, 1999); Charles R. Stark, *Groton, Conn., 1705–1905* (Stonington, CT: Palmer Press, 1922); John Avery, *History of the Town of Ledyard, 1650–1900* (Norwich, CT: Noyes & Davis, 1901); Carol W. Kimball, *The Groton Story* (Stonington, CT: Pequot Press, 1965); Charles F. Burgess, *Historic Groton: Comprising Historic and Descriptive Sketches* (Moosup, CT, 1909); Richard Anson Wheeler, *History of the Town of Stonington* (New London: Day Publishing, 1900); Charles Allyn, *The Battle of Groton Heights* (New London, 1882); Pliny LeRoy Harwood, *History of Eastern Connecticut* (New Haven: Pioneer Historical Publishing, 1932); and Charles W. Burpee, *The Story of Connecticut* (New York: American Historical, 1939).

For more genealogical information on Ledyard's ancestors, see Cass Ledyard Shaw, *The Ledyard Family in America* (West Kennebunk, ME: Phoenix Publishing, 1993); Frances Ledyard Ivy, *The Ledyard Family of Connecticut* (Columbus, MS: Lowndes County Department of Archives and History, 1979); Lucius Barnes Barbour, *Families of Early Hartford, Connecticut* (Baltimore: Genealogical Publishing, 1977); Ruth Lawrence, *Genealogical Histories of Ledyard, Cass, Livingston, Prince, and Allied Families* (New York: National Americana Society, 1925); *Ledyard-Cass Biographical Records* (New York: Press Association, 1924; Charles B. Moore, *The New York Genealogical and Biographical Record*, vol. 7, no. 1 (January 1876); *Connecticut Church Records: State Library Index* (Hartford: Connecticut State Library, 1934); and John Austin Stevens, "The Ledyard Family," in *The Magazine of American History*, vol. 7 (1881).

3 **birth to her tenth child:** All dates are adjusted for New Style by year (if between the first of January and the twenty-fifth of March) but keep the Old Style day until after September 1752. Until that month. Americans followed the Julian calendar, with the new year beginning on March 25 rather than January 1 and with the date being eleven days behind the Gregorian calendar. In September 1752, when America switched calendars, Wednesday the second was followed by Thursday the fourteenth.

3 **grand house in New London:** The house, built in 1678 by Hempstead's father, is still standing today at the corner of Hempstead, Jay, Truman, and Coit Streets in New London. It is owned by the Antiquarian and Landmarks Society of Connecticut.

3 **"baptized in infancy":** John Ledyard's exact birth date is not known. It was traditional to baptize a baby the first Sunday after birth, so he was born in late October or the first few days of November. Thomas Coit, the principal New London physician at the time, probably helped in the delivery. On the same day as his baptism, John's parents officially joined the church and "publicly owned their baptismal Covenant." In June 1788 John Ledyard told his cousin Isaac Ledyard that he was "now in as full bloom & vigour as 37 years will afford any Man." Perhaps Ledyard meant

that he was in his thirty-seventh year, i.e., thirty-six, but it is possible, though unlikely, that the reason his parents eloped in May 1750 was that his mother was pregnant with him and that he was born in the autumn of 1750. If so, the phrase "baptised in infancy" would have been a fallacy visible to all the congregation.

4 **prosperous time for the Ledyards:** See Helen Augur, *The Secret War of Independence* (Boston: Little, Brown, 1955).

5 **buried in the northeast corner:** Charles Ledyard's epitaph on his gravestone reads: "Happy the Babe who Privledged by Fate to Shorten Labour and a lighter weight received by yesterday." In 1881 John Austin Stevens, a Ledyard descendent, reported on a sixth child of Abigail and John Ledyard, a boy named Ferdinand "who died young." Although possible, there is no extant evidence of this child, nor was Ferdinand a family name.

5 **Youngs of smallpox:** A Ledyard family rumor, first mentioned decades later in letters of Ann Bruce, Youngs Ledyard's granddaughter, was that Benedict Arnold, sailing as supercargo on Youngs's ship, poisoned Youngs. Although it was true that Arnold had grown up in nearby Norwich and ran an apothecary in New Haven and knew about medicine, in the spring of 1762 he was in England getting stock for his store.

5 **morass of legal dealings:** John Ledyard, III, had bought the house from his father with money from the sale of land in Southold originally owned by his deceased mother. One Ledyard family member told Jared Sparks in January 1822 that "an unlawful act of Fraudulency deprived the widow and her children of their rightful estate." A few years later Ledyard's half sister Phoebe Ledyard Denison, told Sparks that the deed had been deposited with Ebenezer Avery in Groton. "This deed was soon missing by some mysterious process," Sparks wrote in his interview notes. "Esq. Ledyard, the traveller's grandfather, believing that his grandchildren would be a charge to him, took measures to obtain the deed, destroy it, & thus bring the property again into his possession."

6 **he moved to Hartford:** William DeLoss Love, *The Colonial History of Hartford, Gathered from Original Sources* (1914; repr., Hartford: Centinel Hill Press, 1974).

Chapter 2—Saucy Enough

10 **verge of failure:** For more on the history of Dartmouth, see Isaac Parsons, *Memoir of the Life and Character of Rev. Joseph Vaill* (New York: Taylor & Dodd, 1839); George T. Chapman, *Sketches of the Alumni of Dartmouth College* (Cambridge: Riverside Press, 1867); Baxter Perry Smith, *The History of Dartmouth College* (Boston: Houghton, Osgood, 1878); Frederick Chase, *A History of Dartmouth College and the Town of Hanover, New Hampshire*, edited by John K. Lord (Cambridge: John Wilson, 1891); Leon Burr Richardson, *History of Dartmouth College* (Hanover: Dartmouth

College Publications, 1931); James Dow McCallum, *Eleazar Wheelock: Founder of Dartmouth College* (Hanover: Dartmouth College Publications, 1939); Ralph Nading Hill, ed., *The College on the Hill: A Dartmouth Chronicle* (Hanover: Dartmouth College Publications, 1964); and Robert B. Graham, *The Dartmouth Story: A Narrative History of the College Buildings, People, and Legends* (Hanover: Dartmouth Bookstore, 1990). See also W. Deloss Love, *Samson Occum and the Christian Indians of New England* (Pilgrim Press, 1899; repr., Syracuse University Press, 2000); Bernd Peyer, "The Betrayal of Samson Occum," *Dartmouth Alumni Magazine*, November 1998; Francis Lane Childs, "A Dartmouth History Lesson for Freshman," *Dartmouth Alumni Magazine*, December 1957; and Jere R. Daniell, "Eleazar Wheelock and the Dartmouth College Charter," *Dartmouth Alumni Magazine*, 1969.

15 **according to Dartmouth lore:** The Richard Hovey poem begins: "Oh, Eleazar Wheelock was a very pious man:/He went into the wilderness to teach the Indian,/With a Gradus ad Parnassum, a Bible and a drum,/And five hundred gallons of New England rum/Eleazar was the faculty, and the whole curriculum/Was five hundred gallons of New England rum."

15 **purpose of Dartmouth:** "In the United States of America as in Russia we have made our efforts to convert our Tartars to think and act like us, to what effect?" wrote Ledyard in his diary while traveling in Siberia in 1787, giving a less palatable reason for rejecting Dartmouth's early mission. "When I was at School at Mount Ida there were many Indians there: most of whom gave some hopes of Civilizing: and some were sent forth to preach, but as far as I observed myself and have been since informed they all, like the ungained Sow returned to the mire."

17 **secretly obtained his legacy:** Philip Freneau wrote that Ledyard "sold a small patrimony which had yet remained to him, on Long Island."

18 **particularly large flourish:** Ledyard loved New Year's Day. One year while he was living in Hartford, a newspaper published a poem of his on January 1 that began: "As is man's life, so is the first of January/Short, fleeting and completely momentary."

19 **paddled south:** See Edwin M. Bacon, *The Connecticut River and the Valley of the Connecticut, Three Hundred and Fifty Miles from Mountain to Sea: Historical and Descriptive* (New York: G.P. Putnam's Sons, 1906); Lyman S. Hayes, *The Connecticut River Valley in Southern Vermont and New Hampshire* (Rutland, VT, 1929); and Marguerite Allis, *Connecticut River* (New York: G.P. Putnam's Sons, 1939). Jobab, in "Ledyard," which appeared in *The Scrapbook: Conducted by a Literary Club of Undergraduates of Dartmouth College*, vol. 1, no. 1 (October 1837), wrote: "That small bark carried with it as proud and lofty aspirations, as beautiful and airy imaginings, as noble and godlike ambition as ever burned in mortal breast." The John Ledyard legend included an impossible length of canoe for his escape from Dartmouth. The rumor, spread first by Henry Seymour in his interview with Jared Sparks, was that Led-

yard's dugout was fifty-feet long. For one person, a fifty-foot dugout would be extremely difficult to maneuver, especially in fast water. In all likelihood, Seymour meant fifteen feet. Equally mythical was the suggestion that Ledyard simply floated down the river, daydreaming and reading his Ovid. His Dartmouth classmate James Wheelock wrote in November 1821 that at Bellows Falls "even this hazard he almost tho' unintentionally ran—for, as was said, before his arrival at the falls, his mind was so abstracted, either by sleep, reading, or intense thought, that his bark got almost to the very fall, before he thought of his perilous situation. . . ."

21 **"vile, far-spent Volunteers":** Wheelock could have a venomous quill. Francis Quarles complained about Wheelock's letter of reference when he transferred to Yale: "You could not (everyone said that saw it) wrote any thing more prejudicial to my caracter unless you had accused me of murder."

23 **where the stump had been:** The plaque reads: "In 1772, a Freshman in Dartmouth College, on This Spot Felled a Giant Pine, from Which He Made a Canoe and in It Descended the River to Hartford, Connecticut. He Was a Traveller among the Indians, an Associate of John Paul Jones, an Officer under Captain Cook. Traversing all Oceans and Penetrating Remote Lands. He Foresaw and Foretold the Riches of the Pacific Coast and the Advantages of Commerce with the Far East. When About to Cross Africa He Died in Egypt, at the Age of Thirty-Seven. He, too, Heard the Voice Crying in the Wilderness. HE WAS THE DARTMOUTH SPIRIT." See *Quincy* [Mass.] *Patriot-Ledger*, 16 July 1963.

Another plaque, on Velvet Rocks near the so-called Ledyard Trail on the Appalachian Trail, read, "On or near this spot John Ledyard and some of his companions passed a night in the winter of 1771–72—thus anticipating the founding of the Dartmouth Outing Club."

23 **in the nude:** Many letters to the editor after an article by Brad Parks, "Different Strokes" in the May–June 2002 *Dartmouth Alumni Magazine,* referred to various times when canoeists got naked in Hartford (see, for example, November–December 2002), but the tradition was formalized after two courageous members of the 1991 trip paddled through Hartford in the nude. Another event involving nudity and the Ledyard Canoe Club is the annual Ledyard Challenge. Dartmouth undergraduates swim from the canoe club dock to Vermont and run back via Ledyard Bridge, all while wearing nothing but shoes. For more on Trip to the Sea, see Evan A. Woodward, "The Ledyard Cruise," in *Dartmouth Alumni Magazine,* May 1925 and "From Dartmouth to the Sea," *Life,* 11 May 1959.

23 **patron saint of freshmen:** "We'd treat him fine if he could come back now, wouldn't we," Frost asked in a 1945 letter to Ernest Hopkins, the president of Dartmouth. "I often go down to read his inscription on the stone by the river." Frost ended his 1955 commencement address with a reading of his poem "Departmental" and then

concluded: "And remember for me, will you, the one thing, that you've reached the place where you can listen to what anybody says and, you know, just pull it your way with one little, nice pull. That's what makes life."

24 **eighty-four and blind:** See Alice M. Walker, *Mary Mattoon and Her Hero of the Revolution* (Amherst, 1902).

Chapter 3—Before the Mast

27 **sail before the mast:** See Ernest E. Rogers, *Connecticut's Naval Office at New London During the War of the American Revolution* (New London, 1933); Nathaniel Shaw, Jr. *Mercantile Letter Book* (New London: New London County Historical Society; 1765–1783); Robert Owen Decker, *The New London Merchants, 1645–1909: The Rise and Decline of a Connecticut Port* (PhD dissertation, University of Connecticut, 1970); and *The Whaling City: A History of New London* (Chester, CT: Pequot Press, 1976).

27 **floating wooden world:** For an introduction to eighteenth-century blue-water sailing, see N.A.M. Rodger, *The Wooden World: An Anatomy of the Georgian Navy* (Annapolis: Naval Institute Press, 1986); Christopher Lloyd, *The British Seaman, 1200–1860: A Social Survey* (London: Collins, 1968); Dudley Pope, *Life in Nelson's Navy* (Annapolis: Naval Institute Press, 1981); Brian Lavery, *Nelson's Navy: The Ships, Men, and Organisation, 1793–1815* (Annapolis: Naval Institute Press, 1989); Peter Kemp, *The British Sailor: A Social History of the Lower Deck* (London: JM Dent, 1970); and Marcus Rediker, *Between the Devil and the Deep Blue Sea: Merchant Seamen, Pirates, and the Anglo-American Maritime World, 1700–1750* (Cambridge, England: Cambridge University Press, 1987).

27 **in a hemp hammock:** Hammocks were introduced to sailing in 1586 when a British slaver, John Hawkins, noticed the Arawak Indians in the West Indies used a sleeping device called a hammacoes.

29 **happy afternoons at her house:** Perhaps it was Rebecca who is the mother referred to in a letter to the editor written by a Stonington man in the November 1845 edition of *Revolutionary Reminiscence: A Monthly Journal of Literature, Science, and the Arts*. Eells' father was embroiled in a 1767 scandal relating to the funds raised in Great Britain by Samuel Occum and Nathaniel Whitaker. Without the trustees' knowledge, Whitaker gave £100 of it to Eells. Eells, with his son and son-in-law, planned to invest it, with half the profit going to Moor's Indian Charity School and half for himself. Eells did not repay the £100 until 1778.

30 **pride prevented Ledyard:** Peter Simon Pallas, the German professor whom Ledyard befriended in St. Petersburg in 1787, wrote about Ledyard: "When he was sent by his father to Europe, his restless and nearly savage character apparently led him to debaucheries of youth, of which his wandering life is the result."

31 **ships were Whitby cats:** Alan Villiers's description of a Whitby cat was perhaps the most eloquent: "A cat was a stumpy carrier with rather Dutch or Norwegian
lines—applecheeked forward but fine aft, deep in the hull, flat-floored to sit on the
bottom and stand up with minimum ballast. . . . Chief characteristics of the cat to out-
ward view were very bluff bows about the waterline, a straight somewhat unlovely cut-
water without any form of figurehead, and a slim, five-windowed stern. The two
hawseholes cut in the flat 'face' may have given them a sort of feline appearance—there
seems no other reason for their name—though it could have been derived from Ancient Norse and have nothing to do with four-legged cats at all."

33 **all stayed in England:** Woodruff, second in command of the *Columbia,* was
fired by the ship's captain, John Kendrick, a few weeks after sailing, and was sent be-
fore the mast and forced to sleep on the deck. Woodruff managed to flee the ship in
the Cape Verde Islands. See Frederic H. Howay, ed., *Voyages of the 'Columbia' to the
Northwest Coast 1787–1790 and 1790–1793* (Portland, OR: Oregon Historical Society
Press, 1990). In April 1825 Oliver Wolcott, Ledyard's old college roommate, wrote to
Jared Sparks from Litchfield, Conn. and mentioned that Woodruff was "of this Town."
It is not clear whether Wolcott meant that Woodruff was originally from Litchfield or
was actually living there in 1825.

Chapter 4—Their Native Courage

35 **unfurled her sails:** For the primary sources on the third Cook voyage, besides
Ledyard's book, see anonymous [John Rickman], *Journal of Captain Cook's Last Voyage*
(London: E. Newberry, 1781; repr., New York: Da Capo, 1967); W. Ellis, *An Authentic
Narrative of a Voyage Performed by Captain Cook* (London: G. Robinson, 1782); James
Cook and James King, *A Voyage to the Pacific Ocean* (London: G. Nicol and T. Cadell,
1784); James Burney, *A Chronological History of North-Eastern Voyages of Discovery*
(London: Payne & Foss, 1819; repr., New York: Da Capo, 1969); Heinrich Zimmer-
mann, *The Third Voyage of Captain Cook* (1781; repr., Fairfield, WA: Ye Galleon Press,
1988); "Journal of Thos. Edgar" in George Godwin, *Vancouver: A Life 1757–1798* (New
York: D. Appleton, 1931); James Trevenen, *A Memoir,* edited by Christopher Lloyd
(London: Navy Records Society, 1959); J. C. Beaglehole, *The Journals of Captain James
Cook: The Voyage of the Resolution and Discovery, 1776–1780* (Cambridge, England:
Cambridge University Press, 1967) and *Cook and the Russians: An Addendum to the
Hakluyt Society's Edition* (London: British Museum, 1973); George Gilbert, *Captain
Cook's Final Voyage,* edited by Christine Holmes (Horsham, England: Caliban Books,
1982); *The Charts and Coastal Views of Captain Cook's Voyages: The Voyage of the* Reso-
lution *and* Discovery *1776-1780,* ed. Andrew David (London: Hakluyt Society; and

Eleanor C. Nordyke, *Pacific Images: Views from Captain Cook's Third Voyage* (Oahu: Hawaiian Historical Society, 1999).

For biographies of Cook and his voyages, see A. Kippis, *Captain Cook's Voyages* (1788; repr., New York: Alfred A. Knopf, 1924); Christopher Lloyd, *Captain Cook* (London: Faber & Faber, 1952); Alan Villiers, *Captain James Cook* (New York: Charles Scribner's Sons, 1967); Richard Hough, *Captain James Cook* (New York: W.W. Norton, 1994); Tony Horwitz, *Blue Latitudes: Boldly Going Where Captain Cook Has Gone Before* (New York: Henry Holt, 2002); Nicholas Thomas, *Cook: The Extraordinary Voyages of Captain James Cook* (New York: Walker, 2003); Anne Salmond, *The Trial of the Cannibal Dog: The Remarkable Story of Captain Cook's Encounters in the South Seas* (New Haven: Yale University Press, 2003); and J. C. Beaglehole's entire oeuvre—*Cook the Writer* (Sydney: Sydney University Press, 1970); *The Death of Captain Cook* (Wellington, NZ: Alexander Turnbull Library, 1979); and *The Life of Captain James Cook* (Palo Alto: Stanford University Press, 1974).

For accounts of aspects of the voyage, see E. H. McCormick, *Omai: Pacific Envoy* (Auckland, NZ: University of Auckland, 1977); J.C.H. King, *Artificial Curiosities from the Northwest Coast of America: Native American Artifacts in the British Museum Collected on the Third Voyage of Captain James Cook* (London: British Museum, 1981); Marshall Sahlins, *Islands in History* (Chicago: University of Chicago Press, 1985) and *How "Natives" Think About Captain Cook, For Example* (Chicago: University of Chicago Press, 1995); Gananath Obeyesekere, *The Apotheosis of Captain Cook: European Mythmaking in the Pacific* (Princeton, NJ: Princeton University Press, 1992); Lynne Withey, *Voyages of Discovery: Captain Cook and the Exploration of the Pacific* (Berkeley: University of California Press, 1987); G. E. Manwaring, *My Friend the Admiral: The Life, Letters and Journals of Rear-Admiral James Burney* (London: George Routledge, 1931); *National Geographic*, February 1924 and January 1927; *National Geographic*, February 1924 and January 1927; Clifford Geertz, "Culture War" in *New York Review of Books*, 30 November 1995; Maurice Holmes, *Captain James Cook: A Bibliographical Excursion* (New York: Burt Franklin, 1952); and Adrienne L. Kaeppler, *Artificial Curiosities: Being An Exposition of Native Manufactures Collected on the Three Pacific Voyages of Captain James Cook, R.N. at the Bernice Pauahi Bishop Museum* (Honolulu: Bishop Museum Press, 1978).

For histories of European exploration in the Pacific, see Greg Dening, *Mr. Bligh's Bad Language: Passion, Power and Theatre on the Bounty* (Cambridge, England: Cambridge University Press, 1992); James Burney, *A Chronological History of the Voyages and Discoveries in the South Sea or Pacific Ocean* (London: Luke Hansard & Sons, 1816); J. C. Beaglehole, *The Exploration of the Pacific* (London: A & C Black, 1934); Bernard Smith, *European Vision and the South Pacific* (Oxford: Oxford University Press, 1960) and *Imaging the Pacific in the Wake of the Cook Voyages* (New Haven: Yale University Press, 1992); Jonathan Lamb, Vanessa Smith, and Nicholas Thomas, *Exploration and*

Exchange: A South Seas Anthology 1680–1900 (Chicago: University of Chicago Press, 2000); Margarette Lincoln, *Science and Exploration in the Pacific: European Voyages to the Southern Oceans in the Eighteenth Century* (London: Boydell Press, 1998); Jonathan Lamb, *Preserving the Self in the South Seas 1680–1840* (Chicago: University of Chicago Press, 2001); John Dunmore, *Pacific Explorer: The Life of Jean Francois de La Perouse 1741–1788* (Palmerston North, NZ: Dunmore Press, 1985); Joan Druett, *Rough Medicine: Surgeons at Sea in the Age of Sail* (New York: Routledge, 2000); *The Quest and Occupation of Tahiti by Emissaries of Spain during the Years 1772–1776*, translated and edited by Bolton Glanvill Corney (London: Hakluyt Society, 1913); George Robertson, *An Account of the Discovery of Tahiti*, edited by Oliver Weaver (London: Folio Society, 1955); Peter Whitfield, *New Found Lands: Maps in the History of Exploration* (New York: Routledge, 1998); O.H.K. Spate, *Paradise Found and Lost: The Pacific Since Magellan*, vol. 3 (Minneapolis: University of Minnesota, 1988); Robin Fisher, *Contact and Conflict: Indian-European Relations in British Columbia, 1774–1890* (Vancouver: University of British Columbia Press, 1977); Robin Fisher and Hugh Johnston, *Captain James Cook and His Times* (Seattle: University of Washington Press, 1979); V. L. Denton, *The Far West Coast* (Toronto: JM Dent, 1924); Warren L. Cook, *Flood Tide of Empire: Spain and the Pacific Northwest, 1543–1819* (New Haven, CT: Yale University Press, 1973); and the works of Glyndwr Williams, *The Prize of All Oceans: The Dramatic True Story of Commodore Anson's Voyage Round the World and How He Seized the Spanish Treasure Galleon* (New York: Viking, 2000); *The Great South Sea: English Voyages and Encounters 1750–1750* (New Haven: Yale University Press, 1997); *Voyages of Delusion: The Quest for the Northwest Passage* (New Haven: Yale University Press, 2002); and *Pacific Empires: Essays in Honour of Glyndwr Williams*, edited by Alan Frost and Jane Samson (Vancouver: University of British Columbia, 1999).

35 **one of London's debtor prisons:** For more on the King's Bench and the Fleet prisons, see James Zug, *Squash: A History of the Game* (New York: Scribner, 2003).

37 **donated a peacock and peahen:** The Earl might have also given Cook a pair of tortoises which were left in Tonga. One tortoise became, if the story is correct, Cook's last surviving shipmate, as he lived until May 1966.

38 **most elaborate one:** Henning Henningsen, *Crossing the Equator: Sailors' Baptism and other Initiation Rites* (Copenhagen: Munksgaard, 1961).

39 **picturesque village:** Mai and Charles Clerke, perhaps as a unique way of signing a guest book, scratched their names on a windowpane at the house of the deputy governor-general in Cape Town. In the 1850s the building became the property of South African Bank, which later transferred the pane to a local museum, where it was lost. Bunting Hayden-Whyte, the music historian, once penned a paradelle poem about the graffiti.

48 **"dreaming no doubt of love":** Perhaps referring to his relationship with Rebecca Eells of Stonington, Ledyard added, "Love like this is not to be found in those countries where the boasted refinements of sentiment too often circumscribe the purity of affection and narrow it away to mere conjugal fidelity."

48 **fusillade of grapeshot:** Carrying native passengers was a common practice. On the first voyage, Cook had taken two men, Tupaia, a brilliant high priest, and his servant Taiato, from Tahiti, but both men had died from malaria at Batavia. Bougainville, the French navigator who reached Tahiti a year after Wallis, brought Ahutoru from Tahiti home to Paris. Ahutoru returned with Marion but died of smallpox en route in Madagascar. Hitihiti, a Borabora youngster, sailed with Cook on the second expedition, but opted to be dropped off at home after six months at sea rather than continue on to England. De Surville kidnapped a Maori chief, Ranginui, who died of scurvy on the way to South America.

Chapter 5—Dancing Through Life

59 **"convey'd to endless generations":** When a French ship visited Tongatapu in 1793, astonishingly there was hardly any venereal disease on the island.

62 **the *Aguila* sailed home:** One seaman on the second voyage, a Basque lieutenant named Don Juan Ruiz de Apodaco, became the Viceroy of Mexico and New Spain.

64 **got his hands tattooed:** See R.W.B. Scutt and Christopher Gotch, *Art, Sex and Symbol: The Mystery of Tattooing* (South Brunswick: A.S. Barnes, 1974).

65 **internal Tahitian power struggle:** The only actual fighting occurred in mid-September when, according to William Griffin, the *Resolution*'s cooper, Lieutenant Williamson, fought a duel with Molesworth Phillips over an unknown cause. Both missed when they fired. No one else mentioned the duel.

Chapter 6—Soothed a Homesick Heart

84 **just a single village.** Contact with Alaskan natives was stumbling and misinterpreted. One day in Prince William Sound, Ledyard and John Gore and a few other officers went bird hunting in the *Resolution*'s pinnace. Several boats of Indians greeted them, but Gore, afraid the Indians wanted to fight rather than trade, ordered a hasty retreat to the ship. When the sailors realized that the Indian's intentions were not hostile, they reversed course and headed towards the Indians. But it was too late. As Ledyard wrote with haunting simplicity, the Indians "turned their boats about and were soon out of sight."

Chapter 7—Grief on Every Countenance

91 **handful of firsthand accounts:** There was also William Bayly, *The Original Astronomical Observations* (London, 1782), but it did not concern itself much with the events at Hawaii.

Beaglehole, a figure who loomed over mid-twentieth-century Cook studies, did not appreciate Ledyard's point of view. He called Ledyard's 1783 *Journal* a "nonsensical account" and "a worthless production" and believed that it was Ledyard's patriotism that spurred him "to slip in a few episodes discreditable to the British." Beaglehole, however, was no enthusiast of the able seaman and marines. He was almost repulsed by the common sailors, as he wrote in the introduction to the two-volume third voyage journals: "They were also no great respecters of the blood of other people, they had no great plans in view, were not gifted with foresight, got into a scuffle with remarkable facility—were in fact ignorant, irresponsible, and often stupid."

92 **Ledyard stood alone:** See James J. Jarves, *History of the Hawaiian or Sandwich Islands* (Boston: Tappan & Dennet, 1843) and Ephraim Eveleth, *A History of the Sandwich Islands* (Philadelphia: American Sunday-School Union, 1839).

96 **the legendary waves:** Samwell, in his diary entry of 22 January 1779, gave a long and apt description of surfing which concluded: "Thus these People find one of their Chief amusements in that which to us presented nothing but Horror & Destruction, and we saw with astonishment young boys & Girls about 9 or ten years of age playing amid such tempestuous Waves that the hardiest of our seamen would have trembled to face, as to be involved in them among the Rocks, on which they broke with a tremendous Noise, they could look upon as no other than certain death. So true it is that many seeming difficulties are easily overcome by dexterity & Preseverance."

97 **returned to the bay:** Ledyard wrote, "our Indians were extremely fatigued though they had no baggage, and we were well convinced that though like the Stag and the Lion they appear fit for expedition and toil, yet like those animals they are fit for neither, while the humbly Mule will persevere in both."

98 **"hove the wood and images back":** Ledyard's account of the fence incident is a centerpiece of a long debate over the causes of Cook's death. It does not square with the other journal keepers. Zimmermann wrote that the people "had shown signs of a secret annoyance," but King said in his private journal that the Hawaiians were indifferent to the whole matter and actually assisted in the removal of the fence. Ledyard, seemingly present at the scene, used the incident as an explanation for Cook's death, but, despite his criticisms, he still found the Captain a worthy leader. In 1788 he wrote in his diary that he admired "his Abilities & good Sense, [that he was] accustomed to think for himself & rely upon his own Opinion. It rendered him equally penetrating, cautious & bold."

101 **biggest stories of the century:** Jared Sparks agreed that it could not "be inferred with certainty from anything Ledyard says, that he was in that part of the fray. But the confidence and particularity with which he speaks would seem to indicate actual observation." See J. Kenneth Munford, "Did John Ledyard Witness Captain Cook's Death?" in *Pacific Northwest Quarterly,* April 1963.

Chapter 8—Not Short of Mutiny

111 **as leaky as ever:** Captain V. I. Shmalev at Petropavlovsk reported to Moscow in 1780 that the sailors had told him that "they suffered great exhaustion from the ice and cold air. Thus, during the whole month of July they lived in danger and despair; and finally, in great need."

111 **prevent any unauthorized versions:** The official admiralty instructions, issued on July 6, 1776, read that Cook upon arrival in England must be "taking care, before you leave the sloop, to demand from the officers and petty officers, the logbooks and journals they may have kept, and to seal them up for our inspection; and enjoining them, and the whole crew, not to divulge where they have been, until they shall have permission so to do." Evidently, the admiralty did not think the crew would keep journals. James King, writing in the official 1784 account of the voyage, knew otherwise. "The execution of these orders seemed to require some delicacy, as well as firmness. I could not be ignorant, that the greatest part of our officers, and several of the seamen, had amused themselves with writing accounts of our proceedings for their own private satisfaction, or that of their friends, which they might be unwilling, in their present form, to have submitted to the inspection of strangers. On the other hand, I could not, consistently with the instructions we had received, leave in their custody papers, which, either from carelessness or design, might fall into the hands of printers, and give rife to spurious and imperfect accounts of the voyage, to the discredit of our labors, and perhaps to the prejudice of officers, who, though innocent, might be suspected of having been the authors of such publications."

113 **each square inch:** "The fur of them were more butiful than any fur I had ever seen," wrote William Clark after seeing sea otter pelts when the Lewis & Clark expedition wintered over at the mouth of the Columbia River. "It is the richest and I think the most delightfull fur in the world at least I cannot form an idea of any more so, it is deep thick silky in the extream and strong."

Chapter 9—Crooked Billet

118 **tedium of a soldier:** Ledyard made a lasting friend at Plymouth, William Davids, a captain in the marines. Davids offered to join Ledyard on his African expedition in 1788 and Ledyard wrote to him from Alexandria.

119 **north coast of Long Island:** Perhaps they sailed via Newfoundland, as Ledyard wrote in his diary in 1788 about once seeing ice north of Belle Isle Strait.

121 **sailed off with Mann:** Jerusha was named after her mother, Jerusha Howell Moore, Micah Moore's first wife. She returned at the end of the war, died at age twenty-one, and was buried at Mattituck.

121 **"All my comfort":** "Who can but admire and wonder at the facts related of the heroism and courage which marked the eventful lives of our Revolutionary mothers and wives, in the dark years of that sanguine war," wrote local historian Augustus Griffin in 1857. "What hours of anguish! What floods of tears must they have shed beneath their lonely roofs, during that eight years of desolation, unheard-of cruelty and injustice inflicted on our country by the heartless foe."

122 **earning the nickname:** It was claimed in an 1832 article in the *New York Sun* that a nephew of William Ledyard's was found by the British in the fort's gun room and bribed his way to freedom. Another legend was that the only reason the Hempstead house in New London survived the battle was because Arnold found a hot meal on the dining room table and sat down to eat. In 1830 the town of Groton honored the memory of those slain by building a stone obelisk, which was extended in 1881 to its present height of one hundred and thirty-four feet. William Ledyard's sword resides at the Bill Memorial Library in Groton in the winters and at the Fort Griswold Memorial in the summers. The Avery house is still extant, but was moved in 1971 to its present site below the fort. In 1836 the town of North Groton was renamed Ledyard in honor of William Ledyard; the high school's nickname is the Colonels. Today Ledyard is the home of Foxwoods, one of the largest casinos in the world. See *Narrative of Jonathan Rathbun* (New London, 1840).

123 **eschewed ordinary professions:** Jared Sparks wrote of Ledyard's personality: "The peculiar frame of his mind and temper was such, that nothing would have been more idle, either in himself or any other person, than to think of chaining him down to any of the dull courses of life, to which the great mass of mankind are contented to resort, as the means of acquiring a fortune, gaining a competence, or driving want from the door. That he must provide for himself by his own efforts, was a proposition too forcibly impressed upon him to be denied; but there seemed not a single propensity of his nature, which inclined him to direct these efforts in the same manner as other people, or to attain common ends by common means. Poverty and privation were trifles of no weight with him, compared with the irksome necessity of walking in the same path that all the world walked in, and doing things as all the world had done them before. He thought this a very tame pursuit, unworthy of a rational man, whose soul should be fired with a nobler ambition."

124 **"exclusive right of publishing":** In October 1781 the Connecticut assembly had granted a special five-year copyright for Andrew Law, who had published in New

Haven a collection of church hymns. See, Hellmut Lehmann-Haupt, *The Book in America: A History of the Making, the Selling and the Collecting of Books in the United States* (1937; repr., New York: R.R. Bowker, 1939); Lawrence C. Wroth, *An American Bookshelf 1755* (Philadelphia: University of Pennsylvania Press, 1934); and Charles Evans, *American Bibliography*, vol. 6, 1779–1785 (New York: Peter Smith, 1941).

128 **a verbatim sentence:** Ledyard mentioned Hawkesworth in a discussion of circumcision practices, chiding him for assuming circumcision had no religious basis. Ever the reporter, Ledyard did note that during the circumcision "the Otaheitean has only an oyster-shell; and the member is a delicate, a nervous and sensible member."

128 **deserved the blame:** Ledyard rarely mentioned his 1783 *Journal* in writing. In November 1784 he asked his cousin Isaac to give Captain Abonville, whom he met in Lorient and who carried his letters to America, "two setts of my *Journal.*" In 1786 he gave a copy to Thomas Jefferson. When he asked for it back, Jefferson told Ledyard, "I am sorry it is not in my power to send you your book. Very soon after I received it from you I lent it to Madame de la fayette, who has been obliged to lend it from hand to hand & has never returned it."

128 **Because of his appropriations:** See F. W. Howay, "Authorship of the Anonymous Account of Captain Cook's Last Voyage," in *Washington Historical Quarterly* 12, no. 1 (January 1921).

129 **dedicated the book:** Ledyard, at his florid best, wrote in his dedication that Trumbull was "a testimony of that original urbanity and dignified familiarity which distinguishes the magistrate from the tyrant—the people from slaves, and is still the boon of which every son of this country participates. Such virtues, like the rose in the bud, are lovely in ordinary life; but when transferred to the bosoms of the fair and great, become by the contrasting change more perfectly beautiful."

130 **visited his beloved cousins:** Isaac had trained as a doctor in New York under Dr. John Bard, a pioneering hygienist in New York. During the war Isaac served as a surgeon's mate in the Hairy Caps, a New York infantry division captained by his brother Ben and known for their furry hats. He was eventually stationed at West Point. Ben, leading the Hairy Caps, had his sword shot off during the Battle of Fort Washington and his horse killed from under him in the Battle of Monmouth. In 1779 he retired due to ill-health and returned to Matawan, New Jersey and his wife and four children to run a salt works and general store.

During his visit, Ledyard roasted a pig Tahitian style in the ground with hot stones, drank rum, played with Ben's children, and vigorously flirted with "Good Nel of the Point," Eleanor Forman. According to a Philip Freneau biographer, Mary Austin, Ledyard once stealthily rode up behind Forman. She "suddenly felt herself embraced most warmly," and then Ledyard rode off. "Her feeling of indignation cooled down later on, upon learning that the author of the affair was her wild-fun-loving relative; for no one could be angry with Jack Ledyard."

Ben Ledyard's brother-in-law Samuel Forman, then eighteen, was bowled over by his famous relative and jumbled up Ledyard's biography when he later wrote that Ledyard's "history at that time was very interesting. He was well educated, wrote a good hand—he was lively, talkative, sensible & facetious. I believe that he took French leave of his family & left College & took a canoe & descended Connecticut River & found his way to London & became acquainted with the great Captain Cook, the Navigator. I believe he went two Voyages & was with him when he was killed at Otaheit by the natives!" When Ledyard left, Forman wrote, "I brushed his Coat as he put it on."

130 **every day in the summer:** See David McCullough, *John Adams* (New York: Simon & Schuster, 2001), Ron Chernow, *Alexander Hamilton* (New York: Penguin Press, 2004); and Russell F. Weigley, ed., *Philadelphia: A 300-Year History* (New York: W.W. Norton, 1982).

132 **"first Conveyance some Cash":** Freneau commented that Ledyard "knew [his cousins] would prevent this Embarrassement—as readily at least as any one but himself would the case reversed. But while with them he so totally devoted himself to freindly Enjoyments, thus no Pecuniary Consideration could approach him."

133 **barely any thought of directly trading:** For more on the origins of the China trade and the fur trade, see E. James Ferguson, John Catanzariti, Elizabeth M. Nuxoll, Mary A. Gallagher, et al, eds., *The Papers of Robert Morris* (Pittsburgh: University of Pittsburgh, 1978); Philip Chadwick Foster Smith, *The Empress of China* (Philadelphia: Philadelphia Maritime Museum, 1984); Jean Gordon Lee, *Philadelphians and the China Trade 1784–1844* (Philadelphia: Philadelphia Museum of Art, 1984); Clarence L. Ver Steeg, "Financing and Outfitting the First United States Ship to China," *Pacific Historical Review* XXII, no. 1 (February 1953); Josiah Quincy, *The Journals of Major Samuel Shaw* (Boston: Wm. Crosby and H.P. Nichols, 1847); Tyler Dennett, *Americans in Eastern Asia: A Critical Study* (New York: Farrar, Straus & Giroux, 1979); Carlos A. Schwantes, ed., *Encounters with a Distant Land: Exploration and the Great Northwest* (Moscow: University of Idaho Press, 1994); Foster Rhea Dulles, *China and America: The Story of Their Relations since 1784* (Princeton: Princeton University Press, 1946) and *America in the Pacific: A Century of Expansion* (Boston: Houghton Mifflin, 1938); John Kuo Wei Tchen, *New York before Chinatown: Orientalism and the Shaping of American Culture, 1776–1882* (Baltimore: Johns Hopkins Press, 1999); James R. Gibson, *Otter Skins, Boston Ships and China Goods: The Maritime Fur Trade of the Northwest Coast 1785–1841* (Seattle: University of Washington, 1992); Samuel Eliot Morison, *The Maritime History of Massachusetts, 1783–1860* (Boston: Houghton Mifflin, 1921); Colin G. Calloway, *One Vast Winter Count: The Native American West before Lewis and Clark* (Lincoln, NE: University of Nebraska Press, 2003); Samuel B.

Woodhouse, "The Voyage of the Empress of China," *Pennsylvania Magazine of History and Biography*, no. 63 (1939); and Robert Kingery Buell and Charlotte Northcote Skladal, *Sea Otters and the China Trade* (New York: David McKay, 1968).

For two books that have a romantic view of Ledyard, see Sydney Greenbie and Marjorie Barstow Greenbie, *Gold of Ophir: The China Trade in the Making of America* (New York: Wilson-Erickson, 1937)—"The world was surfeited with gaudy promises. But Ledyard still had the faith born of experience, transfigured by youth and genius"— and Agnes Danforth Hewes, *Two Oceans to Canton: The Story of the Old China Trade* (New York: Alfred A. Knopf, 1944), which is dedicated "To The Shining Memory of John Ledyard."

For more on the people involved, see Clarence L. Ver Steeg, *Robert Morris: Revolutionary Financier* (New York: Farrar, Straus & Giroux, 1954); Frederick Wagner, *Robert Morris: Audacious Patriot* (New York: Dodd, Mead, 1976); and Robert F. Jones, *The King of the Alley: William Duer—Politician, Entrepreneur, and Speculator 1768–1799* (Philadelphia: American Philosophical Society, 1992).

134 **hit the papers:** On 9 September the *Pennsylvania Packet* picked up on the *Salem Gazette* story. News of the impending launch of the Ledyard trip impelled a rival group of Boston merchants to start their own China venture. In December 1783 the *Harriet* sailed from Boston with an entirely different plan of profiting from the China trade. Isaac Sears, the *Harriet*'s owner, hoped to take American ginseng to Europe where he could supply European ships going to China. When severe winter weather prevented the *Harriet* from leaving early enough in the fall, Sears sent her to Cape Town to intercept the Canton-bound ships. There she off-loaded her ginseng cargo at a good price.

136 **fiercest winter:** David M. Ludlum, *Early American Winters, 1604–1820* (Boston: American Meteorological Society, 1960).

137 **filed lawsuits:** When Lafayette contacted Parker in 1822 on behalf of Jared Sparks, Parker was unapologetic, writing only that Ledyard had "offered his services to a company of merchants in New York to conduct an Expedition to the North west Coast of America to prucure furs, especially Sea Otter Skins for the Chinese market, & he was the first person who proposed this trade to the merchants of the U. States."

138 **sailing for Spain:** Freneau commented: "Having as in duty bound made the first offering of his service to his native country, he hastened to Europe where genius had more friends and Enterprize a better friend to prosecute his plan."

Chapter 10—Bought for a Bagatelle

139 **unique aura:** Jared Sparks described Ledyard in his typical style: "His manly form, mild but animated and expressive eye, perfect self-possession, a boldness not ob-

trusive, but showing a consciousness of his proper dignity, an independent spirit, and a glow of enthusiasm giving life to his conversation and his whole deportment."

144 **"barbarous amusement":** Ledyard wrote: "Riley has not those characteristics you might suppose. His education is contracted: he is capricious, severe, & arrogant: ordinary in his person, and extremely forbidding in his address—en fine, as Marplot says." Marplot, a character in the 1709 play *The Busy Body*, by Susannah Centlivre, was an officious meddler. There are streets in Havana, Madrid, Barcelona, and Cadiz bearing Riley's name.

145 **smugly told his brothers:** While in Lorient, Ledyard complained about not receiving letters from his family. He tried to face the lack of news positively, as he wrote to his cousin Isaac: "I am determined to Sit down—not despondingly, dejectedly, or supinely—what a vile row of adverbs, but contemplatively, chearily, industriously—do but see the Contrast!—and yet these are adverbs too."

149 **Paris was an explanation:** G. K. Chesterton popularized this proverb in 1908. See Simon Schama, *Citizens: A Chronicle of the French Revolution* (New York: Alfred A. Knopf, 1989) and Patrice Higonnet, *Paris: Capital of the World*, translated by Arthur Goldhammer (Cambridge: Harvard University Press, 2002).

150 **mismatched pair:** See Saul K. Padover, *The Complete Jefferson: Containing his Major Writings, Published and Unpublished, Except his Letters* (New York: Tudor, 1943); Julian Boyd, ed., *The Papers of Thomas Jefferson* (Princeton: Princeton University Press, 1950); James A. Bear Jr. and Lucia C. Stanton, *Jefferson's Memorandum Books: Accounts, with Legal Records and Miscellany, 1767–1826* (Princeton: Princeton University Press, 1997); Douglas L. Wilson and Lucia Stanton, eds., *Jefferson Abroad* (New York: Modern Library, 1999); Marie Kimball, *Jefferson: The Scene in Europe, 1784–1789* (New York: Coward-McCann, 1950); Dumas Malone, *Jefferson and the Rights of Man* (Boston: Little, Brown, 1951); Fawn Brodie, *Thomas Jefferson: An Intimate History* (New York: W.W. Norton, 1974); Andrew Burstein, *The Inner Jefferson: Portrait of a Grieving Optimist* (Charlottesville: University Press of Virginia, 1995); Willard Sterne Randall, *Thomas Jefferson: A Life* (New York: Henry Holt, 1993); Joseph J. Ellis, *American Sphinx: The Character of Thomas Jefferson* (New York: Alfred A. Knopf, 1996); Foster Rhea Dulles, *Americans Abroad: Two Centuries of European Travel* (Ann Arbor: University of Michigan Press, 1964); E. M. Halliday, *Understanding Thomas Jefferson* (New York: Harper-Collins, 2001); and Howard C. Rice Jr., *L'Hotel De Langeac, 1785–1789* (Monticello, VA: Thomas Jefferson Memorial Foundation, 1947) and *Thomas Jefferson's Paris* (Princeton: Princeton University Press, 1976).

152 **"save half a Crown":** To explain how Ledyard was able to charm so many famous people, Philip Freneau wrote: "He was, unquestionably, a presentable, courteous, and charming man, one of those whose blandness and decision of character passes them into the ranks of the wealthy and educated as a matter of course."

153 **the legendary Benjamin Franklin:** See Alfred Owen Aldridge, *Franklin and his French Contemporaries* (New York University Press, 1957); Susan Mary Alsop, *Yankees at the Court: The First Americans in Paris* (Garden City, NY: Doubleday, 1982); Claude-Anne Lopez, *Mon Cher Papa: Franklin and the Ladies of Paris* (New Haven, CT: Yale University Press, 1966); Ronald W. Clark, *Benjamin Franklin: A Biography* (New York: Random House, 1983); Walter Isaacson, *Benjamin Franklin: An American Life* (New York: Simon & Schuster, 2003); and Bernard Bailyn, *To Begin Anew: The Genius and Ambiguities of the American Founders* (New York: Alfred A. Knopf, 2003).

153 **frequent dinner companion:** See Harlow Giles Unger, *Lafayette* (New York: John Wiley, 2002) and Louis Gottschalk, *Lafayette between the American and the French Revolution, 1783–1789* (Chicago: University of Chicago Press, 1950).

157 **bright star in the Parisian firmament:** See Janette Taylor, *Life and Correspondence of John Paul Jones* (New York: A. Chandler, 1830); Lincoln Lorenz, *John Paul Jones: Fighter for Freedom and Glory* (Annapolis: United States Naval Institute, 1943); Samuel Eliot Morrison, *John Paul Jones: A Sailor's Biography* (Boston: Little, Brown, 1959); and Evan Thomas, *John Paul Jones: Sailor, Hero, Father of the American Navy* (New York: Simon & Schuster, 2003).

159 **suffered a third strike:** Jared Sparks mentioned a fourth attempt on Ledyard's part after the Jones company failed. He apparently approached a "mercantile company in Paris." "Some progress was made," wrote Sparks, but "several months were passed in unavailing efforts to conquer obstacles, which seemed to thicken as he advanced, and in vainly striving to enlighten ignorance and overcome prejudice, till his perseverance could hold out no longer."

Chapter 11—More Shirts than Shillings

161 **fever about furs:** Diplomacy briefly became the next stream John Ledyard paddled. John Lamb offered Ledyard a job as his secretary. Lamb, his dramatic entrance at Jefferson's house notwithstanding, was on his way to Algiers to ransom the twenty-one American sailors of the *Dauphin* and *Maria* who had been captured by the dey, put in chains and forced into hard labor. Such an offer seemed providential at first. "I shall inter this hobby at Paris and attend Mr. Lamb to Africa," Ledyard told Isaac. But knowing Lamb's "unhappy Vulgarity" of manner and dogmatic opinions, Ledyard declined the job. It was a good decision, for Lamb's mission to Algiers was a disaster. He offered $200 per man for ransom; the dey wanted $6,000 for a master and $1,500 for an able seaman. Lamb confided in the British consul in Algiers, which led to the conniving consul urging the dey to seize more American ships. Lamb left in disgrace and the Americans remained captives for another decade.

162 **a willing listener:** For more on Jefferson and the history of western exploration, see Donald Jackson, *Thomas Jefferson & the Stony Mountains: Exploring the West from Monticello* (Urbana: University of Illinois Press, 1981); Anthony F. C. Wallace, *Jefferson and the Indians: The Tragic Fate of the First Americans* (Cambridge: Harvard University Press, 1999); Bernard DeVoto, *The Course of Empire* (Boston: Houghton Mifflin, 1952); Peter S. Onuf, *Jefferson's Empire: The Language of American Nationhood* (Charlottesville: University Press of Virginia, 2000); and William H. Goetzmann, *New Lands, New Men: America and the Second Great Age of Discovery* (New York: Viking, 1986). For a less rigorous, more romantic discussion of Ledyard and his role in the settling of the west, see Fred Lockley, *Oregon Trail Blazers* (New York: Knickerbocker Press, 1929) and Jeannette Mirsky, *The Westward Crossings: Balboa, Mackenzie, Lewis & Clark* (New York: Alfred A. Knopf, 1946).

164 **unofficial Russian representative:** In April 1816 Jefferson reminiscenced about Paris in a letter to John Adams: "Did I know Baron Grimm while at Paris? Yes, most intimately. He was the pleasantest, and most conversible member of the diplomatic corps while I was there: a man of good fancy, acuteness, irony, cunning, and egotism: no heart, not much of any science, yet enough of every one to speak it's language. His forte was Belles-lettres, painting and sculpture. In these he was the oracle of the society, and as such the empress Catharine's private correspondent and factor in all things not diplomatic. It was thro' him I got her permission for poor Ledyard to go to Kamschatka, and cross over thence to the Western coast of America, in order to penetrate across our continent in the opposite direction to that afterwards adopted for Lewis and Clarke: which permission she withdrew after he had got within 200 miles of Kamschatska, had him siesed, brought back and set down in Poland."

165 **foot tattooed on his arm:** He also explained to Ledyard a simple way of measuring the breadth of a river. When John Quincy Adams later heard of these tattooing plans via Nathaniel Cutting, he wrote in his diary that "whatever benefit his success might have procured to mankind, his journal upon his skin would not, I think, have been worth much."

165 **for the first time in five months:** Philip Freneau explained the apparent lack of letters in the winter of 1785–1786 as a part of Ledyard's nature: "In his great designs, generous, as they were, the beneficence, the Pride, or the avarice, of his fellow creatures, furnished the fund, on which he relied for success. It was usual, with him, when his heart was elated, by prospects uncommonly bright, or depressed by the reverse, to remain silent; leaving it to events, to speak for themselves,—On such importance occasions, or else, and especially in the latter case, to indulge in a careless, shandian kind of style, and in that sprightly humour, sooth his own anxiety, and conceal it from his friends, towards whom, his tenderness, served generally, as an interdiction, to any melancholy narrative of himself—so that when he appeared in this style, it maybe

presumed of him, that his situation at that time, was either distressing, or eventful. The L'Orient, failure must have had more bitterness, in it, that almost any thing, he endured, in his travels; and it is expected must have caused some debate in himself, of perservering, in his designs; for he seems, on his arrival in Paris, to have retired within himself, and to have shut out comfort, at least, if not hope. He must have remained some months, in all the severity of want, with its consequent indignities, whilst he was brooding over new schemes of adventure."

166 **"man was much hurt"**: After copying this letter into his notebook, Jared Sparks added in the margin: "Suppose the man had fallen on his forehead & been killed—that the horse had recovered & run off—that he had been found about him—at that hour. here w^d have been a singular adventure truly. a pedestrian from Connecticut &c &c."

168 **dashed to London:** Ledyard left Paris so quickly that, as he wrote a year later, "When I left france my accounts were not closed & from y't day to this I know not whether I owe france or france me."

168 **christened by Sir Joseph:** See John Keay, *The Honourable Company: A History of the English East India Company* (London: HarperCollins, 1991). Besides the John Company, as the EIC was called, fur traders also had to contend with the South Sea Company, which controlled the waters along the western littoral of North America. Few fur traders bothered to obtain a license from the South Sea Company.

For more on London, see John Brewer, *The Pleasures of the Imagination: English Culture in the Eighteenth Century* (New York: Farrar, Straus & Giroux, 1997).

170 **Cook man nonpareil:** see Harold B. Carter, *Sir Joseph Banks 1743–1820* (London: British Museum, 1988) and *Sir Joseph Banks (1743–1820): A Guide to Biographical and Bibliographical Sources* (Winchester: St. Paul's Bibliographies, 1987); Joseph Banks, *The Letters of Sir Joseph Banks: A Selection, 1768–1820*, edited by Neil Chambers (London: Imperial College Press, 2000); John Gascoigne, *Joseph Banks and the English Enlightenment: Useful Knowledge and Polite Culture* (Cambridge, England: Cambridge University Press, 1994); and Patrick O'Brian, *Joseph Banks: A Life* (Chicago: University of Chicago Press, 1987).

172 **"some damned riddle":** Henry Beaufoy wrote in 1790 that Ledyard's plan was "frustrated by the racpacity of a Custom-house Officer, who had seized and detained the vessel for reasons which on legal inquiry proved to be frivolous."

174 **practising seriously on your fiddle:** Devoto, in endnotes to *The Course of Empire*, ruminates at length about the chances of Ledyard crossing North America.

176 **"wearing Armenian dress":** "A Relative," *The Life and Adventures of the Celebrated Walking Stewart: Including his Travels in the East Indies, Turkey, Germany & America* (London: E. Wheatley, 1822). Stewart, in a Ledyard-like style, told the directors of the East India Company in his letter of resignation that he "was born for higher

pursuits than to be a copier of invoices and bills of lading to a company of grocers, haberdashers and cheesemongers."

177 **treason trial in Richmond:** See Curtis Carroll Davis, "The Curious Colonel Langborn: Wanderer and Enigma from the Revolutionary Period" in the *Virginia Magazine of History and Biography* vol. 64, no. 4 (1956).

177 **fifty-mile shortcut:** In the spring of 2002 two Dartmouth undergraduates, Peter Bohler and Peter Brewitt, hiked and biked much of the Ledyard's route around the Gulf of Bothnia. For more on Lapland, see Ornulv Vorren and Ernest Manker, *Lapp Life and Customs: A Survey* (Oxford: Oxford University Press, 1962) and Halliday Sutherland, *Lapland Journey* (New York: Dodd, Mead, 1938).

179 **marshy delta:** See Anthony Cross, *By the Banks of the Neva: Chapters from the Lives and Careers of the British in Eighteenth-Century Russia* (Cambridge, England: Cambridge University Press, 1997), *Russia under Western Eyes 1517–1825* (New York: St. Martin's, 1971), and *St. Petersburg, 1703–1825* (Basingstoke, UK: Palgrave Macmillan, 2003); W. Bruce Lincoln, *Sunlight at Midnight: St. Petersburg and the Rise of Modern Russia* (New York: Basic Books, 2000); Arthur L. George, *St. Petersburg: Russia's Window to the Future, the First Three Centuries* (New York: Taylor Trade, 2003); Henri Troyat, *Catherine the Great*, translated by Joan Pinkham (New York: E.P. Dutton, 1980); Anna M. Babey, *Americans in Russia 1776–1917: A Study of the American Travellers in Russia from the American Revolution to the Russian Revolution* (New York: Comet Press, 1938); James R. Masterson and Helen Brower, *Bering's Successors, 1745–1780: Contributions of Peter Simon Pallas to the History of Russian Exploration toward Alaska* (Seattle: University of Washington Press, 1948); and Carol Urness, ed., *A Naturalist in Russia: Letters from Peter Simon Pallas to Thomas Pennant* (Minneapolis: University of Minnesota Press, 1967). A number of animals today bear Pallas' name: there is a Pallas cat, warbler, gull, sandgrouse and reed bunting.

182 **robbed of fifty rubles:** While in Russia, Ledyard followed the Gregorian Old Style calendar. I have kept all the dates from leaving St. Petersburg to returning to London in Old Style, eleven days behind the U.S. calendar.

Chapter 12—Double Relish

185 **eat and spend the night:** See an account of the usual kibitka route across Russia in the meticulously detailed itinerary in Martin Sauer, *An Account of a Geographical and Astronomical Expedition* (London: T. Cadell & W. Davies, 1802; repr., Richmond Publishing, 1972).

For more on Siberia, see: Gavriil A. Sarychev, *A Journey Through the Northeastern Part of Siberia,* (London, 1806); L'Abbe Chappe D'Auteroche, *A Journey into Siberia* (London: T. Jefferys, 1774); John Bell, *A Journey from St Petersburg to Pekin: 1719–22*

(New York: Barnes & Noble, 1966); M. De Lesseps, *Travels in Kamtschatka during the Years 1787 and 1788* (London: J. Johnson, 1790); Edward D. Clarke, *Travels in Russia, Tartary and Turkey* (New York, 1813); Hubert Howe Bancroft, *History of Alaska 1730–1885* (San Francisco: A. L. Bancroft, 1886); Emil Lengyel, *Siberia* (New York: Random House, 1943); Marc Raeff, *Imperial Russia, 1682–1825: The Coming of Age of Modern Russia* (New York: Alfred A. Knopf, 1971) and *Catherine the Great: A Profile* (New York: Hill & Wang, 1972); Orlando Figes, *Natasha's Dance: A Cultural History of Russia* (New York: Henry Holt, 2002); James Forsyth, *History of the Peoples of Siberia: Russia's North Asian Colony 1581–1990* (Cambridge, England: Cambridge University Press, 1992); Benson Bobrick, *East of the Sun: The Epic Conquest and Tragic History of Siberia* (New York: Poseiden Press, 1992); Galya Diment and Yuri Slezkine, eds., *Between Heaven and Hell: The Myth of Siberia in Russian Culture* (New York: St. Martin's, 1993); Alan Wood, ed., *The Development of Siberia: People and Resources* (New York: St. Martin's, 1989) and *The History of Siberia: From Russian Conquest to Revolution* (London: Routledge, 1991); and Walther Kirchner, *Commercial Relations Between Russia and Europe 1400–1800: Collected Essays* (Bloomington: Indiana University Press, 1966), *Studies in Russian-American Commerce, 1820–1860* (Leiden: E.J. Brill, 1975), *and A Siberian Journey: The Journal of Hans Jakob Fries, 1774–1776* (London: Frank Cass, 1974).

For travel writing, see Anna Reid, *The Shaman's Coat: A Native History of Siberia* (New York: Walker, 2003); Jeffrey Tayler, "White Nights in Siberia," *Atlantic Monthly*, December 2000; *New York Times Magazine*, September 14, 1997; Colin Thurbon, *In Siberia* (New York: HarperCollins, 1999); and Sharon Hudgins, *The Other Side of Russia: A Slice of Life in Siberia and the Russian Far East* (College Station, TX: Texas A&M University Press, 2003).

187 **immigrated across the Bering Strait:** See Calloway, *One Vast Winter Count.*

200 **"a sense of delicacy":** A year later De Lesseps, the Frenchman who left the La Perouse expedition and traveled across Russia, noted that Billings was "carefully avoiding in conversation every thing that might lead to [gossip]. I admired the delicacy and prudent of M. Billings in this respect." De Lesseps said of Irkutsk: "Its population is numerous and its society brilliant; the multitude of officers and magistrates who reside there, have introduced the modes and customs of Petersburg."

Chapter 13—Common Flag of Humanity

204 **being a French spy:** See Nina N. Bashkina et al, *The United States and Russia: The Beginning of Relations, 1765–1815* (Washington: Smithsonian Institution Press, 1980); and S. B. Okun, *The Russian-American Company*, edited by B. D. Grekov, translated by Carl Ginsburg (Cambridge: Harvard University Press, 1951). Iakobi was so upset by Ledyard that in February 1788 he ordered Shelikhov's men in Alaska to raise

Russian flags "where in 1784 an English boat had stopped and the crew had made a rich haul."

Catherine II also had no love for America. According to Samuel Smucker, writing in 1859, Ledyard "would afterward report his observations in the United States, which country she detested as the hotbed of jacobinism and red republicanism."

In August 1823 Marquis de Lafayette wrote to Jared Sparks about Ledyard's arrest. He called Catherine II's conduct "illiberal, not for want of taste for that kind of discoveries. . . . she has been in the affair of Ledyard actuated by a narrow minded policy & her measures respecting him were particularly ungenerous."

Sparks also received via Lafayette, a letter from Comte de Segur, the French ambassador to Russia. "The Empress who spoke to me on the subject herself, observed that she would not render herself guilty of the death of this courageous American, by furthering a journey so fraught with danger as that he proposed to undertake alone across the unknown & savage regions of North western America." Segur did not necessarily believe her, as he added, "Possibly this pretext of humanity advanced by Catherine only disguised her unwillingness to have the new possessions of Russia on the western coast of America seen by an englightened citizen of the United States. The above however were the reasons she advanced to me." Commenting on this, T. M. Eddy wrote in 1854, "We suspect Ledyard would have preferred the savage attentions of North-West American tribes to the tender mercies of the Empress." Sparks voiced his suspicions in the biography, quite ably, considering the dearth of sources, that Ledyard was arrested because of his interest in the fur trade. He argued that Markovskii and Iakobi were in league together to delay Ledyard and that they wrote to Catherine II to ask for his arrest.

In 1800 Peter Simon Pallas told English traveler Edward Clarke that "the sudden recall of the unfortunate Ledyard. . . it is said, would never have happened but through the jealousy of his own countrymen, whom he chanced to encounter as he was upon the point of quitting the eastern continent for America and who caused the information to be sent to Petersburgh which occassioned the order for his arrest." There were no Americans in Siberia at the time. Perhaps Pallas had mistakenly assumed that Ledyard was British or that Billings was American. But Billings could not have been the culprit. He did not meet Ledyard until the middle of November, far too late for any report of his to reach St. Petersburg in time for an arrest order to be issued in the middle of December—it took the mail about forty days to travel from St. Petersburg to Irkutsk and another three weeks to Yakutsk. In commenting on the arrest of Ledyard, James Burney wrote: "If the Empress had understood the characters of the two men, the commander of the expedition would probably have been ordered to Moscow, and Ledyard instead of being denied entertainment in her service, have been appointed to supply his place."

207 **never relinquish them:** Reflecting the notion that Ledyard had not really given up the fur-trading scheme, the 2002 edition of the *Encyclopedia Britannica* wrote that "Ledyard conceived the daring scheme of attracting interest in the commercial possibilities of the Pacific Northwest by walking eastward across Russia."

208 **abandon many of his personal papers:** In a report written that night, Iakobi told Catherine II that he had arrested Ledyard "without giving him any offense" and sent him to Moscow "for examination." Iakobi added, "I did not neglect to give instructions to the police officers assigned to him as to what sort of treatment he should be given on the journey."

211 **"How sweet are thy embraces":** The *Columbia Magazine* in June 1791 wrote, copying from Henry Beauford, of Ledyard's situation at the Polish border: "Misery and hardship had now become familiar to him. Though it is scarcely possible to conceive a human being capable of sustaining the accumulated misfortunes he experienced on this occasion, yet he bravely struggled with and finally surmounted them all. In the midst of poverty, covered with rags, invested with the usual accompanment of such clothing, worn with continual hardship, exhausted by disease, without friends, without credit, unknown and full of misery he found his way to Koningsburg."

211 **came to Vilna:** On March 24/April 4 Ledyard switched back from Old Style to New Style in his diary.

212 **nine men gathered:** See Henry Vincent Rutherford, "Sir Joseph Banks and the Exploration of Africa, 1788 to 1820" (PhD dissertation, University of California, 1952) and Robin Hallet, ed., *Records of the African Association* (London: Thomas Nelson & Sons, 1964). The Sir Joseph Banks collection at Sutro Library, San Francisco State University, contains records of the African Association relating to Ledyard. See also Fergus Fleming, *Barrow's Boys, The Original Extreme Adventurers: A Stirring Story of Daring, Fortitude and Outright Lunacy* (New York: Atlantic Monthly Press, 1998) and *Journal of The Royal Geographical Society*, vol. 50 (1880).

212 **"Sensible of this stigma":** Or, as Henry Rutherford wrote in his dissertation on the African Association, they were "to remove from the escutcheon of science the stain of ignorance on the subject of Africa."

214 **"enterprising character":** *Times* of London, 21 August 1788.

214 **paint Ledyard's portrait:** See Emil Hultkrans, *Carl Fredrik von Breda: Sein Leben and Sein Schaffen* (Stockholm: Centraltryckeriet, 1915). Joseph Acerbi, who saw Breda exhibiting in Stockholm in February 1799, wrote "Mr. Breda is happy in seizing and taking likenesses: he possesses the art of giving an historical air to his pictures by means of the accessories of architecture, landscape and drapery. His colouring is brilliant, but perhaps too glowing: his attitudes are sometimes a little unnatural and overstrained, his designs not always correct, nor is his drapery easy. He works a great deal and very rapidly: his pictures are often, strictly speaking, nothing more than sketches.

In his personal deportment and manners he is very mild, amiable, and not in the least assuming. He has a collection of pictures, some of them very fine ones." Joseph Acerbi, *Travels through Sweden, Finland, and Lapland to the North Cape in the Years 1798 and 1799* (London: Joseph Mawman, 1802).

216 **a single copper coin:** See Damon G. Douglas, "James Jarvis and the Fugio Coppers" in *The Colonial Newsletter*, July, September, and December 1969.

Chapter 14—I Go Alone

221 **"propriety of the choice":** On 10 April 1789 Thomas Paine told Thomas Jefferson that Sir Joseph Banks also had received a letter from Ledyard dated 15 November 1788. "Sir Joseph is one of the society for promoting that undertaking. He has an high opinion of Ledyard, and thinks him the only man fitted for such an exploration."

221 **"sic transit gloria Mundi":** One of Cleopatra's Needles stands on the Thames in London and the other is in Central Park in New York. The American one, at sixty-nine feet, is one foot higher than its British counterpart.

222 **on the back of a donkey:** For more on Egypt, see Max Rodenbeck, *Cairo: The City Victorious* (New York: Alfred A. Knopf, 1999); J. Christopher Herold, *Bonaparte in Egypt* (New York: Harper & Row, 1962); Anthony Sattin, *Lifting the Veil: British Society in Egypt 1768–1956* (London: J.M. Dent & Sons, 1988); and James C. Simmons, *Passionate Pilgrims: English Travelers to the World of the Desert Arabs* (New York: William Morrow, 1987). For Baldwin, see the *Times* of London, August 21, 1788; and George Baldwin, *Political Recollections Relative to Egypt* (London: T. Cadell, Jun. & W. Davies, 1801).

223 **population of a quarter million:** Ledyard estimated there were 700,000 citizens in Cairo.

224 **drank it on the top of the pyramids:** The African Association's attitudes towards Baldwin and Rosetti, perhaps because of Ledyard's fate, became hostile. When Frederick Hornemann went to Cairo in 1797, Sir Joseph Banks was not happy to hear he was friendly with either man. He told Hornemann the African Association was "seriously sorry" and that "the only advice I ever gave you in strong language was to avoid by all means suffering either of those Gentlemen to know your intention."

226 **"oppressed and critical situation":** See *Times* of London, July 12, November 27, and December 16 and 18, 1788.

228 **Temper boiled over:** In 1790 Beaufoy explained Ledyard's frustration: "The bilious complaint with which he was seized has been attributed to the frowardness of a childish impatience—Much more natural is the conjecture, that his unexpected detention, week after week, and month after month, at Cairo (a detention which consumed his finances, which therefore exposed to additional hazard the success of his

favourite enterprize, and which consequently tended to bring into question his hon-our to the Society) had troubled his spirits, had preyed upon his peace, and subjected him at last to the disease that proved in its consequences the means of dragging him to this grave." In Alexandria in January 1792, William George Browne, an African ex-plorer, wrote that "Ledyard, the man employed by the Society on the Sennar expedi-tion, was a very unfit person; & tho' he had lived, would not have advanced many leagues on the way, if the judgement of people in Egypt concerning him be credited." Jared Sparks blamed the sun and Egyptian heat: "During his residence at Cairo, his pursuits had made it necessary for him to be much exposed to the heat of the sun, and to other deleterious influences of the climate, at the most unfavorable season of the year."

Epilogue

230 **in the form of a poem:** See *The North-American Calendar and Rhode-Island Almanack for the year of our Lord Christ 1802* (Providence).

230 **in its Africa section:** See James Hardie, *The American Remembrancer and Universal Tablet of Memory* (Philadelphia: Thomas Dobson, 1795) and William Allen, *American Biographical and Historical Dictionary* (Cambridge: W. Hilliard, 1809).

231 **struggled to discern:** In February 1800, Isaac Ledyard, in a speech for a me-morial service for George Washington, said: "In our reflections upon departed friends, especially of eminent men, every thing relating to them in life acquires an enhanced estimation, and is rendered peculiarly interesting."

231 **ran newspaper advertisements:** In December 1821 Richard Bartlett, one of Sparks' correspondents in New Hampshire, wrote of the confusion the ads sowed: "Poor Mr Dan¹ J. Ledyard of N.Y. seems to be in great agony lest 'the gentleman in N.H.' should do some violence to his deceased kinsman's reputation, but I have hu-manely put his heart at ease by assuring him that 'JS' are the initials of your name & that I act only as your friend & agent."

231 **brother-in-law:** For more on Freneau, see Mary S. Austin, *The Poet of the Revolution: A History of His Life and Times* (New York: A. Wessels, 1901); Fred Lewis Pattee, *The Poems of Philip Freneau: Poet of the American Revolution* (New York: Rus-sell & Russell, 1963); and Jacob Axelrod, *Philip Freneau: Champion of Democracy* (Austin: University of Texas Press, 1967).

232 **"answer the public expectation":** Ledyard's mother, Abigail Moore, died in March 1805 at age seventy-seven. George Ledyard died in April 1814, Thomas in Sep-tember 1815, and Fanny in January 1816. In June 1895 the Fanny Ledyard chapter of the Daughters of the American Revolution (based in Mystic) laid a tablet of Groton gran-ite on her grave in Southold. See *Brooklyn Eagle*, 17 June 1895. Not much is known

about Ledyard's three stepsisters. Abigail, known as Nabby, married Captain Jonathan Landon and lived in Southold. Julia married Matthias Case and also lived in Southold; she died in September 1855. Phoebe married Ebenezer Denison and lived in Stonington. Isaac Ledyard died in August 1803, and his brother Ben died that November. Lewis Case Ledyard, the lawyer and founder of Carter Ledyard & Milburn, was Ben's great grandson.

Ledyard's portrait—actually the pen and ink copy of the Breda portrait—went missing at some point. In January 1790 he sent the portrait to Ledyard's mother, Abigail Moore "for the amusement of my Aunt." It appeared to be in Philadelphia with Philip Freneau at the turn of the century. In April 1822 a Ledyard relative, Mary Youngs Hempstead, wrote to Jared Sparks, saying the portrait and the original *Life & Letters* manuscript was "supposed to be lost in the deluge of Sickness [yellow fever] which took place there [in Philadelphia] about that time. The Family were never Satisfied that Dʳ Ledyᵈ used all the vigilence which ought to have been on the occasion (they however may have been in an error) yet if I am not mistaken they never knew the name of the Publisher, what Street he lived in—whether he had property—any Heirs—or adminstrators—with whom such manuscript and Likeness might remain as uninteresting things, nor did I ever hear they was ever advertised for."

232 **agent for the French:** A third expedition, secretly organized by Henry Knox, the secretary of war, was mounted in 1790. An army lieutenant, John Armstrong, reached the Mississippi before turning back.

232 **into a comfortable obscurity:** For more on Sparks, see Herbert B. Adams, *The Life and Writings of Jared Sparks: Comprising Selections from his Journals and Correspondence* (1893; repr., Freeport, NY: Books for Libraries Press, 1970).

233 **ran newspaper advertisements:** In December 1821 Richard Bartlett, one of Sparks' correspondents in New Hampshire, wrote of the confusion the ads sowed: "Poor Mr Danˡ J. Ledyard of N.Y. seems to be in great agony lest 'the gentleman in N.H.' should do some violence to his deceased kinsman's reputation, but I have humanely put his heart at ease by assuring him that 'JS' are the initials of your name & that I act only as your friend & agent."

233 **reviewed his book:** See, for example, C. Cushing, *North American Review*, October 1827 and October 1828; *American Quarterly Review*, March 1828; *New-York Mirror*, 24 May 1828; *Christian Monthly Spectator*, June and July 1828; *American Quarterly Review*, June 1828; John Barrow, *Quarterly Review*, July 1828; *Spirit of Pilgrims*, September 1828; and *Southern Review*, November 1828. An excerpt appeared in *The Boston Book: Being Specimens of Metropolitan Literature* (Boston: Ticknor, Reed & Fields, 1850). See also Maria Lydia Childs, *Biographical Sketches of Great and Good Men* (Boston: Putnam & Hunt, 1828).

234 **a household name:** In 1831 a twenty-horsepower steamboat named the *John Ledyard* captivated New England when it motored up the Connecticut from Hartford to Windsor, Vermont, in a record thirty-four hours and then proceeded to Wells River, farther north on the Connecticut than any steamboat had ever gone. The *John Ledyard* was then used on a scheduled route on the Connecticut. In 1840 at the bicentennial ball for the founding of Hartford, a local newspaper noted that one woman's outfit included Ledyard's mother's shoes. In 1855 a California monthly ran a profile of Ledyard's mother: "A true American wife and mother; formed herself, as she moved in her appointed orbit, the sun of the domestic circle, kindly by it own refulgence the noble aspiration, the generous impulse, and warming into life and vigor the budding virtues, that time was to fructify and call into action."

235 **touch the spirit of John Ledyard:** There are three towns in the United States named Ledyard. The Connecticut town, formerly a part of North Groton, is named after Ledyard's uncle William, the slain hero of Fort Griswold. The town in upstate New York is named after Ledyard's beloved cousin Ben. The town in northern Iowa was named by William Larrabee, Iowa's twelfth governor, for Ledyard, Connecticut, where he was born in January 1832.

Credits

The following institutions kindly granted me permission to quote from manuscript materials in their archives: Rauner Special Collections Library at Dartmouth College, the New-York Historical Society, Houghton Library at Harvard University, the Connecticut Historical Society Museum, Hartford, Connecticut, and the Library of Congress.

Maps

Captain Cook's Third Voyage was produced in 1977. John Ledyard's Route was produced in 2004 by Carl Mehler. Both are used with permission of National Geographic Society.

Illustrations

Courtesy of Dartmouth College Library: 1, 4, 5, 6, 7, 8, 9, 10, 11, 12, 13.

Image 1 was sketched by an artist named Updyke.

Image 5 was sketched by Jose Cardero in 1792 and originally appeared in Josef Espinosa y Tello, *A Spanish Voyage to Vancouver and the North-West Coast of America,* trans. Cecil Jane (London: Argonaut Press, 1930).

Image 6 was painted by John James Audubon and lithographed by John T. Bowen. It originally appeared in John James Audubon and John Bachman, *The Viviparous Quadrupeds of North America* (New York: J.J. and V.G. Audubon, 1845–48).

Images 7, 8, 9, 10, 11, 12 were created by John Webber and originally appeared in James Cook and James King, *A Voyage to the Pacific Ocean* (London: G. Nicol and T. Cadell, 1784). Image 9 was engraved by William Angus, 10 was engraved by William Sharp, 11 was engraved by John Keyse Sherwin, 12 was engraved by William Byrne. William Bligh also contributed to images 7 and 8.

Courtesy of the Whitaker Historical Collection, Southold Free Library: 2, 3.

Courtesy of the National Maritime Museum, London: 14. It was originally titled "The Resolution and Discovery in Ship Cove" and sketched by John Webber.

Index